Praise for Scott Nadelson

The Next Scott Nadelson: A Life in Progress

A poignant meditation on love, literature, and the pains as well as the perverse pleasures of loneliness. Nadelson chronicles his life in progress with the wry, warm honesty of an old friend catching up after many years. He reminds us that the world can be simultaneously huge and miniscule, that what we read and see and remember is at once nothing and everything, that wholeness is much greater than any sum total you can imagine.

MEGHAN DAUM, author of *Life Would Be Perfect If I Lived In That House*

The Next Scott Nadelson: A Life in Progress is an endearing self-portrait filled with wisdom, humor, and refreshing honesty. Nadelson examines moments in his life marked by failure and disappointment, yet nothing fails or disappoints in this fine modern memoir. A great read.

DINTY W. MOORE, author of *Between Panic & Desire*

In *The Next Scott Nadelson*, the title figure is honest, open, and searching, and his presence on the page is truly consoling: his patient excavation of his life will help readers understand their own.

DAVID SHIELDS, author of *Realty Hunger: A Manifesto*

Aftermath

Aftermath is a sophisticated, emotionally complicated collection with an exhilarating undercurrent of danger.

MARGOT LIVESEY, author of *The House on Fortune Street*

Seamlessly Nadelson opens a window to the workings of the human heart.

NORTHWEST BOOK LOVERS

I emerged from the book, as if from a movie, so lost in and convinced by the vivid screen, that the world felt a little sun-bleached in comparison.

DEBRA SPARK, author of *Good for the Jews*

A novel could bring him the attention he deserves, though an artful, accomplished writer like Nadelson ought to be able to sustain a respectable career on stories alone. Ms. Treisman and others often forget that many writer's writers are finally pulled from the edges of obscurity. The career of Andre Dubus – who wrote long stories and novellas, published with a small but respectable outfit, and crafted two exquisite books of personal nonfiction – might be a guiding example for Scott Nadelson. Perhaps *The New Yorker* should pay attention to him. Perhaps you should.

THE COLLAGIST

Nadelson is master of the anticlimax. *Aftermath* is an often-despairing testament to the elusiveness of closure, the infinite and insurmountable distance between even intimate lovers, but also to the human capacity for growth.

PORTLAND MONTHLY

Nadelson creates characters so endearingly flawed that regardless of our actual similarities, we relate to each of them. Each page documents our own fears, insecurities, and heartbreaks. Each sentence becomes the moment we first remember hope failing. Perhaps Nadelson's greatest accomplishment, however, is that the collection as a whole is uplifting … [the] realization that losses are universal – is comforting.

PLOUGHSHARES LITERARY MAGAZINE

Nadelson is interested in the grey area between major life events, the fumbling and wrong turns, the ambiguities of heart and purpose that have become the hallmarks of young adulthood. His stories strike just the right balance between funny and sad, between the high shtick of aging Jewish parents and the raw emotion of young people experiencing their first major personal disasters.

EUGENE MAGAZINE

The former Oregon Book Award winner's prose is elegant in its unpretentiousness. The depth of his insight is stunning. The breadth and detail of his knowledge of the ordinary lives of men and women in widely varying walks of life is astonishing.

JEWISH REVIEW

The Cantor's Daughter

My first choice [*Samuel Goldberg & Sons Fiction Prize for Emerging Jewish Writers*] is *The Cantor's Daughter*, which I found moving and original without being clearly derivative from any specific style.

DAPHNE MERKIN, panelist, former *New Yorker* essayist and cultural critic

An enticing collection.

DIANA ABU-JABER, author of *The Language of Baklava* and *Crescent*

The stories in Scott Nadelson's *The Cantor's Daughter* seethe with psychological insight.

CAI EMMONS, author of *His Mother's Son*

Nadelson, a tireless investigator of the missed opportunity, works in clear prose that possesses a tremolo just below the surface.

STACEY LEVINE, author of *My Horse and Other Stories* and *Dra--*

This is a thoughtful collection, compassionate yet unsparing in its observations. "Only connect," reads the oft-quoted passage from E.M. Forster's *Howards End*. If only the characters in these stories could.

THE OREGONIAN

Authentic ... Careful stories about suburban New Jersey Jews turn on the inescapable mix of love and destruction ... Nadelson bears unflinching witness to his characters' darkness.

PUBLISHERS WEEKLY

Nadelson tells his stories in unpretentious prose in which the writer is mostly invisible, a quality he has further refined in this second collection. Nadelson's prose is sturdy but not flashy, almost workmanlike. As a mason lays bricks, he stacks one sentence upon another until slowly, a story emerges.

THE PORTLAND MERCURY

A strong literary work of fiction, a quiet book that has much potential.

THE JEWISH WEEK

Nadelson's best trick is slipping complex emotions and startling revelations between smooth and steady sentences, as a mother mixes in peas with the mashed potatoes so her child will eat his vegetables unwittingly.

WILLAMETTE WEEK

Saving Stanley: The Brickman Stories

- Winner of the H.L. Davis Award for Short Fiction at the 2004 Oregon Book Awards
- Winner of the GLCA 2005 New Writers Award

These extremely well-written and elegantly wrought stories are rigorous, nuanced explorations of emotional and cultural limbo-states. *Saving Stanley* is a substantial, serious, and intelligent contribution to contemporary Jewish American writing.

DAVID SHIELDS, author of *Enough About You: Adventures in Autobiography* and *A Handbook for Drowning*

Scott Nadelson's stories are bracing, lively, humorous, honest. A splendid debut.

EHUD HAVAZELET, author of *Like Never Before* and *What Is It Then Between Us*

Scott Nadelson's fine first story collection achieves a rare balance between compassionate comedy and an unswerving attention to the dark trials of family life

MARJORIE SANDOR, author of *Portrait of My Mother, Who Posed Nude in Wartime* and *The Night Gardener*

Equally powerful with narrative and dialogue, he is a writer in full possession of both his material and his craft.

SUSAN THAMES, author of *I'll Be Home Late Tonight*

It's thrilling to watch a young talent reach out and grasp the essence of an art form, particularly a form as rich and nuanced as the short story. Smart, funny, and heartbreaking, *Saving Stanley* is an uncommonly exciting debut.

TRACY DAUGHERTY, author of *Five Shades of Shadow* and *Axeman's Jazz*

I wish I could write such sentences.

JOSIP NOVAKOVICH, author of *Salvation and Other Disasters* and *Apricots from Chernobyl*

Library of Congress
Cataloging-in-Publication Data

Nadelson, Scott.
The next Scott Nadelson : a life in progress / Scott Nadelson.
p. cm.
ISBN 978-0-9834775-6-3 (alk. paper)

1. Nadelson, Scott.
2. Authors, American–21st century–Biography.

I. Title.
PS3614.A34Z46 2012
814'.6–dc23
[B]

9 8 7 6 5 4 3 2 1

Hawthorne Books
& Literary Arts

2201 Northeast 23rd Avenue
3rd Floor
Portland, Oregon 97212
hawthornebooks.com

Form:
Adam McIsaac, Bklyn, NY

Printed in China

Set in Paperback

For Iona

ALSO BY SCOTT NADELSON

Saving Stanley: The Brickman Stories
The Cantor's Daughter
Aftermath

The Next Scott Nadelson

A Life in Progress

Scott Nadelson

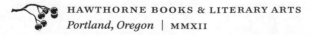

HAWTHORNE BOOKS & LITERARY ARTS
Portland, Oregon | MMXII

Contents

Everything is not enough
And nothing's too much to bear
Where you've been is good and gone
All you keep's the getting there

TOWNES VAN ZANDT

Life is easy to chronicle, but bewildering to practise.

E. M. FORSTER

Preface

THIS IS WHERE I'M SUPPOSED TO OFFER A DISCLAIMER of some kind, explaining that what follows is a work of memory and meditation and therefore shouldn't be taken as statement of fact; that other people may remember certain events differently; that I've changed names for the sake of privacy; that I have otherwise been scrupulous in my effort to remain accurate, restraining from all temptation to embellish, exaggerate, or invent.

But because I believe so strongly in the power of embellishment, exaggeration, and invention – not to mention temptation – I won't make any claims about accuracy, restraint, or scruples. Instead, I'll say that these pieces are as true to me as anything I've ever written, and that the Scott Nadelson who appears in them is as close to the person who walks around in the world with that name as possible – as close, that is, as is possible for a combination of sentences to stand in for an actual human being.

And then, to make myself sound sophisticated and well-read and maybe the slightest bit sly, I'll quote Borges: *I do not know which of us has written this page.*

I

The Next Scott Nadelson

A FEW YEARS AGO, WHEN I WAS STILL LIVING IN PORTLAND, single and shadowed by a persistent and unaccountable sense of failure, I gave a reading in a downtown bookstore. It was late winter, and I didn't expect anyone to show up. The store, tucked away on a side street, with only a small sign to mark it, was run by a mother and daughter who maintained one of the best collections of literary magazines in the city and an enormous poetry section. To no one's surprise, they were struggling to stay in business. I didn't think they were helping their cause by inviting me to read, but of course I accepted without hesitation.

Six months earlier, in the summer of 2004, I'd published my first collection of stories, about a Jewish family in suburban New Jersey, and it had been received with the kind of silence most books receive, especially first books by unknown writers. Since then it had won a couple of small awards and gotten a few positive reviews, particularly in the Jewish press, but still I had a hard time convincing myself I'd done something worthwhile, that I'd ever do something worthwhile. This, I can see now, had less to do with the story collection than with my life generally. The previous June, a week before the book came out, and a week after wedding invitations had arrived in the mailboxes of our friends and family, my fiancée fell in love with someone else. I was left reeling and broke, living in a furnished attic apartment whose ceiling was infested with squirrels. Not long after, my car's brakes went out, and I discovered my cat was dying. Everything was falling apart, as far as I could tell, and for the past six months I'd been stumbling around in a fog of sadness that refused to lift even when I received an invitation to do a reading. How excited could I get, after all, knowing I'd be one more nail in the bookstore's coffin?

But to my surprise the reading drew an enthusiastic crowd, more than two dozen people, most of whom had seen my name in the local Jewish paper. They listened attentively, clapped, and asked questions about how much of the book was autobiographical, to which I replied that I'd promised my parents not to say. Afterward, an aging hippie wearing a yarmulke woven with the colors of the Jamaican flag came up to me and growled, "You're the next fucking Philip Roth." I smiled and thanked him and didn't bother to remind him that Philip Roth had published his first book at twenty-six and won the National Book Award, that by the time he was my age – thirty-one – he was beginning *Portnoy's Complaint* and was soon to be a household name. I was happy enough to take the compliment, more pleased actually than I wanted to admit, and I signed the old hippie's book warmly and shook his hand.

He wasn't the first person to make the Roth comparison. It was inevitable, I suppose, for a young, male, Jewish writer from New Jersey, especially one who wrote about family and generational conflict. Most of the reviews in the Jewish press had mentioned Roth, usually saying something along the lines of *Scott Nadelson isn't Philip Roth – he's not as fierce, or as funny, or as Jewish – but he's not terrible*. Even my father had joined in, saying I must have read *Goodbye, Columbus* every morning before sitting down to write.

The fact was, I didn't know much of Roth's work. Unlike my father, a devoted fan who read every new title as soon as it hit the shelves and who was outraged every year when the Nobel went to someone else, I'd only ever read three of Roth's books. It was true that *Goodbye, Columbus* had meant something to me when I was in college, as had *Portnoy* and *The Ghost Writer* in the years following. Roth had certainly been an early inspiration for my picking up a pen, but really, I thought, he wasn't so relevant anymore, not to someone of my generation, whose response to the pushy, loudmouthed Jews he'd grown up around wasn't to agonize and torture himself but to pack up and move west, as I had ten years earlier.

It was true, too, that for the past ten years I'd dated only non-Jewish women, and that I'd almost married one, but this was simply coincidence. I'd been attracted to plenty of Jewish women when I was younger – girls from my Hebrew school and youth group, olive-skinned soldiers I'd seen on my two trips to Israel – and I wasn't opposed to getting romantically involved with one now, though it wasn't a priority, either. I wasn't some pathetic Portnoy running away from his mother. In fact my mother had been as excited as anyone about my wedding and had treated my ex-fiancée as a daughter, though she did lecture me about the importance of tradition and of not forgetting my roots; she couldn't bear the idea of her grandchildren not celebrating the holidays and singing all the songs I'd sung as a kid, though I hadn't sung any for more than a dozen years.

Still, the old hippie's words had an unexpected impact on me, and my fog of sadness lifted enough that when the bookstore owner – the daughter, a small, bright-eyed girl a few years younger than me, with punky hair and sleek glasses and a sweet, lopsided smile, certainly not a Jew – thanked me and praised my work, I invited her to have a drink at a bar around the corner.

She'd love to, she said. Only her boyfriend's band was playing in a few hours, and she had to help him load his gear into the club, but thanks again for such a great reading…

"Of course," I said, and even then the fog of sadness only hovered above me, keeping its distance. Not only was this the first forward step I'd taken in six months, the first time it occurred to me that I *could* take a step forward, but I saw in the daughter's expression a little thrill of flattery, maybe even of attraction, a look that said that if she didn't have a boyfriend whose band was playing in a few hours she *would* have a drink with me, that given different circumstances who knew what might have happened. The look even seemed to suggest that circumstances might not always be the same, that she might, after all, not always have a boyfriend. "I hope it's a good show," I said, though of course what I really hoped was that the band would flop, that the daughter would recognize her mistake in turning me down. I gave her a smile I wanted her to take as acknowledgment of her look, a signal that should circumstances change she shouldn't hesitate to let me know.

Only when I'd left the store and walked a block alone, my book under my arm, passing the bar where the daughter and I might have shared a quiet drink under different circumstances, only when I pictured us in there together did the sadness return, and the anger that always came reluctantly but with terrible force, the fog enveloping me so completely that soon I was blind with despair and rage. Not because she had a boyfriend and turned down my invitation, but because she might one day *not* have a boyfriend, because one day she and I *might* have a drink together, and then who knew what would happen? Maybe we'd love each other and plan to get married and then change our minds after sending out the invitations. Maybe I'd be the one to fall in love with someone else this time and cancel the wedding—who knows? Worse than imagining what might happen between us was recognizing that everything was so uncertain, every moment bursting with possibilities. The thought infuriated me. It made me want to kick things, as I'd recently kicked the hollow-core bathroom door in my attic apartment, leaving a hole I'd have to repair if I ever moved out.

I cursed myself for having taken that step forward, cursed the old hippie for his compliment, cursed Philip Roth. By the time I made it back to my attic, I decided I'd never leave again.

I'D BEEN SO unprepared for suffering that when it blindsided me the previous June I went down in a heap, with no chance to catch my balance. It had never occurred to me my fiancée might fall in love with someone else, especially not after we'd mailed our wedding invitations, though when she told me, she said I should have seen it coming, that I couldn't possibly have failed to recognize how unhappy she'd been, and really, wasn't it at least partly my fault for not understanding her needs? Her words stunned me so completely that I didn't argue. I just made teary phone calls to my friends and family, packed my clothes and books – I didn't own any furniture – and brought my cat to the attic atop a narrow old Victorian whose roof sloped so steeply I had to sit down to pee.

The apartment's best feature was a grimy skylight over the bed. I spent whole days staring at it in the weeks and months after I'd moved out of my ex-fiancée's condo, lying on sheets she'd insisted I take, no matter how many times I refused them. She knew I didn't have money for good linens, and she couldn't bear the thought of me sleeping in cheap K-Mart sheets with a ridiculously low thread count – I might as well sleep on canvas – and anyway, she couldn't imagine sleeping with someone else in the sheets we'd shared. She sobbed as she said this, tossing things out of the linen closet, making a heap in the middle of the bedroom floor. "Take whatever you want," she said. "Take it all." She was getting new sheets, she was starting everything fresh.

The sheets were light yellow and incredibly soft, inappropriate for a bachelor's apartment, I thought, inappropriate for a person in so much pain, though if she hadn't given them to me I might not have bothered with sheets at all, not even with a low thread count, not even canvas. I would have just slept on the bare mattress. That would have been appropriate, stripped down as I was, my nerves so exposed even the air felt abrasive.

Nevertheless I used the sheets. For months I hardly got out of them, listening to squirrels scurrying in the ceiling, watching the seasons change through the grimy glass overhead, blue skies giving way to clouds and then to rain. I thought I'd just lie there until the sheets shredded beneath me, until they turned to dust, and I'd watch the seasons turn and turn and turn, until I no longer knew which summer I was in, or which winter, because, really, why should I care?

To my surprise I did care, and not long after the reading in the downtown bookstore, I found myself spending less time in those sheets, which had begun to fray at the edges and had even torn along one seam. Two and a half seasons were enough, and now the fog of sadness that had enveloped me so completely, that I thought would never lift, dispersed so quietly I was shocked to find it mostly gone.

Now it was early spring. Wet cherry blossoms plastered my car, and red-headed finches frolicked in the eaves outside my windows. Ordinarily the birds would have driven my cat crazy. She would have taken up vigil on a windowsill, pacing and making odd bird-like sounds, sounds more envious than threatening, as if she wanted to join in their merriment rather than eat them. But now she hardly ever left her spot on the couch, curled up on a sweaty T-shirt I'd long since given up hope of retrieving, just as I'd hardly left the bed for the few months prior. It was as if we'd traded off keeping watch on the place, sentinels on extended guard duty, and just as she'd kept up a cheerful front while I'd slept my long, dreamless sleep, a constant reminder that life still persisted even if I denied it, now I paced in front of her, occasionally scratching her head, coaxing her with treats, telling her she'd be feeling better any day now, while she glanced up at me with huge mournful eyes, her emaciated face giving no sign that she believed me, that she had any hope for the days to come.

Part of me worried my sadness had rubbed off onto her, that the months I'd spent in bed had brought her to this state, though rationally I knew that sadness didn't bring on diabetes, which was what had caused her to lose half her body weight and made her drink a gallon of water a day. Every twelve hours I injected her with insulin, pulling up the loose scruff on the back of her neck, which smelled faintly of cotton candy, though the needle robbed her of all sweetness. She didn't protest, didn't register any pain, but still I felt cruel and guilty every time I pressed down the plunger, more so since the shots weren't doing any good. Her sugar levels were erratic, the vet told me. She must be insulin-resistant. Diabetes had killed my maternal grandmother, when I was too young to know her well, and now I was sure that the disease was a plague on my family, that the vet was wrong about what had caused it – it wasn't the cheap grocery store cat food loaded with carbohydrates but my genetics, or more likely, my terrible luck, my habit of misfortune, my uncanny ability to make everything I touched fall apart. Even though I hadn't sired the cat, she was after all my family, maybe the only family I'd ever have, and now I was losing her, too.

So I was left to watch the finches alone. They danced under the eaves, chirping, diving to pick up sticks and bits of trash, the red-headed males weaving and singing, the brown females watching coyly, and then pairs disappeared behind the gutters to do intimate things I could only imagine, with piercing envy, as I listened to the rustling of wings and the soft clanging of aluminum.

And they weren't the only ones doing intimate things. My downstairs neighbor, whom I'd met only a few times in passing, a short, roundish, plain-looking girl with crooked front teeth, who always wore corduroys and fleece jackets and workboots, had recently begun bringing someone home to bed, and to my surprise and horror and fascination, she turned out to be a loud and energetic lover, with a range of noises I could hear plainly through the floor, beginning with a soft, squeaky moan that might have been the bed springs, then rising to a series of staccato cries – Oh shit oh shit oh shit – and finally ending with a guttural nonsensical shout that sounded to me like Mamele! Mamele! but might have been her lover's name, or more likely just a vocalization of a pleasure I couldn't imagine at all, though I tried to replicate it in my own bed, my hand a sad substitute for the plain girl a few feet below me. Her partner didn't make any noise at all, not until they'd finished, and then he started what sounded like a monologue, a low rumble of words I couldn't make out, without any answer from the girl, who must have exhausted herself with all that shouting.

I tried to picture them, to imagine how they were lying together, whether her head was on his chest or shoulder, whether his hand moved up and down her spine, and I tried to imagine what the girl's silent partner did to provoke her noises, whether he moved in response to her cries, or whether her cries were sparked by each of his movements. What an odd thing, crying Oh shit oh shit while he moved inside her, as if it were all too much to bear, as if she were afraid of what was coming next. I wondered if her partner thought it was strange, too, if it evoked an image in his mind – as it did in mine – of someone hunched on a toilet seat, and if he ever felt an aching desire to run to the toilet the moment after he pulled out of her, as I sometimes used to when I pulled out of my ex-fiancée, the urge for one release following another, and if he held back for the sake of his lover, as I always did.

But of course I couldn't know any of these things, any more than I could know what the finches did behind the gutters, and all I was left with instead was my spent penis in my hand and a sticky mess on my belly.

IT WAS ACTUALLY my penis that re-awoke to the world first, before the rest of me was ready to rise from that long, restorative slumber. Every morning that past fall and winter I'd open my eyes to the muted light through the grimy skylight, the drifting clouds, the drumming rain, and for a moment I wouldn't be sure where I was. It was almost a blissful feeling, until my mind caught up with my senses, and I remembered the attic and the furniture that wasn't mine, and the wedding invitations that had gone out in June, and the cheerful responses that came back in the mail the very same day that I had to call all my friends and relatives and tell them to cancel their flights and hotel reservations, to return their gifts, to put off polishing their shoes or pressing their suits. And then I'd shake my head and think, This isn't my life I'm remembering, this hasn't happened to me, and I'd pull the blanket over my head and keep it there until my cat pawed at me, begging for the cheap grocery store food that was destroying her body.

But now the cat didn't paw at me anymore, and though I watched the same grimy skylight and drifting clouds, and remembered the same wedding invitations and phone calls, I woke every morning with an inexplicable erection that lingered even after I got up to urinate, and that threatened at unexpected moments throughout the day, as I wandered through the grocery store or stood at a bank teller's window. With it came a dreamy, directionless desire that didn't fit with the belief that this wasn't my life I'd awoken to, that I should just keep my eyes closed until I could no longer remember wedding invitations and teary phone calls, or that several miles away my ex-fiancée was in bed with someone else. It seemed unfair for a part of my body to rebel, standing up straight when the rest of me was hunkering down, and I resented my penis with all its selfish, unrestrained appetite, for forgetting that I'd given up wanting anything.

Or if I did want anything, it was never to want anything again. Wanting was what had landed me here in the first place, though now, some mornings as I heard my downstairs neighbor clinking dishes in her kitchen, I was unreasonably hungry. I imagined making myself eggs and pancakes and sausage, though all I usually ate for breakfast was half a bowl of cereal and two cups of black coffee. Damn you, I thought, glancing down at my erection. Leave me alone.

Didn't it know what kind of trouble it was asking for, what it would take to satisfy its craving? Didn't it realize that to make it happy I'd have to meet another woman whose smell made my throat close up, whose laughter made me want to pick her up and swing her around? Didn't it realize I'd not only have to meet this woman but coax her into loving me – or at least liking me –

enough to take off her clothes, that I'd have to buck up to my own shyness, my worry that I wouldn't satisfy her, that I'd be too clumsy or too quick, that she wouldn't like the sound of my breath in her ear or the way I kissed her nipples or stroked her hair? Didn't it know she might impulsively ask me to marry her in the middle of a restaurant on Valentine's Day, and then just as impulsively decide that marriage was too conventional for her, that she'd never wanted to be anyone's wife, that she'd fooled herself into believing she could sign on to something so permanent, into believing her heart was capable of remaining constant, that she could reign in its need to wander, to explore, to experience what the world had to offer? Didn't it know she might love me for three years and then fall in love with someone else?

Didn't it know it was asking too much?

It didn't know, or if it did, it didn't care. For the first time I understood the demand for prostitution, a perfectly rational service for heartbroken men with unwanted erections, and if I wasn't terrified of disease and of being ripped off and beaten by a drug-addled pimp, I might have called one of the dozens of escorts who advertised her services in the back of the local weekly paper.

Instead I perused the dating websites. This was something my mother had been encouraging for months, though she referred only to the Jewish sites, telling me about her friend's daughter who'd met the man of her dreams online – an Israeli, no less – and had just gotten married. As excited as she'd been about my wedding, I'd always known her enthusiasm was at least partially a mask for disappointment. I would have been the first person in our family – including my brother and all my cousins – to have married a non-Jew. Even though my mother was from Philip Roth's generation – in fact, she was ten years younger than Roth – she hadn't rebelled the way Roth had, and neither had my father. They might as well have been from Roth's parents' generation. Even though they were mostly secular, attending services only on the High Holidays, all their friends were Jewish, and whenever they left the east coast they seemed lost somehow, their Brooklyn and New Haven accents growing thicker, puzzled looks crossing their faces, as if only then did they realize they were living in a predominantly Christian country. I suspected that my mother was secretly relieved that my ex-fiancée had left me, that she'd even seen it coming, though of course she never said so directly. What she did say was, "Relationships are easier when you understand the other person's background. There's a solid foundation from the beginning." Then she tried to set me up with her bridge partner's niece, who'd just moved to Portland.

My father didn't weigh in on the dating question at all. When my mother handed him the phone, he talked sports and then told me about *The Plot Against America*, which he was reading for the second time. "Haunting," he said. "You really believe it could have happened here. Just imagine. There wouldn't be a single one of us left in the world. The guy's a genius." There was no reason to put much stock in my father's judgment of good writing. He'd spent his career as a chemist in the pharmaceutical industry, and hadn't even written articles for science journals since graduate school. But still, he was a voracious reader, especially now that he was retired, and I felt compelled to tell him what the old hippie in the bookstore had said. For a second he didn't answer. When he did speak, he sounded more worried than amused. "Those are big words to live up to, kiddo. You've got a lot of work ahead of you." Then, before he hung up, he said, "Mom wants me to remind you to call Jackie's niece. She's expecting to hear from you."

I didn't for a second believe that my break-up had anything to do with my ex-fiancée's ethnic or religious make-up – English and Irish Protestant, with a touch of lapsed-Mormon – but given what I'd suffered as a result, my mother's words lingered in my mind enough for me to wonder if dating a Jewish woman really would make some kind of difference, if in fact I'd been missing something all along. So I tried her suggestions. But her bridge partner's niece turned out to be a lesbian – her aunt was in denial, she told me over the phone – and the dozen or so local women on the Jewish dating websites were looking for men who owned their own homes, who had a minimum annual income of $50,000, who observed Shabbat or went to shul at least once a month. It's not that I wasn't attracted to any of them – there was a particularly cute one in the mix, though she looked too much like one of my cousins for me to imagine kissing her, or taking off her clothes – but when I moved on to the general dating websites I found myself suddenly aroused at the thought of shopping for a romantic partner. Before long I moved on to porn sites, where the women I looked at all shared my ex-fiancée's light hair and pale skin and high cheekbones, and when I finished, exhausted and ashamed, I thought that maybe fucking Philip Roth had my number after all.

I WENT BACK to the downtown bookstore on a weekday afternoon about two months after the reading. I had no real business downtown, or anywhere else for that matter. My only paid work at the time was a shuffling deck of part-time teaching jobs, and my classes were all at night or online. My days were open, boundless, and to keep myself from taking long afternoon naps or pacing my attic, I hopped on the number 15 bus after lunch most days and made my way across the river, where I'd wander crowded shopping streets or through the park alongside the art museum and the university and stop into coffee shops, slowly coming alive to the world I'd thought I'd given up.

There was a bookstore in my own neighborhood, in the southeast quadrant of the city, and plenty of coffee shops, but by then I was consumed with the idea of cutting loose from all ties, real or imagined, of leaving things behind. On the bus heading west I could pretend I was off to a land new and unfamiliar, a place of fresh starts and rich possibilities, and I could forget momentarily that I had three months left on my teaching contracts, six on my lease, that my credit card was charged close to its limit and my car's brakes were still shot and my cat was still dying. West had seemed like a magical direction when I'd first set out from New Jersey ten years before, and even though the notion of heading west to seek one's fortune was a tired cliché, and even though the bus was filled with clients of a nearby methadone clinic who discussed the best spots to score H or Oxy – nothing, I overheard one say, beat a post-clinic fix – and even though I knew I'd return the same way a few hours later, on the inbound number 15, I always worked up a small glimmer of expectation, a vague hope that I was moving in the necessary and appropriate direction of adventure or discovery or flight.

On my way to the bus, I passed my downstairs neighbor's kitchen window, which looked onto the stairs to my apartment, and lingered for a moment, despite the steady drizzle. The curtain was open, and I could see that her kitchen was everything mine wasn't: clean, orderly, well-stocked. On the counter was a bowl overflowing with fruit. Magnets pinned pictures of friends and family to the refrigerator. An unopened bottle of wine sat on a shelf above the sink. I could see far enough into the rest of the apartment to confirm that it was all this way, her whole life tidy and discreet, no hint that a few hours earlier she'd been shouting Oh shit oh shit oh shit, or Mamele! Mamele! or that she and her lover – a chub like her, I guessed, feeling mean-spirited and faintly superior – had rolled to their backs, a sweaty, tangled mess.

And somehow knowing what this orderly surface belied bolstered the sense of hope I felt as I left my apartment. Maybe I, too, could hide the truth behind a calm exterior. Maybe my morning's shave and shower, my recent haircut, my reasonably clean though mildly wrinkled clothes were enough to mask what was really there to see. Maybe a casual passer-by glancing my way would fail to recognize someone slowly emerging from suffering, someone whose sadness had kept him in bed for most of the summer and fall and winter, whose occasional, reluctant surges of anger had once made him kick a hole in a hollow-core bathroom door.

And I remained hopeful even as I passed my car plastered with wet cherry blossoms – its brake pads worn as thin as those flower petals – even as I reached in my wallet for my bus pass and saw the credit card nearly maxed by veterinary bills, even as the bus stopped in front of the methadone clinic and a dozen gaunt, disheveled addicts filled the seats around me. I was heading west, moving forward into an undetermined future, and now it didn't matter that I'd followed this same route nearly three years ago, driving straight into the sunset to visit my ex-fiancée, who wasn't yet my fiancée but only my lover, and though now it was gray and drizzling, I could picture the way I'd driven nearly blinded by the fire of the horizon, how I'd squinted to see the car in front of me, afraid I'd accidentally drive off the bridge before I could get to her. It was as hard to believe that this had once been my life as the one I was living, that I'd once arrived full of confidence at my ex-fiancée's condo in the northwest quadrant of the city, a tidy, orderly space well-stocked with food, and that we'd fall into a sweaty, tangled heap on her bed, the fulfillment of my fantasies, only in my fantasies I was so much more assertive than I was in reality, never intimidated by the responsibility of it all, never worried that I'd be too quick or too clumsy, never so eager to satisfy that often enough I satisfied myself before either of us was ready.

By the time the bus neared the bridge, the hope I'd felt outside my neighbor's window was fading. That sense of failure crept up on me again, and despite my shower and shave and haircut, I was suddenly sure everyone could see the suffering plainly on my face, that my not-quite-clean and somewhat wrinkled clothes gave me away entirely. In front of me one of the clients of the methadone clinic was complaining about his back pain, and I caught a snippet of a story about how he'd injured it on a job site, something to do with a crane and a concrete pipe. He'd been married then and had a house, but his disability checks didn't cover the mortgage, and he'd lost it. His wife took the kids. Why shouldn't he fill himself with H or Oxy, I thought, even if the state was paying for his methadone treatment? Didn't a person deserve to do whatever he had to to make himself feel better? In the face of suffering, shouldn't everything be fair game, including hiring a prostitute or looking at pornography?

Just before the bridge the bus passed a series of brick warehouses, the last belonging to a liquidation company that had in its window a handwritten sign: School Desks $10. And past the sign, behind the sooty window, was a jumbled stack of little desks with little chairs attached, the kind whose wooden top flips open so you can store your books and pencils and ruler inside. It looked as if there were hundreds of them, the entire top story of the warehouse, floor to ceiling. Who would buy so many desks? Who would buy even one?

I had an image of some commuter seeing the sign and having a sudden vision of his future, an ecstatic, bewildering moment in which he'd decide to give up his miserly corporate job to start a school for needy children, bankrolling it with his 401(k), the price of the desks the first down payment on a life full of meaning. How satisfying to be that person, to live only for greed and consumption and then to discover a charitable spirit and make up for past sins. How easy and enviable! Why didn't we all want to be Scrooge, and have the best of both worlds? Why be compassionate from the start, full of feeling and goodwill, with no potential for change, no ecstasy, no means to fund a school?

The handwriting on the sign was shaky and childlike, as if one of the little people who'd once occupied the desks had written it, and I pictured a row of dirty children waiting quietly for their school to open. But of course no corporate miser was going to slow down before the bridge and notice the sign; I saw it only because I was on the bus and didn't have to concentrate on driving. And anyway, there weren't real-life Scrooges out there waiting to be transformed, because Scrooge was the most unrealistic character in all of literature. His story was ridiculous, Christian and sentimental. Give me a good Jewish story, I thought, full of wrath and undeserved pain, Job and Lot's wife and the seduction of Samson, the dirty children left to fend for themselves.

Of course I couldn't help but picture myself among them, my books and papers stuffed so carelessly inside my desk that it never closed properly, my clothes always a little crooked, my hair fraught with cowlicks, my smile shy but eager, and I wondered what had happened to this little Jewish boy, so bright-eyed and full of hope, so open to whatever might come. How could he be thirty-one and on a bus surrounded by heroin addicts, his marriage failed before it even started, his cat dying, his only set of sheets torn and frayed?

The bus hit the bridge and surged upward, into merging traffic, toward a wall of downtown office buildings full of people with purpose to their days, families to go home to. Below, the river rippled around pylons. The addict who'd injured his back and lost his house had fallen asleep. I pulled the cord for my stop.

THE DAUGHTER WAS out when I arrived at the bookstore, but I chatted briefly with her mother, who at first didn't recognize me or remember my name when I offered it, and I resisted the impulse to ask if any copies of my book had sold since the reading. I told myself I didn't care that the daughter was out, that I hadn't come in because of her. Rather, I wanted to break up my routine of wandering through parks and sitting in coffee shops, to show my support for the struggling store, and to convince myself that failure wasn't the defining feature of my life, that despite my attic apartment and wrinkled clothes and canceled wedding, I might consider myself something of a success.

The mother was friendly enough, and even acted pleased to see me when I reminded her I'd read there two months earlier, though she obviously still struggled to recall who I was. But she was in the middle of putting in an order, so I left the counter and scanned the literary journals and then wandered over to the fiction section, browsing alphabetically, taking my time getting to the Ns. And then I felt a little zing of pride to see my book tucked in there so happily, right between Nabokov and Naipaul. With such weighty, serious company, how could anyone fail to think that it, too, must be weighty and serious, that it must be worth the price listed on the tag? I pulled out a copy and reread the blurbs on its back cover and reassured myself that someone had believed it was worth paying for, that someone believed it belonged on a shelf, though maybe not in the company of Nabokov or Naipaul. When I replaced it, I left it sticking out an inch, as if that might entice someone into picking it up, or as if it might snag like a burr onto someone's clothing and ride with him to a new home.

Then I sidled down to the Rs, thinking, as I had for the past two months, of the old hippie's words. The next fucking Philip Roth. I counted the Philip Roth books. Eighteen, and the store didn't carry all his titles. There was no point in being envious, but I consoled myself anyway by thinking that someone who produced so much had a higher percentage of garbage in his work than someone who labored over each book for years, and that it was harder to find the gems when you had to wade through pages and pages of dreck. Not that I knew much of Roth's dreck, since I'd read only the three books. What came to mind instead was the precision of those early stories, the rebellion, the anger that seemed to come to their author easily, swiftly, though of course it had probably cost him plenty of effort, and I wondered if that was what my father loved about Roth's books, since he, like me, was slow to anger even when it was justified. It was two months after my ex-fiancée left me before I kicked a hole in the bathroom door, and then only because my therapist told me it was dangerous to keep my anger bottled up, that it was bad for my health. I deserved to feel it, she said, and deserved to express it, though when, a week later, I told her how I'd expressed it, she said shouting would have done just as well and would have been less expensive.

Whether or not Philip Roth had anything to offer me, I'd avoided his books soon after deciding I wanted to write myself.

He was standing in my way, I thought. You couldn't be a Jew from New Jersey and write fiction without changing your name and taking on a new identity, without moving to the Balkans and writing about war and suffering in Bosnia and pretending that the people you knew best were Semsa and Huse Kovacevic of Sarajevo and not Lois and Harold Kornreich of Morristown. I spent several years writing about Edinburgh, where I'd lived for six months after graduating college, and though my Scottish characters were wooden and cartoonish, saying things like "Ach, you wee beasties!" and smashing each other over the head with beer glasses, I felt a certain freedom in trying to disappear into another culture, imagining I was treading across relatively untouched ground.

And it was disheartening to discover that if I was capable of writing at all, it was only about those Morristown Kornreichs. No one would ever come up to a young Jewish writer from New Jersey and say, You're the next fucking Scott Nadelson, no matter how many books I wrote, no matter how successful I was. The phrase didn't even sound as good. The alliteration wasn't as punchy, and neither was the rhythm. This other young Jewish writer from New Jersey would just be the new next fucking Philip Roth, one more in a long series of next fucking Philip Roths, all of us lined up from now to the end of time, or until New Jersey was swallowed up by the rising sea, and none of us would really be the next fucking Philip Roth, because there was only one fucking Philip Roth, now and forever.

I picked up a copy of *Portnoy* and studied the photo on the jacket, gripped by the sense of failure that had plagued me for the past nine months. I decided now that it had less to do with a canceled wedding and an attic apartment than with this photo of the thirty-something fucking Philip Roth, whose nose was bigger than mine, shoulders broader, arms hairier, who was altogether more Jewish than I was. I was happy that my hairline hadn't begun to recede as early as his had – was that the cost of all his anger? – but still I felt inadequate. As fiercely as he'd rebelled, as furiously as he'd ridiculed his own people, they loved him for it. He gave my father exactly what he wanted, a reflection of the world he knew so well, providing the anger and outrage my father didn't have to feel himself. And maybe this was why the old hippie's words had had such an effect on me – I, too, wanted to be the revered outlaw, the heretic who received invitations to speak at every JCC in the country, though by the time I started writing there was no longer much to rebel against or much to ridicule that hadn't been ridiculed a hundred times before.

The truth was, even though I didn't read his books, I'd always had a fantasy that my work would somehow reach Philip Roth, that he'd recognize something special in it and take me under wing, as his character Nathan Zuckerman is taken under wing by the older, more prominent I.E. Lonoff in *The Ghost Writer*, as Roth himself had been taken under wing by Lonoff's real-life model, Bernard Malamud (or, depending on which critic you believe, I.B. Singer or Henry Roth). But of course Roth had probably played Lonoff to some other Nathan Zuckerman by now, maybe a dozen other Zuckermans, all those next fucking Philip Roths who were far more prominent than I was.

I was sick of fucking Philip Roth anyway, sick of seeing his name in reviews of my book, sick of hearing about him from my father, and I put down *Portnoy* and went on to his neglected European relation, Joseph Roth, who'd written nearly as many books in half the time, though the store carried only one. I preferred the photo on the back of *The Radetsky March*, of a squat, froggy man with a shaggy mustache. There was nothing to envy here, nothing to struggle against, and I decided it was much better to be neglected, nearly forgotten, read only by the initiated. No one would ever call a young Jewish writer from Galicia the next fucking Joseph Roth, though what an admirable thing to be, how preferable to being one more in a series of next fucking Philip Roths, writing one more failed imitation of *Goodbye, Columbus*. To write a failed imitation of *The Radetsky March*, now that was something worthwhile, something to strive for, and when I heard the bell on the shop's front door jingle, I took a copy of Joseph Roth's masterpiece and headed for the counter, though I already had one at home.

THE DAUGHTER HAD returned. I knew it as soon as I heard the jingle, and knew, too, that she was the only reason I'd come back to the store, that I'd been fooling myself to think otherwise. No one else had come in since I'd arrived, and I worried the store wouldn't survive much longer, that the daughter would disappear before circumstances could change. At the counter she was shaking rain out of her glistening hair and wiping her glasses. She took off her jacket, and on her upper arm was a tattoo I hadn't noticed before, of a rose strangled by its own thorns, dripping blood. It was just coincidence that she shared some features in common with my ex-fiancée, I told myself. I would have been attracted to her even if she didn't have the pale skin, the light hair, the high cheekbones, even if she were dark and Jewish, because what drew me to her was the look she'd given me, the bright, lopsided smile, the way she'd praised my work and talked hesitantly about her boyfriend's band. Of course I didn't know anything about her, but I had the feeling that we had something in common, a potential spark that went deeper than skin or cheekbones. I wasn't Alexander Portnoy, after all, and this wasn't 1969.

When she put her glasses back on, she seemed startled to see me there, smiling stupidly at her, holding out *The Radetsky March* and a literary journal I'd grabbed on my way to the counter. She greeted me warmly, said how nice it was to see me again, and told me she was still thinking about the story I'd read two months earlier. All good signs, I thought, along with the lopsided smile she gave me, and I tried to detect a hint of that suggestive look she'd offered the night of my reading, some sign that circumstances had changed. She hoped I was working on a sequel to my book, she said. A novel, maybe? In fact, I was working on more stories, unrelated to those in the first book, but nodded anyway. "I can't wait to read it," she said.

I couldn't believe I hadn't noticed the tattoo before, though I remembered clearly that she'd worn a tight black T-shirt the night of the reading and that her arms were long and wiry and elegant. It bothered me not to have noticed, because I suspected this was a pattern in my life, that despite being a writer and priding myself on paying attention to details, I was always looking in the wrong direction, oblivious to what was actually there to see. Should I have known, as my ex-fiancée told me, that her falling in love with someone else was inevitable, that I should have seen it coming from miles away? Had my heartache been forecast, and I'd simply missed the signs? And if so, did it matter? Would it have been any less awful if I'd known what was on the way?

The daughter looked younger than I remembered. Twenty-five, maybe, or twenty-six. Too young for me, really, though if there was a spark that went deeper than skin and cheekbones, I supposed age shouldn't matter, either. I wondered what a bleeding rose choked by its own thorns might mean to her, what it could possibly symbolize to a twenty-five-year-old whose fiancée likely hadn't left her for someone else a month before her wedding, who likely didn't have a broken car or a dying cat. The image struck me as powerful and mysterious, an insight into beauty and pain that was beyond her years, and if I wasn't already drawn to her face, I would have been drawn to that rose. It suggested that we did in fact have something in common, that we might understand each other, and even though she looked too much like my ex-fiancée for me to trust her, I was glad I'd come back to see if circumstances had changed. She must have caught me eyeing the tattoo, because her fingers went to it, just for a moment, touching it lightly and then moving down her arm, a graceful, inviting gesture that suggested someone older, experienced, aware of her power and poise, even if she wasted it on one of the hundreds of scruffy Portland kids pretending to be a rock star.

I handed her my books, hoping she might recognize *The*

Radetsky March, that she was one of the few who'd read it, and in recognizing it, she'd recognize something in me, too, something more profound than what she'd heard in my story, something beyond a failed imitation of *Goodbye, Columbus*. I wanted her to say that she thought she was the only one who read Joseph Roth, and wasn't it a shame he was so neglected. But she rang up the books without any sign of recognition. I asked if she'd ever read *The Radetsky March*, and when she shook her head, that sandy hair gleaming against her pale neck, I said, "Oh, you should. It's fantastic. He's the real Roth. Much better than Philip."

She smiled again, but with restraint, and I realized I'd said the wrong thing. Was she, too, a devotee of fucking Philip Roth? Did she like my story only because it reminded her vaguely of him? Was that why she'd been flattered by my invitation to have a drink, why she'd given me a suggestive look? Had she pictured herself in a bar with the hairy-armed author of *Portnoy*, whose fierceness was matched only by his popularity? Did she hope to end up in his next novel about an angry Jew running away from an overbearing mother and lusting after cute shiksas with high cheekbones and bleeding rose tattoos?

When she handed the books back, I asked, casually, how her boyfriend's band was doing, trying to suppress the longing in my voice. "Great," she said, and took a step backward, crossing her arms so that one hand covered her tattoo. "They just cut a deal with Touch & Go."

"I'll have to check them out," I said, trying to sound sincere, and the look she gave me then was a pitying one, that said that circumstances wouldn't change, or that if they did, I wouldn't be part of new circumstances, and really, it would be better for everyone if I quit imagining the drink we'd have together, if I quit hoping for possibilities that didn't exist, if I quit expecting a happy life. I glanced down at the photo of Joseph Roth on the back of the book I already owned, and his sour, froggy face gazed up at me in disappointment. Didn't I know already how hard the world was, how unforgiving? How many times did I have to learn it?

I paid the daughter, took my change, and slipped the book under my arm.

BY THE TIME I headed back to the bus, after wandering through the park and stopping at a coffee shop, it was nearly four o'clock. The eastbound number 15 was scattered with office workers going home early, all of them well-dressed and nicely groomed, and they gave me a wide berth, as if I were one more ragged client of the methadone clinic whose shave and haircut and slightly wrinkled clothes hid nothing of his suffering.

I was impatient to get back to my apartment, to bury myself in the frayed sheets. West was the wrong direction for me, I decided. Maybe after all these years it was time to backtrack, to trace my steps and discover where I'd made a wrong turn. Maybe I really belonged in New Jersey, in those monotonous suburbs I hated, surrounded by pushy loudmouths Philip Roth had once written about with such precision, who all seemed stuck in 1969. Maybe if I lived there, I could write about someplace else, Scotland or Galicia or the war-torn Balkans, though as the bus crossed the river, passing the warehouse full of school desks no one would ever buy, rolling slowly in the direction of my father, who was beginning *The Plot Against America* for the third time, and my mother, who was scheming to set me up with a friend's lesbian niece, I knew I wouldn't go any farther than the Victorian on Portland's east side.

When I got there, my downstairs neighbor was in her kitchen, scrubbing dishes in the sink, and she waved a soapy arm as I passed her window. And behind her was her lover, chopping vegetables at the counter. To my surprise, he wasn't a chub at all. His arms were sleek and muscled, his skin dark. Not the dark of a Jew, but of an Indian or a Pakistani. And it struck me as bizarre that of all the women in this city he'd chosen a plain white girl who wore corduroy and fleece, though I suppose it wasn't bizarre at all, just as ordinary and mysterious as my being attracted to a bleeding rose tattoo. I wondered whether his family knew about her, and whether they told him outright how much they disapproved or just pretended to accept her rather than show their disappointment. Did they tell him that he and this white girl could never fully understand each other, that relationships were easier when you and your partner shared a similar background? Did he answer that nothing so trivial could matter, since they gave each other such pleasure, since he never had to worry whether or not he was satisfying her, since her cries told him all he needed to know?

Within half an hour of entering the apartment, just after I injected my cat with the insulin that took away her cotton-candy smell but did nothing else, I heard those cries again, and at first I was furious. They were tormenting me on purpose. They'd seen me pass and decided to set their dinner aside and harass the lonely shlub upstairs, to rub his face in their ecstasy. But somehow the girl's cries didn't sound superior or boastful. They were defensive, rather, as if she needed to prove to me how much pleasure her lover was giving her, how well suited they were to each other.

And then I wondered if her cries had something to do with his parents, and their different backgrounds, and the gulf between them that could never be bridged, the ways in which she could never know him. It was an appropriate response: Oh shit oh shit oh shit. But it wasn't just about being lovers with someone from a different background, it was about being lovers with another human being, the gulf that always existed, that could never be bridged, no matter how open you were, no matter how honest. In all his raving, this was what Portnoy never said, though I was sure fucking Philip Roth must have realized it at some point, and maybe he'd even written about it, though I'd never know since I refused to read his books. It didn't matter if you were in love with a shiksa or another Jew; there were so many things you could never know about another person, even with his penis inside you, even with her straddling you and moving her hips in rhythm with your thrusts. Crying oh shit oh shit oh shit was the only thing you could do when you really thought about it. It covered everything that needed to be said, and now I wanted to cry out, too.

But then the girl's cries changed, growing faster and fiercer. They no longer sounded like Mamele! Mamele! but just blind, thoughtless utterances, empty of pleasure, empty even of desire. The cries were angry, or pained, and I imagined her expression, mouth working furiously, chin puckered, a sharp vertical line appearing between her eyebrows. She was angry that the pleasure would soon come to an end, I guessed, that nothing lasted forever, and I was angry for her. Why did everything worthwhile have to be so fleeting?

As soon as it was over, her lover started talking in his low rumble, and I imagined he was saying something about his family, preparing her to meet them, maybe, or explaining why they'd been so cold to her when she had met them. And I imagined she was inconsolable, wondering how they could ever stay together when there was such a gulf between them, even if they gave each other such pleasure, and thinking that maybe it was easier to move on from person to person, to let her heart wander, rather than have to face that same gulf every day for the rest of her life. And her lover kept remembering her cry, Oh shit oh shit oh shit, and didn't want to talk at all. What he really wanted was to get up and go to the toilet, to release everything at once, and the longer he held back the harder it was to hide his frustration.

Or more likely he was just talking about his job, or about a TV show, or about the dinner they hadn't finished preparing, and she was lying on his chest, drifting in and out of sleep, unable to raise her head, just as my cat was unable to raise hers from my old T-shirt when I scratched her behind the ear and began to tell her again that she'd soon be feeling better, that everything would soon be okay. This time I couldn't stand the words. I'd never believed them, and I was tired of being dishonest. Instead I pleaded with her not to die, just as I'd pleaded with my ex-fiancée not to leave me even though she'd fallen in love with someone else. And here was my real failure, I thought: believing I had any influence over things that were beyond my control, that I was to blame for the world being so unfair.

Soon, my neighbor's lover quit talking. Even the finches were quiet now. The only sound was rain drumming on the skylight. I tried to read *The Radetsky March*, but couldn't get past the first line: "The Trottas were a young dynasty." It was so simple and perfect, I thought, capturing the essence of the entire book in a single stroke, the nostalgia for a lost world whose underpinnings were entirely flimsy. I couldn't imitate it if I tried. I just read it again and again, thinking about my father and the old hippie and the lovely bookstore owner with her lopsided smile and enticing tattoo, all wanting what I couldn't give them. Nothing I'd ever written or thought or felt was original, I knew, but I'd go on writing and thinking and feeling those things all the same. They were mine, and they were all I had.

I put the book aside and went to my computer, where I browsed the personal ads again, and soon found myself back on the porn sites, looking at more pictures of women who resembled my ex-fiancée. My penis didn't care that I wasn't Portnoy and this wasn't 1969; no matter how much I wanted to wallow in despair, it would continue to prod me onward, into new attempts at living or into further humiliation. The couple downstairs had gone back to making dinner, laughing and clattering pots and pans. The finches began singing again in the eaves. My cat teetered to her water bowl to slake her unquenchable thirst, and I reminded myself that suffering was as fleeting as anything else, no different than pleasure or contentment or love. Whether it faded, or you overcame it, or you lived with it until you died, one way or another it ended.

2

Three Muses

FOR JUST OVER A YEAR IN MY LATE TWENTIES, I WORKED as a fundraiser for a literary nonprofit in Portland. The organization had a number of programs, including fellowships and awards for local writers and a creative writing program in public schools, but its flagship was a lecture series that brought luminaries such as Salman Rushdie and Isabel Allende to speak to halls packed with wealthy patrons and book lovers, where they offered words of wisdom or funny anecdotes that shed light on the mysterious genius that filled their books and made them famous enough to stand on brightly lit stages around the world.

I wasn't much of a fundraiser – I could write decent grant proposals, but I was too shy to schmooze potential donors, and I hated organizing cocktail parties and informational luncheons – but I enjoyed being part of the international literary scene, no matter how tangentially, imagining myself close enough to the heart of contemporary letters that I could catch the rhythm of its pulse. I also had a crush on the organization's marketing director, who was a few years older than I, worldly and sophisticated, with a smile that made me stupid. We'd become friends soon after I started the job, sometimes catching lunch together or a drink after work, but while the friendship was tinged with gentle flirtation, I saw no chance for it to turn into something more. For one thing, she had a boyfriend, a flight instructor with thick shoulders and a limp he'd gotten from a crash a few years earlier, when one of his students overshot a runway. The plane had gone up in flames, the student had died, but despite a fractured spine, somehow the boyfriend had dragged himself to safety.

If that weren't enough to discourage me, I also knew the marketing director and I lived in different worlds. She owned a condo in Northwest Portland, a neighborhood of rapid yuppie development, full of boutiques and tapas bars and French bakeries. She had her hair done in a salon near our office that charged a hundred bucks to walk in the door. Most weekends she flew off to visit friends and family in San Francisco, Salt Lake City, Jackson Hole.

I, on the other hand, lived in a rented Southeast basement, with a ceiling low enough that I could touch it without fully extending my arm. The two rooms were scattered with the cheapest second-hand furniture I could find: a rickety card table, folding chairs I'd bought at a church rummage sale, pressboard bookshelves that sagged under the weight of a few dozen paperbacks. I cut my own hair, badly, with electric clippers, and on weekends I worked my way through the collected stories of Mavis Gallant, Wright Morris, William Goyen, Peter Taylor – all those neglected or forgotten masters – and struggled to put together stories of my own. Not only did I not fly planes, but I was suddenly afraid to ride in them; the last time I'd gone back to New Jersey to visit my parents I'd panicked during landing, thinking we were heading straight into the Meadowlands, and when we were on solid ground I discovered that I'd dug my fingernails so deeply into my arm I'd actually drawn blood.

For the past few years I'd been teaching part-time at local community colleges, making less than twenty-thousand dollars a year, and until now I'd never had a real salary. I'd been trying to dedicate myself to writing, sacrificing all other pleasures for the sake of some half-formed vision of a life given over to art and ideas. But my teaching career was getting me nowhere, and I hadn't been able to sell the collection of stories I'd finished – in fact, I hadn't published a single one of those stories in a magazine or journal. So when a job came open at the literary organization, I told myself that dedication didn't have to be absolute, that I could compromise enough to stop worrying about how I'd pay my rent. I'd keep the job five years at most, I decided, and save up enough to write for another three. My first month on the job I bought a new stereo, but otherwise I didn't change my lifestyle at all. Anything I didn't spend on groceries I hoarded in a savings account, not ending the life I'd envisioned for myself, I thought, only postponing it until it was financially feasible.

In the meantime, the fundraising job kept me so busy, and filled me with such anxiety – how in the world would I bring in half a million bucks by the end of the year? – that I hardly wrote at all. This in turn filled me with greater anxiety, for how could I return to the life I wanted in five years if I abandoned it completely in the interim?

I expressed my anxiety in a muted way to the marketing director, who herself had been a writer and editor in New York for several years. She'd had some serious success, editing and publishing a couple of well-received anthologies, but ultimately came west when the pressure of earning a living and the threat of disappointment overwhelmed her. Her job, too, was a compromise, one in which she felt only slightly more settled than I did, and over lunch or drinks we talked about the difficulty of a creative life, its enormous risks and small rewards, and we agreed that being involved in a literary undertaking was less of a comfort than we'd hoped, since we spent more time with budgets and layouts than we did with books. There was real intimacy to our talks, and she began to confide in me, telling me about troubles with her boyfriend, whom, to her amusement, I called "the fighter pilot." She told me more than I wanted to know about him, including that his spinal injury had blunted feeling in his genitals. As a result his erections lasted for hours, and so did their sexual escapades, which they quit only when they were too exhausted to carry on. Still, he didn't give her everything she needed. He was often distant, emotionally closed, and he found excuses not to introduce her to some of his closest friends. He refused to come to any literary events – he liked reading, but he was sure writers were far more interesting on the page than in person. I tended to agree, though I didn't tell the marketing director so.

She also told me about her substantial and sometimes sordid romantic history, giving accounts of long-term relationships and one-night stands, with men and women, every one fraught with passion and drama and eventual discontent. To me, who could count the number of people he'd slept with on a single hand, with a finger to spare, this all sounded wonderfully alluring, part of a world I'd read about but never experienced. In my fantasies I took the pilot's place – my shoulders thick like his, my erection everlasting – but still I couldn't quite imagine myself taking up a spot in the marketing director's long, lurid list of present and former lovers.

By early fall, when our lecture series was set to open, I was in such a state of distress – panicking over my fundraising goals and my nonexistent writing, distracted by my longing – that I stopped sleeping. Sleep had always been tricky and unpredictable for me, and it didn't take much to throw me off. Now I lay in bed staring at my low ceiling until deep into the morning hours, listening to my upstairs neighbor play video games – he worked at a bar until two, played till six, and slept all day. Overhead, electronic explosions rumbled until light seeped through my blinds, and I went to work bleary-eyed and fuzzy-headed, just conscious enough to add a few paragraphs to the grant proposal I was writing and to check items off lists for the events I was organizing. The office was busy enough that no one noticed; phones were constantly ringing, people were running in and out, my boss, the organization's executive director, was always searching for a missing clipboard with the lecturers' flight information and hotel confirmation numbers. The marketing director had no time for lunch – she was meeting with reporters at all the local papers – but she occasionally stopped by my desk to tell me about the flight instructor's latest offense. "He can't handle women getting emotional in bed. Sometimes sex makes me cry. Is that really so scary?" Of course it isn't, I said, debating whether or not her question was meant as an opening, whether she was waiting for me to prove myself worthy. She was the only one who noticed my bloodshot eyes and asked, with a wink, if someone had been keeping me up late. "You're not holding back on me, are you?"

"I was up writing all night," I said, and took note of her expression, which was at least partly impressed, though also partly skeptical.

Our first speaker of the season was Stephen Jay Gould, the great evolutionary biologist and popular science writer. I'd never read Gould's work and didn't know much about him, nor did I realize how much excitement he sparked in others until calls started coming in for tickets to his lecture. One man very politely reserved a dozen seats. He was a biology teacher at a nearby high school and planned to bring his most promising students. Before hanging up, he shouted into the phone, "Can't wait to see the guru!" During the week before Gould showed up, I repeated that phrase around the office every chance I got, which made my boss laugh and kept her from noticing how little work I was doing. "Can't wait to see the guru!" I'd call when she was heading toward my desk to ask a question, which she'd immediately forget, instead going back to searching for her clipboard.

The first event I organized was a pre-lecture Q&A with Gould and some students from a local college, whose president was one of our sponsors. My job was to make sure there were soft drinks and cookies ready by the time the students arrived in the hotel conference suite, and to escort Gould down from his room. The guru was cranky by the time I knocked on his door. On the way to the elevator he complained about how many books we'd asked him to sign for our sponsors, and on the way down he complained that no one had told him the Q&A would be with undergraduates. And those undergraduates, munching the cookies I'd ordered, didn't please him with their questions, which were mostly about the controversy between proponents of evolution and proponents of creationism. "There's no controversy," he told them, mumbling into the hand that propped up his chin. "One thing is science, the other is fantasy." When one of the students began to follow up, he shrugged, scowled, and cut her off. "The whole discussion is a waste of time." The room descended into silence, and to break it, I raised my hand and asked if science writing had changed much in the thirty years since he'd first started publishing. "Of course it's changed." He shook his head and closed his eyes, as if he couldn't even bear to look at someone who'd come up with such an idiotic question. The students rustled in their seats. Most were looking down at their laps. "Everything changes," he said.

At that point, the guru must have been acutely aware of change, and also of time and how precious it was. He had cancer, which had metastasized in his lungs and would soon spread to his brain. I didn't know this until much later, and at the time thought that he was simply ungenerous, spoiled by his success and renown. I was paying close attention to these things: If I wasn't writing, at least I'd learn how or how not to be a writer in the world. I couldn't help imagining myself in front of all those wealthy patrons and book lovers, imparting words of wisdom, telling funny anecdotes, with nothing but generosity and patience for undergraduates and their naïve questions.

I wrote Gould off, until later that evening, when he began his lecture. And then I saw that there was in fact something special about him, a reason for high school biology teachers to call him the guru. From the moment he hit the stage he didn't stop moving, pacing back and forth with a wireless microphone, swinging an arm like a conductor to signal the projectionist to advance his slides, talking so fast that people leaned forward to catch every word. He had a parlor trick, whereby he could guzzle a glass of water and keep talking, without taking a breath, and it made the audience howl with laughter. Around me people beamed. A few rows ahead, the marketing director had a hand on her chest. Her eyes were moist, her mouth open, teeth glistening. And as soon as I caught sight of her, Gould won me over completely. Cranky or not, he was a showman, an entertainer, and he made evolution funny, moving, relevant to all of our lives. He spun science into a story about our origins and our future. He turned it into literature.

Eight months later he was gone.

THE SECOND SPEAKER of the year was Edward Albee, who was unlike Gould in every way. He was thin and soft-spoken, polite to everyone who greeted him, incredibly patient with questions, though there was a weariness to his bearing – his eyes, too, were bloodshot, as if he hadn't slept any better than I had for the past month – that made me want to protect him from other people's demands. I didn't want to make him sign books for the sponsors, or make him attend the luncheon in his honor, which we were using as a fundraising opportunity, in collaboration with a local theater company. But he agreed to all these things without complaint. He agreed also to attend the theater company's production the night after his lecture, and to attend the patron party afterward.

On stage he wasn't a performer like Gould, but he spoke confidently, without notes, about his life as a playwright and the relationship of the writer to his audience. He was humble and self-deprecating, and it was hard to believe this was the person who'd penned the fierce, acidic lines of *Who's Afraid of Virginia Woolf*, and whose newest play, set to open in New York in the spring, was about a love affair between a man and a goat. After the lecture, audience members wrote questions for him on notecards, and while Gould had answered only two or three, Albee addressed every last one, speaking for another hour, until his voice was hoarse. When he finally made his way back to his room, he looked beaten and drained, and I worried he was ill and wouldn't show up at the luncheon the next day.

That night I went out for a drink with the marketing director, who'd found Albee's lecture self-indulgent and uninspired. I argued with her, though not very forcefully, claiming that it was valuable to hear anyone of Albee's stature speak about himself, that his life story held lessons for all of us, particularly those of us who wrote. She was unconvinced, and maybe I was, too – not about the value of Albee's lecture, but about his approach to being a public figure, his generosity and patience, his willingness to give so much that it left him with so little.

In any case, we didn't talk about him for long. The marketing director was troubled. She kept turning her wine glass one way and then the other, and hardly took a sip. Her relationship with the flight instructor was sputtering. He seemed to be pulling away, and she didn't know why. Rather than reassure her, I told her she deserved better, that if he didn't appreciate her – she was, after all, smart and beautiful, I said, though I stopped short of calling her sexy – she should move on. But this wasn't the answer she wanted to hear. She started crying, abruptly and openly, without covering her face. I glanced around the bar, hoping no one noticed and thought I was the cause of her distress. "I'm going to end up alone," she said. "No one wants me." It was a ridiculous thing for her to say, and it irritated me, since I spent every night alone in a dank basement while she was in bed with her fighter pilot and the cock that wouldn't quit. But I did my best to comfort her, putting a hand on her back and feeling, with a little thrill and a small bite of shame, the contours of her ribs beneath her shirt, telling her that she'd have no trouble finding someone else, that anyone would be lucky to have her. I wasn't brave enough to offer myself up as an alternative.

Soon she recovered her composure, wiped her eyes, and laughed. I kept my hand on her back. "I'm being silly," she said. "It's not like I'm in love with the guy. I just know I'll miss the sex."

She drove me home that night, and for a few minutes we sat in her car at the curb. I snuck glances at her legs moving beneath her skirt and took in the sweet, buttery smell of her hair cream or skin lotion. She thanked me, and said how nice it was to have a friend who listened so well, and who genuinely cared about her feelings. Her face was puffy from crying, her cheeks red and soft and vulnerable, and she glanced at me through her eyelashes. It was a look I now recognize as expectant and open, waiting for me to take a step. Maybe I recognized it then. But my head was swarming with images of Edward Albee's slumped shoulders and the flight instructor's numb erection, and I was suddenly so tired that my jaw hurt and my eyes were starting to close. I yawned and squeezed her hand and told her I'd see her in the morning. But as soon as I hit the bed I was wide awake, staring at the ceiling, imagining her face above me, her thighs straddling my middle. My own erection was short-lived.

The next day I met Albee at his room. He didn't look any less exhausted than he had the night before. But when I asked if he'd slept well, he nodded and said, "Fine, just fine." I praised his lecture, said how inspiring it was to a young writer like me, and he gave me that weary, patient look that expected new demands on his time and energy. Maybe he thought I was going to ask him to read my manuscript. And maybe I would have if he'd given me the slightest opening, but now I chastised myself for being one more person trying to suck the life out of him. I escorted him to the luncheon, where he made a gracious speech about the importance of regional theater, about the hardworking actors and directors and administrators who kept the dramatic arts a vital part of our culture. He was honored, he said, to have been invited to this evening's performance and looked forward to it wholeheartedly. He did, however, manage a single aside that revealed the limits of his patience, for which I was grateful. "Most plays are far too long," he said, with a little laugh. "I hope you won't keep me up too late tonight."

I saw him one last time the following day. Before heading to the airport he wanted to visit an art gallery where he'd previously bought photographs, and I volunteered to take him. On the way there from his hotel, I asked if he'd enjoyed the play.

"Three and a half hours," he said, and sighed.

And he went to the party afterward?

He did, but no one talked to him. No one even announced his presence. "I'm not quite sure why I was invited," he said. I was outraged, and told him so, but he only shrugged. "You learn to expect these sorts of things." I asked if he had more lectures coming up. Another big sigh. "One more in Santa Cruz, and then I get a break until next month."

We drove in silence for a moment, but then, as if suddenly remembering the need to be polite, he asked about our lecture series, who'd already been, who was coming next. When I said that Edna O'Brien was due in a few weeks, he sat straighter and smirked. It was the most alive I'd seen him. "You know her?"

"Oh yes," he said. "She's quite mad, you know." Then he shook his head and waved a finger in front of his nose. "Don't tell her I said so."

At the gallery he pressed my hand and wished me luck, with the utmost earnestness. He seemed to know how much I needed it.

OF ALL THE writers we were bringing to Portland that fall, Edna O'Brien excited me most. She was the only fiction writer, for one, and years ago I'd read several of her early novels. I'd picked them up in a used bookstore, mostly because of their covers; the 1970s Penguin versions were incredibly sensual, even downright erotic, each one with a nude model in positions of increasing revelation and promise. The titles, too, were sexy: *A Pagan Place*, *The Love Object*, *August Is a Wicked Month*. And though the novels themselves didn't have as much straightforward titillation as I might have hoped for, they were sexy for other reasons – their evocation of Ireland's dramatic landscape, their characters torn apart by repression and longing, their beautiful language, which somehow managed to be at once earthy and magical, with sentences like, "Dan Egan was dead but his name lived on, because there was a tree named after him, a horse chestnut."

I'd read maybe three or four of her books and then somehow forgot about her. And when I was hired at the literary organization and saw her name on the upcoming season's brochure, I had the strange feeling that I'd betrayed her, failing to maintain her in my personal canon, while others of her countrymen – William Trevor, Frank O'Connor – had taken her place. Before her visit I read her newest novel, *Wild Decembers*, and her work was just as I remembered it, romantic and heart-breaking, moodily poetic: a dispute over land made mythic, a tractor described in terms that made it sound more beast than machine. Her author photo was just as dramatic. Big black eyes, red lips, an enormous mane of ginger hair. I looked up her biography online and discovered that she was seventy-one. I hardly believed it.

Albee's comment about her surprised me, but when I relayed it to my boss, she gave a knowing laugh. She'd been on the phone with Edna – I could think of her only as Edna – at least a dozen times over the last month. Lately their conversations had been about Edna's flight out of Portland. Before going back to London, she was heading to Tucson. For another lecture? I asked. No, for swimming lessons. I didn't ask the next and most obvious questions: Why go to Tucson for swimming lessons? Didn't someone in England teach people how to swim? The sticking point was that she wanted to fly first class. My boss had an arrangement with the airlines to upgrade our speakers coming to Portland and going home, but it didn't cover the extra leg. Edna wasn't satisfied. "Ah, really now," my boss said, mimicking Edna's musical brogue. "Couldn't you cajole them a bit?"

The request struck me as perfectly reasonable – or at least reasonable enough for someone who'd written as many great books as Edna had – and it annoyed me to hear my co-workers belittling our speakers. Was this just a job for them? Didn't they care at all about being close to the heart of contemporary letters? Whether my boss caught my annoyance or not, she did invite me to come to dinner with Edna after the lecture. Usually these dinners were reserved for board members and big donors, but Edna insisted that she wanted only a quiet meal afterward, that too much agitation affected her sleep. "Just yourself and a few of your kind people," my boss said, and this time I laughed, though her Irish accent was a lousy one, making Edna sound like a leprechaun with a bad cold.

The day of the lecture I could hardly sit still. All afternoon I pretended to proofread a grant proposal, going over the same lines without seeing anything more than dark marks on a white page. Dark marks on a white page – that was all Edna O'Brien's novels were, and Edward Albee's plays, and Stephen Jay Gould's scientific narratives, and my own unsold manuscript, and yet these marks mattered so much to me I could hardly sleep at night, and sometimes, looking at my bookshelves, or at the computer I'd hardly touched for months, I had to stifle unexpected, unaccountable sobs.

Just before I left the office to head to the lecture hall, I got a call from the marketing director, who'd been gone most of the day, helping to set up the evening's events. She was crying. It was all over with the flight instructor. He'd spent the night, and she thought things were going fine – I could picture only that numb, perpetual erection, which in my imagination had grown enormous, the length of my forearm – but this afternoon he called and said he couldn't go on, his heart wasn't in it, it wasn't fair to either of them. She was inconsolable, saying again that she'd end up alone, that if nothing had worked out by now – she was thirty-one – nothing ever would. Again I did my best to comfort her, knowing she could replace the flight instructor the instant she wanted to, but still I didn't let myself imagine I could really be the replacement. I was no more than a friendly ear, I told myself, as enticing as a eunuch.

Soon she calmed down and asked if I wanted to get a drink

after the lecture. I'd love to, I said, except that I was going to dinner with Edna. But maybe afterward ...

"Call if you're not too tired," she said, and hung up.

When the lights went down in the lecture hall, my boss introduced Edna warmly, without any hint of her earlier ridicule, and though I chafed against the hypocrisy, I also welcomed her words and found myself nodding along. Edna stepped onto the stage and gave a delighted smile, seeming astonished to hear such a roar of applause, to see so many people waiting for her words. Unlike either of the first two speakers, she sat on a stool behind a lectern, with a little lamp on top, which cast a dramatic glow over her face and lit up her radiant hair. I was sitting toward the back of the hall, but even from so far away I caught the gracefulness of her movements and posture, and recalling the sexy covers of her early novels, I thought again that she couldn't have been over seventy, that I must have read the date wrong, or else the biography I'd read was mistaken. She looked just like her author photo, or at least I imagined she did, though I was too far away to see for sure.

Her lecture was titled, "Irish Writers and Their Muses." It was complex, formal, and fascinating, a mixture of biography, literary criticism, and gossip, investigating the lives and work of Yeats, Joyce, and Beckett through their relationships with the women who inspired and infuriated them, and again I found myself doubting Albee's words. This wasn't a madwoman's lecture. Though she read from a prepared draft, her delivery was engaging, even theatrical at times – especially when she read from Joyce's letters to his wife – that musical voice, so much richer than in my boss's imitation, filling the cavernous hall. When she finished she seemed surprised again by the applause, as if she'd so lost herself in her talk that she'd forgotten she was in front of such a large crowd. She smiled, stood, and bowed, and then answered questions from the audience, thoughtfully, with grace and generosity, though unlike Albee she answered only the questions that interested her, slipping some cards discreetly onto the bottom of the stack. She understood that she didn't have to give exhaustively, that we'd be satisfied with a few sharp insights into her life and work. She bowed again, gave a little wave, and floated offstage, her blue dress deep and shimmering, in dark contrast to her flaming hair.

Before going to dinner, I had to stop by the post-lecture reception, where patrons milled around, showing off their expensive clothes and jewelry, sipping donated wine and nibbling donated pastries – and where I was supposed to schmooze, though all I did was lurk at the edges of the party, always moving, so as not to let anyone recognize how paralyzed by shyness I was, how terrible at my job. I spotted the marketing director across the room, talking to an editor from one of the local weeklies, and the longing I felt was painful, nearly crippling. According to Edna, Yeats, Joyce, and Beckett had all suffered deeply in love, but it was the fulfillment of their desires that spurred them to write their greatest masterpieces. What would have happened to them if they'd never gotten what they wanted? Would they have taken jobs as bank tellers or tax collectors or fundraisers?

The marketing director caught my eye and gave me an inquisitive look. I raised a thumb and made an asinine gesture meant to evoke a phone and a finger dialing, and then hurried out to the street.

By the time I made it to the restaurant, my boss and a couple of other staff members had already gotten appetizers. Edna was drinking from a wine glass so enormous I thought someone must have given it to her as a gag, or as some odd gesture toward the guest of honor. A candle in a glass globe lit her face just as dramatically as had the light on the lectern. She stood when the director introduced me, took my hand in both of hers, and gave a big smile and long look, her eyes black and glinting. Up close she didn't entirely resemble her author photograph. Her hair was obviously dyed, her face wrinkled and powdered. She looked her age, in other words, though she was as striking as any seventy-one-year-old I'd ever met, and the years didn't seem to matter to her: Her dress was tight and sleeveless, sheer to midway down her dark bra, nearly as revealing as those photographs on the covers of her early novels.

I praised her lecture even more lavishly than I had Albee's, saying how refreshing it was to hear something so thoughtful and complex, not just another off-the-cuff discussion of her development as a writer. Her smile disappeared. "I thought it was supposed to be a formal lecture," she said. "Do you mean to tell me I could have just talked about myself? Is that what Albee did?"

"It's just that your talk was so sophisticated," I said. "It was pitched at a higher level."

She blinked her big dark eyes, smiled again, and said, "Ah, so you're a writer, too."

I nodded, shrugged, looked down at my shoes, more flattered than I wanted to reveal. "Edward told me to say hello."

"A lovely man," she said, and once again I thought how unjustified his words had been, how mean-spirited and undeserved.

We sat, and while I looked over the menu, Edna returned to the conversation I'd interrupted, which, I quickly gathered, was about her hotel room. The desk clerk had originally put her in a room facing Broadway, though she'd told him specifically she wanted the quietest room they had. "It sounded as if the lorries were driving right through the windows," she said. When she complained, the clerk moved her to a room facing the back of the building. Yes, it was quieter, but there was still the noise of fans on the rooftop next door, and people shouting in a nearby park, and some hotel employee who kept passing by with a hand cart that rattled on the sidewalk. "No, no, it just wouldn't do." She called the desk and had a cot brought up, and then got a housekeeper to help her take the mattress off the bed and prop it against the window. She set up the cot at the other end of the room, leaving just enough space to slip in and out the door. Now, with luck, she'd sleep an hour, maybe two.

All around me were people in suits and slinky dresses eating salmon and flashing credit cards, and for the first time since I'd started the job I felt comfortable in my dress shirt and slacks. The waiter, a dozen years my senior, with a tidy mustache and a hard-lived, hollow face, came by to take my order, bowing slightly, hands behind his back, asking if the gentleman would care for a drink. Normally his solicitousness would have embarrassed me, but now I put on a thoughtful expression, gestured across the table, and said, "Whatever Edna's having." To my delight, the wine came out in just as enormous a glass. Edna glanced at it with approval. Then she talked about the Seattle hotel she'd stayed in the night before. She'd been there several times in the past, and they knew her well enough not to have to ask what room she wanted. They had a special one, very infrequently requested, in a strange corner of the top floor, facing no streets or courtyards, far from the elevator shaft and the housekeeping closet. "No windows at all," she said. "No noise, no light. It's like a tomb. How wonderful."

So maybe she was eccentric, I thought. But mad ... that was still going too far. I mentioned my own sleep trouble, and she gave me a sympathetic look, and even reached across the table and patted my hand. "A shame when it comes on so early," she said. "You must be a bachelor, then." I flushed, and shrugged again, and she stared at me hard with those dark, flashing eyes. "Not for long, I have a feeling." She winked.

For the next hour Edna and I talked mostly about sleep troubles, while my boss and the other staff members had their own conversation, which, when I caught snippets of it, was about movies or television. They seemed relieved to be free of their official duties; they couldn't get away from the heart of contemporary letters fast enough. When the waiter came again they ordered only salads, thinking about their weight or our budget. Edna asked about nearly every dish on the menu, and then told the waiter to surprise her. "Whatever's the best you've got." I ordered something with truffles, and she sat up straighter, her fiery hair glimmering in the dining room's dim light. "Delightful," she said. "The food of kings."

When our food came we discussed sleeping pills and therapeutic pillows and debated the value of earplugs and eye masks, and every so often she'd say, "Ach, I'd sleep in a tomb if I could." I asked about her swimming lessons in Tucson, and she told me at length about her terrible fear of water, how often she imagined herself drowning, how she'd lived within a day's drive of the sea her entire life but had never gone in past her ankles. There was a psychiatrist in Tucson who was supposed to be an expert in phobias, though as she described his methods – a combination of hypnosis, massage, and herbal therapy – he sounded more and more like a charlatan. "I only wish I were flying there first class," she said. "If only you could have cajoled the airline a bit more."

The longer she went on, the more I began to see Albee's point. She may very well have been mad – she was certainly obsessive and neurotic – but I found her madness addictive, and brilliant, and I wanted a dose of it for myself. Faced with her wild, glittering eyes, I couldn't help but picture Albee's slumped shoulders and Stephen Jay Gould's sour, grouchy frown. There was no question which was most appealing. When I asked what she was working on now, her face took on a faraway, dreamy expression, and she told me in great detail about the novel she'd just finished, about a psychotic who terrorizes an Irish village, a story exploring the effect of evil on ordinary people. It was based on real events, and in doing her research she'd delved so deeply into the horrors of insanity and violence she sometimes feared she'd never find her way out. It scared her even now, she said. When she thought about the years she'd spent inside this character's head, she couldn't help but shiver.

But even as she described the difficulty of writing the book, there was deep pleasure in her voice, a suggestion that she wouldn't have traded the experience for anything, that she couldn't have kept herself from writing it if she'd tried. For her, there seemed to be no competition between life and literature; she threw herself into both with equal vigor and equal abandon. And even if I didn't know it then, I took her words as permission to do the same, or at least to make the attempt. As she spoke, what I did know was that I was going to quit this job at the earliest opportunity, that I'd soon go back to teaching part-time and scraping by, that I wouldn't purchase any new furniture or clothes or move out of my basement apartment. I knew I'd soon go back to writing every day, that some things couldn't be compromised, that life had to be lived on my own terms. It felt as if I'd known these things all along, and that Edna had simply reminded me of promises I'd made and briefly forgotten. If only I could have stayed with her in that restaurant forever.

When she finished talking about the book, her face altered again, as if she'd come out of a trance, and her voice sped up. "I don't think I have another one in me," she said. "I'm finished for good now." She was finally wrung dry, she told me, too old to do anything else. It was more neurotic talk, and I didn't believe it any more than I believed the marketing director when she said she'd end up alone. Nor did I think she believed it herself. But I reassured her anyway, told her she had plenty of time, and that, by the way, she didn't look a day over fifty. Those black eyes flashed, red lips spread wide, and I could see the fierce young woman she'd been when she'd written novels racy enough to be banned in her home country and to force her into exile. I could see the woman who'd divorced early and had a reputation for slaying men in swinging '60s London, whose books had been adorned with erotic covers. That woman was right here in front of me, in a tight dress, her breasts half-exposed. For the first time in my life, I was turned on by someone old enough to be my grandmother.

The waiter cleared our plates, and my boss nervously scrutinized the bill. Budgets were no longer my concern. I wished

Edna a good night's sleep, and she wished me the same, and many more. Her mad, dark eyes twinkled with reflected candlelight. When we stood, she hugged me, her arms tight around my back, her blazing hair in my nose. "There's only one cure for it," she whispered. "I'm too old for it now, but you, you've got all the time in the world."

Outside the restaurant, the sidewalk was empty, the street nearly free of cars. The last bus of the evening was coming toward me. I was exhausted, and if I went home and fell into bed, I was sure I'd sleep straight through till morning. Instead, I searched for the nearest pay phone.

Oh, Edna. What trouble you caused.

I'm Your Man

If you want a lover I'll do anything you ask me to.
And if you want another kind of love I'll wear a mask for you.
–LEONARD COHEN

MY FIANCÉE LEFT ME FOR A DRAG KING NAMED DONNY Manicotti.

That sounds like the start of a joke, but it's not. It's my life.

I do find it funny now – from a distance of some years and happily married – and even at the time I recognized how ridiculous the situation was, though mostly I was bewildered and devastated. I'd always prided myself on being someone who appreciated the absurdity of life, who didn't take it too seriously, but there's an enormous difference, I discovered, between reading a Kafka novel or watching a Woody Allen movie and living inside of one.

Because our wedding was only a month away, because invitations had gone out and friends and family had bought plane tickets to Portland, because we'd written vows and picked out table settings and made mixed CDs for dancing, I believed our lives were on a track with a clear trajectory, and if I harbored any doubts about my fiancée or our relationship – she struggled with depression, she had a temper, she didn't like my friends – I buried them under pride in my role as groom and husband-to-be. I hadn't realized how important this threshold would feel to me, how badly I wanted to cross it. It would finally make me an adult, though I was already thirty years old.

My fiancée had recently left her job as marketing director of the literary organization and took a new one as features editor at the local gay paper. In her twenties, when she lived in New York, she'd identified as lesbian and dated only women. Since then she'd come to recognize herself as bisexual and even decided that she preferred being with men. And in the years before we'd met she'd been with a number of them, manly men at that: not only the flight instructor, but also a fisherman and a computer tech who liked fast cars. Too manly, she often said when we first started dating, describing the fights they'd had, the ways in which she'd chafed against their aggression, their attempts at dominance. I was the perfect balance, she told me during our first year together, a straight, sensitive guy who was boyish and bookish but liked the outdoors. She called me an honorary lesbian.

Still, she felt she was missing something from her New York days, a sense of identity that had come with being part of an outsider community. She liked being seen as a radical, a nonconformist, and getting married to a straight guy made her fear losing some essential part of herself. So when the job at the paper came open, she jumped at the opportunity, and I encouraged her, saying that I wanted her to have all sides of herself, that marrying me shouldn't come with unnecessary compromises. I encouraged her to hang out with her co-workers, who frequented a new, hip lesbian club – Tart, I think it was called – that had recently opened across the river. Have fun, I said, relishing the time alone, hours that I didn't have to worry about her depression or think about wedding details.

I first heard about Donny Manicotti a month or two before he turned my life upside down. He was a rising star in Portland, darling of the young lesbian scene, and my fiancée had done a story about his dance troupe, which performed weekly at Tart. He was the alter-ego of a young woman whose real name was Annemarie. She was Filipina, but on stage she dressed as a sleazy Italian tough in a sleeveless undershirt, pencil mustache, and fedora, a parody of the men I'd grown up around in New Jersey, whose children drove IROCs and Monte Carlos and slammed me into lockers during high school for no reason other than that they were bigger than me and that I couldn't fight back. In the pictures that accompanied my fiancée's story, I could see that Annemarie was sleek and sexy, with muscled shoulders and a cut jawline, bare stomach ripped over slim hips. I hadn't known there were such things as drag king troupes, and didn't really understand the appeal of cross-dressing, or of watching cross-dressers, but the idea of a roomful of young women whistling and writhing and getting drunk as a girl named Annemarie danced for them immediately turned me on.

My fiancée admitted that she had a crush on Donny – or really, on Annemarie. "Who wouldn't?" I said, and we both laughed it off as something innocent and expected, well within the boundaries of our bond. We couldn't live a whole life together and not have occasional attractions to other people, could we? When she headed off to Tart for the evening, I'd ask if Donny would be there. "Feel free to give him a kiss," I said. "Just don't fall in love."

BUT SHE DID exactly that. When she came home in the middle of the night and told me, her lips swollen, hair mussed, eyes flashing a crazy kind of light, my first instinct was to say, "But I told you not to." I was too stunned to come up with much else as she cried and apologized and said that she hadn't meant to, but that it just happened, and she couldn't help it now, and really I never should have encouraged her to go out dancing. For a day or so we talked about going to counseling. We even debated whether we could still get married and have an open relationship, and for the briefest moment the idea excited me, as I pictured myself sleeping with new women every week. An image flashed through my mind: my pale fiancée – now my wife – and the dark Annemarie tangled together in the sheets, and me, erection looming, climbing in. But the image didn't last long, because of course I knew Annemarie wouldn't want me coming anywhere near her with that erection, and really an open relationship would have meant me in bed alone, while my wife fucked a guy named Donny in the room next door.

By the time we came to the conclusion that we'd have to call off the wedding, that I'd have to move out of the condo my fiancée owned, she was insisting that our break-up wasn't just a consequence of her meeting someone new. She'd been dissatisfied for a long time, though maybe she hadn't been fully conscious of it until now. Her needs weren't being met, emotionally, sexually. I wasn't a full partner to her, I was too solitary and introverted, I never wanted to go shopping for curtains or think about painting the living room. I gave so much time and attention to my writing that I might as well have been having an affair. Plus, marriage was just too conventional for her, and now she found even the idea of being in a long-term heterosexual relationship smothering. And also, she said, pacing the living room I didn't want to think about painting, she thought she was really more attracted to women after all. The reasons kept coming, so many that I could only nod numbly and mutter, "I guess it's better to figure all this out now instead of in a year."

For three weeks I slept on a hide-a-bed in the guest room, first looking for an apartment and then waiting for it to be vacated, cleaned, and painted, while my ex-fiancée came and went, often spending nights away. I can no longer quite recall what the pain felt like – there are some benefits to memory's limitations – but I do remember that it had a physical component; I imagined that I'd suffered internal bruising, that something had ruptured inside of me, a less-than-vital organ but one that bled a lot. But I also remember wanting it to be *more* physical, wishing for my appendix to actually burst or a tumor to spring up on my spine, anything that would allow me to locate the pain in one place and isolate it, rather than shadow-box with the amorphous anguish that encompassed me like a cloud of poison gas, that was nowhere and everywhere. For the first time I understood those stories of spurned lovers chopping off a finger in order to ease their suffering, though all I could manage was to nick myself shaving.

At least there's no other penis inside her, I remember

thinking often during those three weeks, really believing this saved me, that if I'd been left for another man I would have been completely done in, that I couldn't have survived. Leaving me for a woman somehow didn't translate into betrayal, not then; rather, it struck me as an unexpected but necessary realignment of the world, one I didn't want but couldn't resist or even resent. If my ex-fiancée preferred women, what could I do? I chose to hang onto this reason for our break-up out of all those she'd provided, though when I pictured her and Annemarie together, as I did far too often, I didn't see a slim-hipped, sexy Filipina but a sleazy Italian wanna-be mobster, with a pencil mustache and slicked-back hair, a kid I'd hated in high school, who'd kicked my books and made me do push-ups in the hallway, whom I'd always thought would come to a violent, unhappy end – with which I'd be avenged – but who in fact was now plunging himself between the legs of the woman I was supposed to marry, and he did have a penis, and not even a plastic one, and it was thicker than mine, and had more endurance, and was inside her every moment of every day.

BY THE TIME I moved into my new apartment, I'd come to hate Donny Manicotti. All my anger, all my sadness and pain, I directed at him. Later, my therapist would take note of this, asking why Donny, and not my ex-fiancée, was the object of my rage. The truth is, at the time – a time I now see as one of partial, or maybe complete, loss of sanity – it didn't occur to me to be angry with my ex-fiancée, at least in part because I instinctively agreed with her when she hinted that the break-up was my fault, that I was to blame for failing to meet her emotional and sexual needs, though I didn't want to think about the ways I might have done this, preferring instead to believe that if she hadn't met Donny she would have forged ahead with our wedding, blissfully ignorant to my shortcomings, never realizing her needs weren't being met. Or else, if she did realize it, she would have told me so and asked me to fix it rather than leave me for a girl who dressed up as a boy. And I would have fixed it, or at least tried to fix it, showing myself to be a caring, thoughtful partner for at least a few months before falling back into old patterns. And by then we would have been married, we would have crossed that important threshold, and leaving me for drag kings wouldn't have been quite so easy. And anyway, where was it written that a marriage was supposed to fulfill every single need a person had?

In other words, I blamed myself, but I blamed Donny more. To make it clear, when I say Donny, I don't mean Annemarie. I was somehow able to separate the two in my mind, and while I hated Donny, I felt toward Annemarie a grudging sympathy, imagining she, too, was Donny's victim, and victim also of my ex-fiancée's substantial charms, which, when she let them loose, were hard to fend off. I was quite certain that my ex-fiancée had thrust herself on Annemarie the same way she'd thrust herself on me three years earlier, and that even if Annemarie had had second thoughts about getting involved with a woman engaged to a straight man, the sheer force of my ex-fiancée's will would have overwhelmed them. And now it was Annemarie who'd have to cope with my ex-fiancée's depression and her temper, Annemarie whose friends would be the object of my ex-fiancée's skeptical scrutiny, Annemarie who'd have to worry about whether or not she was meeting my ex-fiancée's needs.

So even though it was she who was now in the bed I'd shared with my ex-fiancée – and I still had flashes of them together, pale body tangled with dark – I recognized Annemarie as a human being: selfish, maybe, impulsive and reckless, but also, like the rest of us, frail and vulnerable and destined to suffer. Donny, on the other hand, was a monster. Or, rather, he was the local embodiment of a monstrousness I'd seen around me since high school, a teenage male aggressiveness that showed no compassion, no humility, that laughed at other people's pain, that was all dick and no heart. And of course this monstrousness wasn't relegated only to teenagers; if it was, it wouldn't be so infuriating, or so dangerous. But I saw it on the news every night –

this was a year after we'd invaded Iraq – and in just about every program on TV, cop shows, law dramas, sitcoms, all of them full of roving dicks wreaking havoc. I'd seen it far more often in New Jersey than in Oregon – once, during a Little League game, I'd watched the opposing coach beat and kick and stomp a thirteen-year-old umpire unconscious for making a questionable call – and that was part of what had kept me out west for so long. But of course the monstrousness was here, too, in suited businessmen downtown, in sports bars and rock clubs, in grocery stores, even, and though I mostly kept it hidden from others, I saw it often enough in myself, particularly while driving on the freeway, where I'd shout and swear at someone who cut me off, or refuse to let a woman in a Jeep merge in front of me – and in these moments it felt as if there were just me and my dick and no one else in the world.

I'd tried to quell this part of myself over the past three years, after hearing my ex-fiancée's stories about the men she'd dated before me, the pilot and the fisherman whose teenage boy dickness had eventually sparked screaming matches and tears, who hadn't been dubbed honorary lesbians, who hadn't lasted more than a few months in her bed. I was sensitive by nature, but during this time I actively worked to nip insensitivity in the bud, and any that remained went underground. Often enough, during my ex-fiancée's bouts of depression, I wanted to shake her or ignore her or tell her to get over herself, I wanted to strip off her clothes and remind her of *my* needs, but instead I comforted and coddled, tiptoeing around her, setting aside dick in favor of heart, or really, a semblance of heart, a mask of compassion that hid impatience and frustration and selfish desire. And as a result, I can see now, I was only partly there in the room with her, present only on the surface, while underneath there was this percolating dick, suppressed or submerged, for the sake, I thought, of love and soon-to-be marriage, for the sake of my future.

I didn't appreciate the irony, then, of Donny Manicotti stepping into the space I'd vacated, an imaginary dick taking the place of my real one, which I'd mistakenly hidden away, thinking it was a liability. It was beyond humiliating to have a parody of manliness supplant the absence of my own, and I couldn't bear the idea that Donny–Annemarie, really, though this I wasn't willing to face–was both more assertive in bed and more willing to talk about his feelings, a fuck machine who was happy to shop for curtains and pick out paint colors. If only I'd known what my ex-fiancée had really wanted, I could have given her the Donny side of myself, the New Jersey side; I could have shown her what a dick I could really be.

The truth was, though, that during my time with my ex-fiancée, I'd been afraid to be myself, in part because it would have opened me up to rejection, in part because it would have meant admitting to myself that I had doubts about our relationship, and about the future I'd envisioned. From a distance I can say with some certainty that if I had shown myself fully, we would have broken up much sooner than we had; I would have said what I often thought, which was that I believed some of her depressive episodes to be self-indulgent, an excuse not to take responsibility for her life; I would have said that her temper made me nervous, always worried I'd say the wrong thing, so that I said only what I thought she wanted to hear; I would have told her that to dislike my friends was to dislike an essential part of me that couldn't be compromised. And maybe it would have been easier if I had said all these things, if we had broken up two and a half years earlier and saved ourselves all this difficulty and pain; but at the time I was so desperate to hang onto the vision of life I'd constructed that I believed anything, everything, was up for compromise.

IN THE FIRST couple of months after I moved out of my ex-fiancée's condo, however, I couldn't see any of this clearly. Being myself was what had caused all this trouble, as far as I understood, and instead I wished only that I could be someone else, the way a sweet girl named Annemarie could become a sleazy asshole named Donny Manicotti. I was obsessed with Donny, I'll admit, but that obsession arose in part from the power I perceived in transformation, in choosing to be a particular way and then being that way, as if identity were simply a consequence of will. I'd often hidden myself, but I hadn't ever done so deliberately, adopting a persona to cover the one that embarrassed me or caused me shame. I studied the pictures on Donny's website, imagining I was doing so out of hatred and rage and the need to vent my fury, and even parked my car outside Tart one Sunday night, when his troupe was scheduled to perform. It's somewhat mortifying to think about now, a jilted, half-crazed man hunched down in a car, drinking from a bottle wrapped in a paper bag, waiting for his ex and her new lover to appear. All I'd transformed into was a sad cliché.

I may have imagined myself starting a confrontation, or following them home, a menacing presence outside the condo, but of course I wouldn't have actually done either of those things. What I really wanted, I think, was to understand the nature of Donny's power and appeal. Why were women drawn to him? There were so many streaming into the club that night – a windowless concrete-block building marked only by a spray-painted purple diamond on its black door, the rest painted an industrial green – most of them in their twenties and early thirties, dressed in their finest, the butch girls in crisp T-shirts and baggy jeans and stiff yellow workboots, the feminine ones in tank tops and billowing skirts and sandals, all laughing and bumping hips and handing over their cover charge. Most of these women didn't even like men, so why pay five bucks to watch a troupe of their own playing them on stage, and not even nice men at that?

> I'll prove the prettier fellow of the two
> And wear my dagger with the braver grace,
> And speak between the change of man and boy
> With a reed voice, and turn two mincing steps
> Into a manly stride, and speak of frays
> Like a fine, bragging youth, and tell quaint lies
> How honorable ladies sought my love,

> Which I denying, they fell sick and died –
> I could not do withall! Then I'll repent,
> And wish, for all that, that I had not killed them;
> And twenty of these puny lies I'll tell,
> That men shall swear I have discontinued school
> Above a twelvemonth. I have within my mind
> A thousand raw tricks of these bragging Jacks,
> Which I will practice.

That's Portia, in *The Merchant of Venice*, just before donning a man's clothes, in what is probably the most famous scene of female cross-dressing in all of literature. These lines, of course, didn't occur to me as I was sitting in the car outside Tart; I was too drunk, then, too forlorn to take solace in Shakespeare. But now, they point to something I'd failed to understand. They were lines Donny himself might have spoken, because of course he wasn't adopting male aggression as much as mocking it, showing his adoring fans that real power rested with them, with their intelligence and savvy and the steadiness that comes from not having a penis.

Portia recognizes that her future husband and his friends are incapable of saving Antonio's pound of flesh, and taking matters into her own hands, she impersonates a lawyer, presenting an argument, brilliant and manipulative, that causes the moneylender Shylock to give up his suit. And she's able to do so because she has men's number. She sees straight through their boasting and their bravado, understands their poses, their need for attention and camaraderie, their displays of violence, and knowing all this she becomes a better man than any of them. She ties Shylock into knots, poor Shylock who only wants the revenge he deserves, for being spit on, for having his daughter taken away, for having his usury fees undercut by Christian generosity, for thousands of years of persecution, honest, bitter Shylock with whom I would have identified hunched down in my car in a parking lot littered with broken glass, taking sips of cheap scotch, if I'd been in any place at all to think about literature then, if I hadn't instead been focused on the women streaming into Tart, wanting to tell them that Donny wasn't anything like a real man but rather a composite of the worst in men, that if even the smallest part of them was attracted to male attributes, I was the one they should come talk to, me who was truly sensitive and bookish with a relatively small measure of dickness I usually kept hidden, me who'd been dubbed an honorary lesbian, who might as well have been a lesbian dressed up as a man, though I did in fact have a penis, and in my bitterness and rage, I would have liked to stick it in as many of those women as I could.

And then I saw my ex-fiancée, running across the street awkwardly in heels, holding her hair against the breeze, wearing a skirt and tight sweater she'd worn on one of our early dates, looking pale and drawn and nervous as she took her place at the back of the line, which now wrapped around the club and inched forward slowly. She was alone. Of course the troupe must have already been inside, going through whatever contortions that transformed them from girls named Annemarie and Jill and Christine into Donny, Tony, Vito. In my ex-fiancée's fidgety stance, her impatient shuffling through her purse, the way she craned her neck to see around the corner of the building, I recognized a familiar agitation, one I knew could easily flare into anger, and I imagined her looking at all the women in front of her and thinking jealous thoughts: *All these bitches better stay away from my man*, or, *They all want Donny, but he's mine*. I couldn't imagine her ever thinking that about me. *They all want Scott, but he's mine*. The idea would have made me laugh if I hadn't been so distraught and depressed, but in my vindictiveness I did appreciate that in leaving me for another woman she'd stepped right into the most stereotypical of heterosexual power dynamics, one of jealousy and competitiveness and the constant threat of infidelity.

At the same time, because I still loved her and didn't yet believe it was possible not to see her as my future – that without her I *had* no future – I also felt sorry for the agitation Donny was causing her, and the potential heartbreak, and a part of me felt a faint twinge of hope, telling myself to bide my time, to wait her out. Soon enough she'd come to discover Donny's true nature, the destructive force of his dickness, and she'd remember that what she really wanted was an honorary lesbian, a sensitive boyish writer who coddled her and pretended never to be irritated with her self-indulgence or frustrated by her temper. And that part of me wanted to call to her now, to tell her that she could avoid all this agitation if she wanted, that the future we'd planned hadn't been erased, only postponed.

But then she turned her head, and though her eyes drifted past without seeing me – my car was tucked between two others, and I was so low in the seat only the top of my head would have been visible – I filled instantly with the deepest shame I've ever felt in my life. I was astonished at myself, sitting in a car outside a lesbian club, with a bottle of booze in my lap, imagining my ex-fiancée returning to me, believing we still had a future together, when she was in fact waiting to see her new lover, a girl named Annemarie who dressed up as a boy named Donny. How undignified. How pathetic. I hunched lower in the car, and soon I was shaking with sobs. I had no pride left, I was done in whether there was another penis inside her or not. Maybe this was a brief return of sanity, or at least of clarity, and I couldn't believe what my life had come to. In fact, I said to myself, I can't believe it, this isn't real, but there I was in the car, crying, and outside a line of women were waiting to get into the club. I could hear their talk and laughter, but I wouldn't look at them again, I wouldn't raise my head until I was sure they were all inside. And then I put the car into gear and rolled away, glass shards crunching under my tires. Behind me Donny sneered and shimmied his skinny hips.

THIS WHOLE TIME I kept in touch with my ex-fiancée, or rather, she kept in touch with me, checking in by phone every few days, coming by my apartment once or twice a week. She did so out of genuine compassion; she really did care about me, she said, our time together had meant so much to her, and she, too, was suffering over the loss. All of this I believed then, and still believe now – she didn't want me to be in pain, she really wished things could have turned out otherwise, and even now, years later, whenever we talk she still expresses sadness over what happened between us. She is, at her depths, a kind and loyal person, and since fully extracting ourselves from the tangle of love and almost-marriage, she has in fact been one of the most supportive friends I've ever had.

But as much as she cared about my feelings, she was also looking out for her own. She didn't want to feel guilty. She didn't want to take responsibility for causing me pain. Whenever I suggested that our break-up was her doing, she reminded me of how I hadn't met her needs, how my devotion to writing had been like my having another relationship, how, really, I'd been just as responsible – if not more so – as she had. And because I couldn't believe our future together was really over, I went along with this line of thinking, agreeing that the break-up had been mutual. I even told other people so, though when I tried to explain this mutuality to my therapist, she cocked her head and looked at me with a sad sort of amusement. "Being devoted to writing is not the same as falling in love with another person," she said, slowly, as if I were new to the language and might not catch her meaning. "It's okay to feel betrayed. It's okay to be angry."

Still, whenever I was with my ex-fiancée, I maintained the illusion that I agreed our break-up was mutual, that we'd had a great relationship that had run its course, that it was the right thing for both of us to move on, that it was sad, yes, something neither of us had wanted, but something that had been inevitable and necessary. And even then a small part of me – the quiet, rational, non-insane part – did believe that it was inevitable and necessary, that I'd dodged a bullet, that if she hadn't left me a month before our wedding, then surely she would have left me a month after, or six months, or a year, and the pain and humiliation would have been ten times worse. But the rest of me, the very insane, despairing part, kept a separate narrative running through my mind, one that said our break-up hadn't been mutual at all, that it was something I'd never have chosen, and also that it was temporary. And I believed that if I could just hide this broken, raging part of myself, my ex-fiancée would sooner or later come to her senses, and we'd find our way back onto the tracks we'd slipped off, we'd once again be rolling down the path to the only future that made any sense to me.

I'm doing okay, I'd say on the phone. It's hard, but I'm managing. I miss you, and I can't believe we can't be together, but it's the right thing, we've got to be who we really are, and I don't regret a second of the last three years.

When my ex-fiancée came to visit me at my apartment, we'd sit close together on the sofa, close enough that our legs touched, and sometimes we'd even put our arms around each other and cuddle, and then – I can hardly believe this even now – she'd tell me about her relationship with Annemarie. It wasn't going well. How could it? My ex had cancelled a wedding to be with her, had projected onto her all her hopes for her needs being met, and yet they hardly knew each other, they were only at the stage of testing out the waters, and there was far too much pressure for Annemarie. They'd be out having a good time, and then my ex would get sad, but instead of comforting her, Annemarie would want to go off and be with her friends. And when they were with her friends, she hardly paid any attention to my ex, she was too busy playing Donny, being pushy and loud and the center of attention, though that wasn't really her, my ex said, inside she was sweet and gentle and even a bit timid – particularly in bed, to my ex's dismay – and it drove my ex crazy to see her acting so out of character, or in character, really, so obviously trying to make up for her insecurities and weaknesses, but failing to recognize that my ex needed her to just be herself. She didn't fall for Donny, after all; she'd fallen for Annemarie.

Now I have to believe that my ex-fiancée must have been

in a state of semi-insanity herself to have told me all these things, and to imagine that I cared. And indeed I did pretend to care, trying to comfort her, rubbing her shoulder, telling her to give it some time; relationships had to develop, and of course not all relationships could be as good as ours had been, which really had been a wonderful relationship, even if it had been meant to last only three years. Inside, of course, I was gleeful in my deluded way, envisioning the fights she and Donny would soon have, and the words she'd say when she asked me to take her back, and the phone calls I'd make to my parents and friends, giving them a new date for the wedding, pretending that the break-up hadn't been terribly serious, just a few pre-marriage jitters, though I knew my parents would see right through my cheerful voice, and my friends would shake their heads and give up on me, because I'd chosen a woman who didn't want them in my life.

When my ex-fiancée showed up at my apartment, crying, late one night while I was lying on my couch drinking and reading, I took her in my arms as I'd taken her in my arms so many times before, and rubbed her hair the way I'd always done when she cried, even those times when I thought she was being melodramatic and self-indulgent, when I wanted to shake her or ignore her or tell her to get over herself. Now, as she told me how mean Annemarie had been to her – no, not Annemarie, I thought: Donny – how insensitive she'd been, how she hadn't understood my ex's needs at all, had in fact misrepresented herself as a kind, caring person, I rubbed her hair and held her and what I really wanted was to strip off her clothes and haul her into my bachelor's bed, I wanted to open her legs and jam myself between them, to show her what she'd been missing.

"I'm sorry," she said, as we settled onto my couch. She wiped her eyes, and tucked her feet beneath her, and lay her head on my shoulder, and my cat, whom she hadn't liked any more than my friends, jumped up and curled beside us. My attic apartment had more charm than the basement apartment I'd lived in when we'd first gotten together, splintered fir floor instead of grimy carpet, dormer windows, a leather couch, skylight over the bed – a classy, if shabby, bachelor pad in which to start over again, in which to pretend we'd never been apart. "I shouldn't have come to you with this," she said. "It's not right."

"Who else would you go to?" I said. "I know you better than anyone."

She could stay, I said, if she didn't want to be alone, if she needed to be away from the condo for a night, to be in a place free of drama and confusion. I may even have said she could have my bed, and I'd sleep on the couch. And I might have even talked her into it, she might have agreed to stay – I can no longer remember – but then her cell phone rang, and of course it was Donny, Donny who'd ruined my life, Donny who'd slammed me into lockers, Donny who got whatever he wanted whenever he wanted it. My ex-fiancée took the call, mouthed thanks, and slipped out the door. I slammed the book I'd been reading so hard onto the splintered floorboards that I broke the spine.

WHEN ANNEMARIE AND my ex finally did break up, after a month or a month and a half of fighting, I feigned sympathy and also indifference, as if this weren't what I'd been hoping for, as if I didn't feel vindicated, as if the news didn't feed my deluded hopes. I continued to act as if our break-up had been inevitable and necessary, as if we'd had a great relationship that had run its course; and if my ex ever hinted at regret or at the idea of getting back together, I'd play dumb and act as if I didn't hear her. I wanted to give it time, to let momentum build, until she decided she could no longer live without me – or, more likely, until one night when we found ourselves heated up and horny, taking off our clothes and diving into bed.

In the meantime we may as well have been dating, seeing each other two or three times a week, going to movies or getting dinner, taking walks in Forest Park, and though we didn't have sex we were as intimate as lovers, sometimes even holding hands in a darkened theater or on a canopied trail, laughing and tickling each other, and during all this time I managed not to say what was on my mind: that she'd broken me and could put me back together if she wanted, that without her I had no future, that I didn't believe for a second that our break-up had been inevitable or necessary – or mutual, for that matter. And maybe I didn't say these things because I thought she felt them, too, or that she could read them in my sad smile or in the contours of my palm when we held hands. Outwardly I appeared perfectly content with our new way of being together. We were the closest of friends, intimate, physical, even – though not erotically so – but not dependent on each other for the fulfillment of all our needs. There were no expectations of buying curtains or choosing paint colors, though now that was exactly what I wanted to do. I had colors in mind and knew where to look for curtains. I'd even started doing push-ups and sit-ups, and though there wasn't yet any definition to my muscles, they were beginning to firm up. I'd be everything my ex had imagined Donny could be, and more.

After one of our walks in the woods, we went back to the condo to have a glass of water, and my ex-fiancée's two cats, whom I'd once thought of as my cats, too, flitted around us, happy, I thought, to be rid of Donny, to have the family together again. I must have followed them into the bedroom, and somehow – I no longer remember this clearly, and can't quite imagine the progression of events – my ex and I ended up on her bed together, our old bed, lying on top of the covers, side by side, holding hands, our faces only inches from each other. We were close enough, in fact, that I could smell the familiar citrus scent of her lotion and could see that her lips were chapped and that a corner of the lower one was swollen. I asked her about it, mostly as an excuse to reach out and touch the lip with the tip of my finger, and what I was thinking was that now would be the moment when I'd kiss that lip again, and soon after, our clothes would disappear, as would the last two months – and it would seem as if none of this had ever happened, as if Donny Manicotti had been a dream, a figment of my imagination, a character in a story I'd scrapped before finishing a draft.

But then my ex-fiancée laughed, and covered her lip with a hand, and said, "Oh God, can you see that?"

She'd gone out to Tart with some co-workers the night before, and God, she'd gotten so drunk, and she and the paper's graphic designer had started making out in the middle of the dance floor, and the designer had accidentally bitten her lip. This was actually the third time they'd hooked up, she told me, with giddy, girlish excitement, as if I'd be thrilled for her, as if I really had become the neuter I pretended to be. The first couple of times she'd thought it was just casual; they were attracted to each other but they'd both recently come out of long relationships and they just wanted to have a good time. But last night they'd gone home together, and now she didn't know, maybe it could be more than just casual, maybe some real feelings were developing. She was still holding my hand as she told me all this, and I couldn't believe it; my cloud of insanity had cleared again, and the rationality that took its place left me flabbergasted and indignant. How could I lie on a bed with this woman who'd destroyed me, who continued to destroy me without any hesitation? I felt the person I'd suppressed for the past two months welling up inside me; it was as if he were exploding through my chest, or leaking out my pores. I wanted to shout and tear the walls down, though all I actually did was pull my hand away and ball it into a fist. But somehow my ex-fiancée didn't notice any change. It was as if she didn't see me at all. She just kept going on and on about the designer, who was so sweet, she said, so gentle and funny and caring. "She's just like you," she said. "Only without the penis."

She didn't want an honorary lesbian. She wanted a real one. Or more precisely, she wanted someone, anyone, other than me. The fact of it sent me reeling. I jumped off the bed and hid my face.

"Are you crying?" she said, with an innocence that could

have arisen only from a set of delusions as crazy as my own. "What's the matter?" she called after me as I fled the condo.

ONLY AFTER THIS did I begin to release the anger I'd kept inside, the anger my therapist told me I deserved to feel, that she said would cripple me if I kept it submerged or displaced it onto Donny Manicotti, who by this time really had become more a figment of my imagination than even a fictional stage character or the alter-ego of an actual person who'd actually slept with my ex-fiancée. And when I finally did begin to let the anger out, it shocked me. I'd never felt it so strongly before, or never allowed myself to feel it, though even then it often came out in my car, the place where anger had always felt most natural. As I drove to my teaching job, I shouted at the top of my lungs, I pounded the steering wheel, I called my ex-fiancée the dirtiest names I could think of, or really just strings of obscenities that turned into nasty gibberish – "fuckingcuntwhorebitchfuckingdykecuntwhore!" – and laid on the horn for ten or fifteen seconds when a woman in a minivan tried to merge in front of me.

My ex-fiancée was just as shocked by the sudden surge of my anger, as well as by its force. It took her completely off-guard, which is understandable since it came after such delay, after I'd hidden it for so long. When I expressed it over the phone, she tried to be angry back, reminding me of all the ways in which I hadn't fulfilled her needs, but now I wasn't willing to listen, I didn't care about her needs, I said, and it was bullshit to equate my devotion to writing with her falling in love with someone else, there was no equivalence, one thing was outright betrayal and the other wasn't. The break-up wasn't mutual, I wouldn't accept responsibility for it any longer, she'd just have to live with the guilt or go on believing a narrative that was hers alone. The very idea that she could destroy the future I'd been counting on and then try to blame it on me sent me into such a rage that I kicked a hole in my flimsy bathroom door.

We didn't speak for a month. I seethed and snarled and

stomped through my apartment alone, I punched pillows and shouted in the shower and threw more books, and my cat, who'd been menaced by my ex-fiancée's cats the whole time we'd lived together, cowered in a corner. I drank and drove fast and looked straight into the face of despair and the blank, empty space where my future had once been. I kept doing push-ups and sit-ups and went hiking up the steepest trails I could find, savoring the burn in my legs. I'd finally entered manhood, I decided, I was now an adult, and it was an awful, brutal place to be, but it felt better than being stuffed down inside a child. Every last ounce of my dickness was out and on display, and I never wanted to hide it again.

One night, in my fury, in my madness – a clear-eyed sort of madness, unlike the muddle of the past two months – I stumbled into a nearby bar. I wanted to fuck someone or something, anyone or anything, the walls, the ground, I would have plunged my dick straight through the earth if I could have. I no longer wanted to be a sensitive, boyish, bookish, honorary lesbian, I wanted to be a man, I wanted to be Donny, I wanted to take whatever I fancied as if I deserved it. I felt the full power of my anger, the freedom to be whoever I chose to be, and for a moment I disconnected from the pain of my ex-fiancée leaving me: that was something that had happened to another person, or else it had happened in order to free me into being the dick I really was. Around me billiards cracked and bottles clinked and smoke billowed, and I walked through the bar in full possession of my irrepressible desire, my boundless capacity for harm, and stopped in front of the first woman who made eye contact and smiled. All I can remember of her now is dark curly hair, thin lips, a blunt chin.

Could I buy her a drink?

She laughed, and thanked me, and said sorry, and fluttered her fingers in front of my face. On one of them, a wedding ring gleamed.

I left the bar and walked home, and if I'd glanced to the

side to catch my reflection in a darkened storefront window – I don't recall doing so – I suppose I would have seen what that married woman had seen: a sensitive, boyish thirty-one-year-old, with narrow shoulders and bony chest, a sweet guy, full of patience, rarely angry, in touch with his feminine side, not terribly aggressive in bed, recently heartbroken, at a loss as to what to do with the rest of his life.

OUR BREAK-UP WAS inevitable and necessary. Our marriage would have been brief and unhappy, and every time I think about the canceled wedding now I do so with relief. It helps that I'm married to a woman about whom I have no doubts, who doesn't have a temper and doesn't get jealous of my devotion to writing. My ex-fiancée and I, still in touch after all these years, can care about each other from a distance now, without judgment or frustration, without fretting over gaps in fulfillment, without wishing for something more or something different. One of the most lucid things she said to me during our months of madness was, "If we stayed together I would have always wanted to change you. But I like who you are too much for that."

And even at the height of my anger, I understood what she meant, and knew that despite all the ways she was making me suffer, there was an element of compassion in her leaving me. When it came down to a choice between love and identity, I wasn't able to make a rational decision, so she did it for me. I'm grateful for it now, and maybe the first seeds of that gratitude were what caused my anger to diffuse so quickly. Or more likely, anger simply isn't an emotion that comes naturally to me, and when I do experience it, I want to be done with it as quickly as possible. My Donny side, my New Jersey side, isn't really a full side, but just a small sliver of my personality, one usually reserved for cursing at people in traffic. Why else would I still be living in Oregon after more than a dozen years?

Whatever the reason, I stopped shouting and throwing things after a month or so. I began answering my ex-fiancée's phone calls again, and we spoke to each other civilly, gently, even, consciously tender with each other's feelings. We both laughed uneasily at the thought of our previous madness. We wished each other well. We started off on our separate paths. On the phone she told me, "I can appreciate who you are so much more now that I don't have to imagine us being together forever."

Who was I, then? Of all others, that was the most crucial question, wasn't it, the only one with which I could head into any kind of fulfilling future. At the time it was also the one I felt least able to answer. It's a question I've struggled with ever since, and it's the reason, I suppose, why I am writing this now.

Here's an answer, of sorts:

About three months after I moved out of my ex-fiancée's condo, I was taking a walk in my neighborhood park. It was a warm, early September afternoon, and because I hadn't been out much lately – I hadn't, in fact, left my bed much – the sunlight on my face had a searing quality, as if it were not only drying the tears I'd recently shed but evaporating some of the skin, too. The grass was brown and crispy, the duck pond murky with algae, the air so free of moisture that it felt strangely effortless to put one foot in front of the other. I wouldn't say I was feeling hopeful, or anything close, but it was the first time in a long while that I wasn't actively resisting the reality I'd found myself inhabiting. It would still be some time before I fully accepted that this was actually my life, but here was an initial inkling that acceptance was even possible.

And when I came around a corner, there in front of me was Annemarie. I recognized her instantly, though she wasn't wearing a pencil mustache or fedora. Her hair was up in short spikes rather than slicked back, a pair of sunglasses propped on top. She wore a tank top and running shorts, and her shoulders and thighs were cut with ribbony muscle. She was on a cell phone, laughing – with a new lover, I thought – and she had a dog on a leash, a big white husky who was sniffing the base of a nearby tree.

I could have turned around and walked the other way. I

don't know why I didn't. Curiosity, maybe, or some sense that this, too, was inevitable and necessary, that I was going to face something I'd been avoiding for too long. It's hard to pin down the strange swirl of emotion I felt as I walked toward her. Anger was certainly in the mix; I no longer thought of Annemarie and Donny separately, but rather as a tag-team of homewreckers. But I also felt an odd sense of giddiness the closer I got, and also of arousal at the sight of those dark, ripped shoulders, those strong hands that had pinned my ex-fiancée's pale body down. And with these feelings came a thought that had been absent from my mind for so long that I'd almost forgotten it, and I welcomed it like an old friend: How ridiculous life was! How wonderfully absurd!

She was looking at the dog, laughing into her phone, and glanced up only when I was a few feet from her. And then she flinched and quickly looked away. But before she did I caught her expression, wide-eyed, with raised brows and tightly pressed lips, a look of horror and guilt and maybe even fear. There was no question that she knew who I was, and this surprised me more than anything. It had never occurred to me that my ex-fiancée would have shown Annemarie pictures of me, but of course she had, and of course she'd probably talked about me and our relationship to Annemarie in just as much detail as she'd talked about Annemarie to me.

We knew far too much about each other for us to be strangers. The giddiness was overwhelming now, it welled up in me just as the anger had welled up a month earlier, it was rising in my chest as a great guffaw. What I felt toward Annemarie then, more than anything else, was simple fellowship over all we shared. Affinity was just plain easier than antipathy. I wanted to clap her on the back or give her a hug. I wanted to ask how she'd dealt with my ex-fiancée's depression and temper. I wanted to know what it was like to dress up as a sleazy tough who didn't care about anyone but himself. I wanted to tell her I'd tried to become Donny, too, and failed.

But instead I pretended I had no idea who she was. Whether she believed it or knew I was pretending, I'm still not sure. In either case, her face relaxed, and she pretended, too. Evasion was easier even than goodwill; it was a gift we were giving each other, or maybe just a gift we were giving ourselves. The dog pulled her forward, and we passed within inches of each other, so close I heard the swish of her running shorts and caught the scent of her sweet, musky sweat, and then her laughter was behind me, fading away.

Leaving Portland

AFTER FIVE YEARS I HAD NOTHING BUT MIXED FEELINGS for the place, and in the late spring of 2004, I was ready to leave for good. My teaching career was going nowhere. My social life was stagnant. It was the second week of June, but still the sky was overcast. The clouds had settled on my shoulders. My teeth felt soggy.

This town is too sleepy, I thought. Too provincial. It lacked the east coast edge of my childhood, the rudeness and friction. There were too many gardeners. Too many bike riders. Too many dog owners. Too many beautiful young families with howling babies.

I'd had all these thoughts before. Every year or so I'd get sick of the rain and study maps and scour the internet for affordable apartments in New York, San Francisco, Chicago. I'd think about going back to school, finding a new career, becoming a nurse, a paralegal, an astrophysicist.

Then the sky would clear, and with light came the predictable transformative moment – a glimpse of Mt. Hood from the freeway, the reflection of downtown skyscrapers on the river, the laughter of good friends on a warm summer night. Suddenly I'd be struck dumb with gawking, Jersey-boy awe, imitating Kyle MacLachlan in *Twin Peaks*: "Look at those amazing trees." And for months I'd wonder how I could have imagined living anywhere else.

But this time was different. I'd really had it. I was getting out for sure. It wasn't just my career or my social life. It was heartbreak as well, canceled weddings and ex-fiancées sleeping with drag kings, an abundance of humiliation, pleading, and pain. Too much alternative lifestyle in this town, I thought. Too much yoga and acupuncture and self-discovery. Too many lesbians.

I couldn't afford to move to New York or San Francisco or Chicago. I'd spent all my money on a suit for the wedding, on engraved rings, on a non-refundable deposit for a honeymoon. Instead I made it only to the other side of town, up three flights of rickety stairs, closer to the clouds. I'd stay here at most a couple of months, I decided, and in the fall I'd move on. I opened Rand McNally at random and circled towns I'd never heard of–Rutland, New Hampshire; Galesburg, Illinois; Enid, Oklahoma.

In July, I turned thirty-one. The sky cleared, and the sunlight hurt my eyes. My attic steamed. I gave readings in empty rooms. A neighbor's dog snarled every time I walked past. Driving down Belmont Street, I came within inches of clipping a kid on a Schwinn and yelled in my best Jersey accent, "Next time I'll run you the fuck over!"

I spent an ugly night in a dive bar with pitchers of Hamm's, and in the morning both my elbows were mysteriously skinned, my sheets spotted with blood.

Fitchburg, Massachusetts. Bay City, Michigan. Beaufort, South Carolina.

I waited for the transformative moment, but it didn't come. I stared at Mt. Hood and shrugged. Oilslicks and floating trash marred the reflection of skyscrapers. The scabs on my elbows split whenever I bent my arms.

The date of my wedding arrived, and my parents flew out to distract me. I drove them to the beach, to the Gorge, to Mt. St. Helens, and they exclaimed over the beauty of the landscape and then tried to talk me into moving back to New Jersey. Their friend had an unmarried daughter I should meet. So pretty, so sweet. Jewish, too. Their exclamations contained hints of accusation, allegations of failure.

My ex-fiancée broke up with the drag king and started dating a graphic designer with a blue mohawk. I accepted a teaching job for the fall but swore I would leave in winter. Fifteen people showed up for a reading, twenty-five for the next. Whenever my neighbor's dog snarled at me, I snarled back.

In the fall, I was drunk most weekends but sober during the week. My students made fun of my wrinkled shirts and bloodshot eyes. They turned in stories with beautiful, transformative moments. Unrealistic, I wrote on their drafts. Reads like fantasy, like fairy-tale.

I contributed what little money I had to John Kerry's doomed presidential campaign. My book won an award, and I read to a nearly packed room. On the last day of fall semester, several of my students thanked me and wanted to shake my hand. One gave me a hug. I agreed to teach a class in winter and determined to head out in spring.

My elbows had healed and scarred over. My road atlas had disappeared under piles of books and student work. Over Christmas break I watched thirty-two movies, all of them hard-boiled crime dramas from the forties and fifties. The wind cut through my attic's splintered window frames.

In January, an ice storm made the streets sparkle. In February, Mt. St. Helens coughed smoke and ash, and I did my best to hide my amazement and wonder. In March, I ironed my shirts and finished a draft of a second story collection.

Ambivalence is sturdier than love, I decided, inertia more reliable than epiphany.

Spring came. Gardens bloomed. I was offered a full-time teaching job for the following year, and I accepted without hesitation. I sold the new book. I went on several dates. My ex-fiancée and her girlfriend made plans to move to San Francisco, and I wished them well.

Wet cherry blossoms plastered my car. My neighbor's dog

frolicked in the rain. Bike riders in waterproofs swerved recklessly through traffic. I opened Rand McNally to a page I'd dog-eared years before, the name "Portland" circled three times in fading blue ink.

Everywhere I turned those beautiful babies howled.

Pal Man

SIX MONTHS AFTER MY FIANCÉE LEFT ME, I BEGAN TO crawl out of the deep depression from which I'd once doubted I'd ever emerge. To my surprise, I found myself oddly restored, with renewed energy, as if awoken from a long, restful sleep. This energy was mostly of the sexual sort, but also creative, political, social. I'd wasted enough time, I decided. I was ready to stop wallowing in self-pity, to engage with life again: to find romance, yes, but also to be part of my community, to recognize my civic responsibility and take an active role in shaping the world in which I wanted to live. My awakening primarily involved reading newspapers again, seeing friends I'd neglected, and signing up for internet dating sites. But I also brought groceries to a food bank, gave fifty bucks to an Israeli peace organization, wrote letters to my senators and congressmen urging them to stop the war in Iraq, to end policies of torture and abuse, to support increased funding for the arts.

By the summer of 2005, soon after I'd turned thirty-two, I felt good enough about my re-entrance into the world, hopeful enough about my future, to sign up for a documentary filmmaking class offered by a local nonprofit. I had a genuine interest in documentary, saw it as a possible means to pursue my socio-political interests, but mostly I needed to get out of the apartment more and meet new people. Meet women, that is, and I figured a class on documentary filmmaking would be as good an opportunity as any, especially since internet dating hadn't panned out so far and because I was too shy to try salsa dancing. And on the first day of class I saw that I'd made a good decision. I was one of only two men in the room, and the women were mostly in their late twenties and early thirties, attractive and intellectual, potentially single.

The class met in an old warehouse in the industrial district of Southeast Portland, a location that had a secretive, romantic air, a meeting place for revolutionaries or dissidents. The teacher was a small, cheerful guy in shorts and flip-flops – my age, maybe a year or two younger – who'd already directed two full-length documentaries for PBS. I was immediately jealous, more so as it became clear that the women in the class were enamored of him, several staying after to ask follow-up questions, walking him to his car. I wanted to believe he was gay but saw nothing to indicate one way or another.

Soon, however, he won me over, too. He stressed the importance of community and collaboration. He didn't want us working alone. "One person's got the camera, another's got the editing software, another's got the idea," he said. I had no camera, no editing software, and not much in the way of ideas. But maybe I could help with writing scripts, I said. I offered myself up to work with anyone who needed a partner, and the teacher called out in his cheerful way, "Who wants a handsome young fellow with writing experience?"

To my delight, several of the women pitched me their ideas. One, who looked too much like one of my cousins to catch my interest, wanted to make a film about civil war reënactments. Interesting idea, I told her, but I'd have to pass. The most attractive woman in the group, a short-haired blonde with a tough, streetwise look and breath that smelled of cigarettes and fruity gum, planned to make a documentary about a luthier. Sounds great, I said, though I had no idea what a luthier was. I told myself I'd look it up when I got home and was ready to sign on, but then she mentioned her boyfriend. He was a musician, she said, so we wouldn't have to worry about the soundtrack. The way she mentioned him didn't make him sound expendable, someone she hoped to replace. I told her I'd think it over and let her know during the next class.

The third woman was cute and Japanese and far too young for me – nineteen or twenty, an undergrad film major at Portland State – but her idea, a Ken Burns-style historical survey of an old building at the edge of Chinatown, sounded dreary. My creative/socio-political energy won out over my sexual/romantic energy, and I turned her down.

I hadn't really noticed the fourth woman until she approached me with her idea. Her name was Laura – or at least that's what I'll call her – and she was dressed in slacks and silk blouse, as if she'd just come from her office job, though the class started at 8 p.m. She may have been plainer than the others, but she spoke with an intensity that made her face come alive, and every time she made a point she jabbed her palm with a nibbled fingernail. She intended to make a film profiling a Palestinian refugee. She knew one, living right here, a friend of a friend. She wanted to do something that mattered, she said, something that explored complex territory. I admired her thoughtfulness, her sincerity, and the shape of her ears. I waited for her to mention a boyfriend. She didn't. "I'll work on it by myself if I have to," she said, her voice taking a dismissive turn, her gaze drifting upward, as if she were now curious about the exposed steel beams overhead. "But if you're interested, I wouldn't mind the help."

Her indifference wounded me, and her tidy appearance made me feel shabby in my worn jeans and T-shirt, conscious of my underemployment – during summer I taught a single class, one night a week, and paid rent with my credit card – and the longing that had become my primary emotion since awakening from my despairing sleep made me say, before I'd quite thought it through, "Count me in."

Immediately her face opened up again, her indifference dropping away, and she gave me a smile that was sweet and awkwardly startled, as if she'd expected me to reject her and couldn't quite believe I hadn't. "I'm so glad," she said, and gripped my arm, firmly. "I think we'll work well together."

I had visions of us editing footage late at night, drinking wine, her nicely shaped ear close to my lips. "I agree," I said.

Our teacher came up to us and asked if we'd made a match. "A perfect one," Laura said, and smiled that same awkward, disbelieving smile.

Before we left for the evening, it occurred to me to say that I hoped she wasn't planning to make a polemic, or propaganda, something that took obvious sides. She looked at me curiously and told me not to worry. "We'll just let him tell his story," she said. And then her voice grew intense again, full of passion, as she described her intention of showing the human side of occupation and conflict, the complexities that people didn't get from reading the newspaper.

Our documentaries were supposed to be seven minutes long. How complex could we really get? I wondered for a moment whether I'd have been better off working on civil war reenactments or old buildings or luthiers. But then she grabbed my arm again. "I'm so excited," she said. "I'll call Samir tonight and set up a meeting."

ONLY AT THE next class session did my concerns begin to crystallize. Laura was in slacks and blouse again, hair down to her shoulders, looking elegant and out of place in the windowless warehouse, her pointy flats raising dust from the concrete floor, her posture stiff as she took a seat on one of the metal folding chairs stenciled on back with the name of a Presbyterian church. This time I asked if she'd just come from work, and looking at me as if I were slightly demented, she answered that she'd been home since four-thirty. Then she told me that Samir didn't want to be in our film. I was surprised to find myself relieved but forced my face into an expression of disappointment. "But it's even better," Laura said, leaning in, her intensity seeming aggressive now, even reckless – still attractive, maybe, but certain to get us into trouble. "He's got a friend who might be willing to do it. He's perfect. He's from Ramallah." She said the word with flawless inflection, accenting the second syllable, her tongue lingering on the *l* sound. "He threw rocks during the first intifada. Now he's in a wheelchair. The Israelis shot him."

Something about Laura had seemed familiar from the start, but only now did it hit me: She reminded me of my ex-fiancée. That's not to say she resembled my ex-fiancée, who in fact looked quite a bit like the short-haired blonde making a documentary about a luthier (which I hadn't yet looked up and which still could have been anything to me, a nuclear technician, or a hairless werewolf). But Laura's intensity was one I recognized, a fierce confidence bordering on self-righteousness that in my ex-fiancée had been unrelenting, that had made me the loser of any argument I was stupid enough to engage in, that had kept me from objecting even when she suggested it was my fault she was leaving me for someone else. Still, it didn't stop me from saying now, "An Israeli."

"Excuse me?" Laura said.

"*An* Israeli shot him. They didn't all do it." Her eyes narrowed, but there was a crack in her fierceness now, a little fissure of doubt, as if she'd just realized she were talking not to someone slightly demented but to a genuine mental patient. "He sounds interesting," I said. "I look forward to meeting him."

Her doubtful look lingered for a moment, but as she began telling me about her new refugee, she grew excited again and seemed to forget what I'd said. His name was Nabil, she told me. He'd been twelve years old when a bullet entered his abdomen and lodged in his spine. He'd spent nearly a year in the hospital. For the next decade, Israeli soldiers appeared at his house every few months, asking questions, threatening to arrest him. One of his brothers was in jail, along with two of his cousins. Now he was twenty-three, a computer engineering student on scholarship at Portland State. He was available Tuesday afternoon to meet with us. Could I make it then? I knew I had nothing scheduled for Tuesday – or Wednesday through Sunday, for that matter – but said I'd have to check my calendar and get back to her.

That evening, all groups were presenting their ideas to the class. Our teacher cheered us on, making nonsensical marks on a flip chart and offering words of encouragement, acting as if each idea were the best he'd ever heard. The woman who looked like my cousin said she and her team were going up to Washington over the weekend to shoot a reenactment of the battle of Chickamauga. "Wash/Chick," the teacher wrote, along with several stars. The short-haired blonde with smoky breath talked about her luthier in great detail, and it took me almost until the end of the presentation to figure out that a luthier was a violin maker. Her boyfriend had already finished the soundtrack. Did he play violin? the teacher asked. Guitar, she said. Interesting choice, the teacher said. On the chart, he wrote, "Violin/Guitar," and more stars.

The Japanese girl described her old building downtown, and its history was in fact fascinating, the site of murder and prostitution and shady business deals. She'd already lined up several interviews and had arranged to shoot in the upper floors, which had sat unused for more than a hundred years and were said to be haunted. She still needed a partner if anyone was interested. She was smart and adorable and looked straight at me. I lowered my eyes and felt myself fill with regret. Beside me, Laura scratched notes furiously into a tidy little journal, paying no attention to the other presenters.

When it was our turn, she strode to the front without waiting for me. I had to hurry to catch up with her, and even then she didn't turn to me before starting to speak. For five straight minutes, she talked about the plight of the Palestinians in the occupied territories, the Israeli blockades and checkpoints, the midnight raids, the terror and poverty. She was impassioned, her broad forehead growing slick, her hands flailing and then closing down into fists. Her voice echoed from the concrete pillars and the aluminum roof. I stood there smiling stupidly at the class in their rickety folding chairs, my nose itching from the dust or the smell of Laura's perfume, remembering how, while visiting Israel as a teenager, I'd gotten choked up singing the Hatikvah, how I'd shed tears when I first saw the Western Wall. I was a solid progressive, a committed pacifist; I believed in a two-state solution and a Palestinian homeland; I had nothing but criticism for the Israeli government's concessions to right-wing pressure. But listening to Laura was like listening to a stranger bad-mouth my family. Only I had the right to point out all our flaws and shortcomings. But I couldn't bring myself to chime in.

To my relief, and embarrassment, the teacher cut her off. His delighted smile was strained. Our time was almost up. What exactly was our film going to be about? Laura spent another two minutes talking about Nabil, detailing his suffering and resilience. "The Israelis shot him while he was running away," she said. "He'll never walk again." On the flip chart, the teacher wrote, "Pal Man," and underlined it twice.

Before going home, I told Laura again that I wasn't comfortable with the film being overtly political. The most persuasive argument, I said, was one that balanced both perspectives and focused on the experience of the individual. I don't know why I didn't just say that I was Jewish and didn't want to make Israelis look like villains, that already I was beginning to feel like a traitor. Maybe I thought she'd already guessed it. In any case, she didn't seem to hear me now. "Tuesday at four," she said, jamming her journal into her purse, and named a coffee shop near the university. "If you can't make it, I'll let you know what he says."

OVER THE WEEKEND I emailed Laura to let her know that I could in fact make it on Tuesday. And wouldn't it be a good idea, I wrote, for us to meet a little early and plan some of our questions? She wrote back three minutes later, full of enthusiasm. It sounded like a terrific idea to her. We could meet at a bar near her office, have a glass of wine. In writing she was relaxed and flirtatious, and remembering her sweet, awkward smile, I tried to excuse her aggression the other night as an overflow of nerves and emotion. Wasn't passion always an admirable thing, even if hers was a little simplistic? Wasn't it something I wanted more of for myself now that I was alive again to the world around me? Once more I imagined late-night editing sessions in a room lit only by the glow of a computer screen, empty bottles scattered around, both of us flushed with wine and summer heat. For the next few days I stopped worrying about the film.

And when we met for a drink, Laura still seemed relaxed, dressed, to my surprise, in jeans and sandals and loose linen shirt, though this time she really had just come from work. Her hair was up in a ponytail, those nicely shaped ears on display. Her casualness made me forget about compiling a list of questions for Nabil, and instead we talked about our summers, where we'd gone hiking and swimming, what bands we'd recently seen, what new restaurants we'd discovered. She told me about a disastrous date she'd been on with a co-worker, who got drunk during dinner and picked a fight with her about politics – spying on U.S. citizens seemed perfectly appropriate to him, so long as it kept us safe – and later abandoned her in a bar, where he met up with three of his buddies in baseball caps. The whole thing sounded so awful and humiliating that I couldn't believe she'd tell me about it, but she related the story lightheartedly, laughing and shaking her head, above all making clear to me that she was single and looking. "I thought I'd quit dating after that one," she said. "But I'm a glutton for punishment."

In turn I described a disastrous date of my own, during which I'd run into my ex-fiancée and her new lover, and realized that in a few days it would be the year anniversary of the wedding that didn't happen. And mentioning it, I felt almost free of the suffering it had caused me, cheerful about my prospects for the future, and Laura and I laughed about the absurdities of dating in your early thirties, the lengths you had to go to to meet people, the awkward conversations you had to have, when really, all you wanted to know was whether or not someone was a good kisser and whether or not you liked his or her smell. Searching for romance was such a distraction, we both agreed. It got in the way of more important endeavors. Knowing that someone was going to be in your bed every night – or at least a night or two a week – made it easier to get things done. We smiled at each other, and drank, and when it was time for us to head to the coffee shop, we'd each finished two glasses of wine. Laura's eyes were half-lidded and sultry, her breath sour. My steps were the slightest bit wobbly. On the train across town we sat close together in a mostly empty car, our legs nearly touching.

Nabil was already in the coffee shop when we arrived. The place was packed with students and bike messengers in spandex shorts, but it wasn't hard to spot him, the only person in a wheelchair. He was at a table full of college kids, laptops and textbooks open in front of them. As soon as Laura saw him she cut across the room, bumping people out of her way, leaving me behind. Once again, I had to hurry after her. She introduced herself and said how pleased she was to meet him, how honored that he was interested in being profiled in her film. "Your story is so important," she said. "I only hope I can do it justice." I had to stick out my hand and say my name. I asked if anyone wanted coffee. Laura ignored me. Nabil asked for a latte. I stood in line as Laura ushered him to a table in the corner.

By the time I joined them, they were deep in conversation, Laura leaning forward, flushed, giggling. Nabil was broad-chested, with thickly muscled forearms resting on the arms of his wheelchair, hands in fingerless gloves. He wore a tight-fitting T-shirt over baggy sweatpants that only suggested the shape of legs, basketball shoes with the laces undone. His hair was black, his eyebrows prominent over a sleepy, sensuous face and big soft lips. If I didn't know he was Palestinian, I could have easily taken him for Jewish, and I remembered that in Israel I could never tell Jews and Arabs apart unless they were wearing something to distinguish them, yarmulkes or kufiyas, headscarves or veils. When I sat, Laura said something I couldn't make out over the din of voices and the hiss of the espresso machine, and I leaned closer to hear. And only when Nabil laughed and responded did I realize they weren't speaking English. This time they both laughed, and Nabil asked where she'd learned Arabic.

"I used to be married to a Saud," Laura said.

I gawked. Laura didn't notice. Was this the source of her passion? Did she just have a thing for Middle Eastern men?

"Not easy to get un-married to a Saud," Nabil said.

"It is if he decides he never really loved you," she said, and fixed on him the awkward, brittle smile she'd given me in class.

I cleared my throat. Nabil turned to me and asked what the film was all about, but before I could say anything, Laura started talking about the propaganda machine of the media and the Israel lobby. She didn't tell him we were students in a class, that we'd never made a documentary before, that, in fact, neither of us had ever picked up a video camera. She didn't tell him the film could be no more than seven minutes long. By now she had her notebook out, the awkward smile gone, the fiercely confident look that replaced it making her face dramatic, sexy, terrifying. Her passion was no less alluring than before, and I could appreciate how much this cause moved her, but every time she said, "The Israelis," I felt implicated and accused. She began firing off questions, and Nabil answered each of them slowly, casually, his voice hardly louder than a murmur, his words undercutting her urgency. "We were just kids," he said, shrugging, when she asked how he'd gotten involved with the resistance. "It was a game, to throw rocks at soldiers. There were always cameras nearby. I wanted to be on TV."

Baristas were banging their tampers on the counter. Bike messengers came rushing in and out, ringing the bell on the shop's door, their skinny, hairy legs scissoring in my peripheral vision. Laura kept jabbing her palm. But nothing disturbed Nabil's composure. He shrugged again when she asked about his injury and hospital time. "It was terrible, of course. But other boys were killed. I'm one of the lucky ones." When she suggested that he must hate the Israelis who shot him, he said, "Do I blame him, whoever he was? No. He was a kid, too. He did what he thought he had to. His government, that's another story."

His words were humble and humbling. Here was someone who'd really suffered, who would never walk again, but he didn't complain, didn't indulge in anger and self-pity, as I had for the six months after my fiancée had left me, believing myself to be cursed, a born victim, someone treated far worse than he deserved. And I found I was less interested in his suffering than in how he'd come through it, how he'd managed in its aftermath. I cut Laura off mid-sentence to ask him what it was like to be in a wheelchair in Ramallah. Were there services for the disabled? Were there ramps at his school? Laura's brow constricted, and she scratched in her notebook. But Nabil sparked to the questions. His friends built ramps for him, he said, into his house, into school, down to their favorite basketball court.

"You played even after your injury?" I asked.

He shrugged again. "Yes, sure. For a while I was on the Palestinian national team."

Now I couldn't stop asking questions. Did he play ball now? How did he like Portland State? How did people here treat him when they found out he was Palestinian? I could sense Laura's irritation but tried to ignore it. The sourness of her breath was overpowering now. The rims of her ears were red. After a few minutes she could no longer hold back. "Do you think there can be negotiated peace with the Israelis? Is armed struggle the only way to end the occupation? Do you support Fatah or Hamas?"

Nabil sighed heavily, as if the questions suddenly made him weary. "I'm not political," he said. "I have Israeli friends. I have Jewish friends." He looked straight at me as he said it. There was no question that he knew what I was, and I could imagine the look on my face, which was a look I'd sometimes seen on the face of a German acquaintance, guilty and burdened and slightly resentful of the burden she, born twenty-five years after the end of the Third Reich, had no reason to bear. Why should I own the bullet in Nabil's spine, when he was the one who'd thrown rocks, when I'd been thousands of miles away, too young to understand what was happening? "I have nothing against Jews, only the Zionists who want to take our land. But I also have a scholarship, and I don't want to lose it. It's dangerous to talk too much about politics. Soon I'll have a degree. I just want to live."

To my surprise, Laura folded her hands and leaned back, satisfied, and didn't press him further. He was willing to be in our film, he said, but now he had to get back to studying. Laura thanked him again, told him how excited she was, said she'd make a film that would show the true plight of his people. He shrugged once more, as if saying, I won't hold my breath. A Jewish gesture, I thought, one that spoke of a long history of disappointment and muted but persistent hope. He shook both of our hands and returned to his fellow students.

The train back to Laura's office was crowded, and we had to stand close together, but now our closeness felt artificial. The wine had worn off, and I had the first hint of a headache. Laura was animated again, even flirtatious, as she talked about her plans for shooting the interview, but when she grabbed my arm, I recoiled.

"We should get footage of him playing basketball," I said. "And wheeling himself into class."

"I downloaded video from the first intifada," she said. "We'll have more images than we can use."

After a few stops, Laura got off the train. I stayed on, heading across the river.

THREE DAYS LATER, I sent an email to the teacher of the documentary class. I was very sorry, I wrote, but I'd have to drop out. My mother was having health problems, and I was flying east for a good part of the summer. I couldn't tell him how disappointed I was not to follow through with my film. I'd already learned so much. When he wrote back, he cheerfully expressed his sympathies, wished me good luck, and said he couldn't refund any of my tuition.

I sent a longer, more heartfelt note to Laura, telling her how awful I felt about letting her down, how I knew she'd make a terrific film. She responded a few minutes later. She was very understanding. She hoped my mother would recover quickly. She told me not to worry about the project, that she'd manage on her own. But she was very sad, she said, not to continue working with me. She was sure we would have made a great team. Most of all she'd been looking forward to spending more time with me. I should get in touch when I came home.

My mother really was having health problems – osteoarthritis that required major back surgery and months of physical therapy – but I had no plans to go east. The lie was disgraceful but easy, and I was relieved the moment I sent the emails. I told myself that going forward with the film was too risky, the subject matter too important, too complex, to be handled badly. It wasn't something to be taken on by first-time filmmakers. It needed more than seven minutes. I didn't want to be responsible for bungling Nabil's story.

All this was true, but I also knew that there were other thoughts lurking beneath the surface of rationality, thoughts to which I didn't want to admit. They had to do with loyalty and tribal bonds and the power of the victor. I felt sorry for Nabil, admired him, and believed that his story deserved to be told, but he wasn't one of my people, we weren't brothers. Choosing sides wasn't dictated by morality or conviction; it was a matter of blood. And just as risky as making a bad film about a Palestinian refugee was the possibility of making a good film, and having my name on it, and having other Jews see me as one who'd betrayed them. I was a coward, in other words, unwilling to stand up for my ideals in the face of scrutiny.

What bothers me most now, though, is to think that I could see no options for dealing with my discomfort other than running away. Being honest with Laura wasn't even something I considered. My only thought was of escape, no matter the consequences, no matter how ashamed it might leave me afterward. It didn't occur to me to wonder how I might be braver or more honorable. And even if it had occurred to me, I can't be sure I would have done anything differently.

The only person who suspected I might have had other motives for dropping the class was the Japanese film student, who wrote to me later that week. She was sorry to hear I had to leave, but just in case it was because I was disappointed with my project or my partner, she'd still love to have my help with her film. She was going to start shooting over the weekend. Did I want to join her? My shame outweighed my regret, and I stuck by my story, flying off that weekend on an imaginary plane. She wrote to me again at the end of the summer, inviting me to the class screening. She was really proud of her film, she said. She'd love to hear what I thought.

Laura invited me, too, but hers was a mass email, sent to all her friends. It was a humble note, expressing her apprehension about having people see her documentary, reminding everyone that this was her first effort and that she was still learning. I was surprised by the tone, but not nearly so much as by the description of her film, which wasn't about a Palestinian refugee, but rather about her obsession with socks. A seven-minute documentary about socks? It sounded fascinating. I wanted to see it.

But by then I'd started seeing someone I'd met on an internet dating site and told myself it wouldn't be appropriate to go to the screening and open myself up to lingering questions about whether or not Laura and the Japanese girl were still single, whether or not they still seemed to have any interest in me. But really, I couldn't face their productivity, their accomplishment, when I was a quitter, who'd accomplished nothing all summer. Even more, I couldn't face them after my lie and expose myself to the suspicion it had unearthed, which I'd since been trying to ignore: that I had no values, no convictions whatsoever, that all along I'd simply wanted something to ease the dull pain of longing and emptiness I'd been living with for more than a year and could no longer bear.

About three months later, single again, I saw Laura on one of those dating websites. In her photograph, she was lying down on a bed, hair spread around her, feet bare, her smile at once shy and ravenous. She didn't want to be cold all winter, she wrote at the top of her profile. Did anyone want to warm her up? I had a terrible urge to write to her but couldn't bring myself to do it. I wasn't worthy of her honesty, I told myself, of her willingness to face further rejection and humiliation. Farther down in her profile, she had a full paragraph about her dedication to ending Israeli apartheid.

AROUND THE SAME time, I went back to the coffee shop where Laura and I had interviewed Nabil. I had no business there, only too much time on my hands. The days were growing short, and I felt hints of the depression that had crippled me the year before. My cat died. My ex-fiancée sent me a photograph of her new apartment in San Francisco, around the corner from Dolores Park, her new lover lounging in a brightly lit bay window, and I felt freshly abandoned, left to fend for myself. Internet dating had led to one awkward situation after another. I decided I should meet women in the real world again, though I didn't know where to find them. The best I could come up with was a coffee shop near the university.

There were in fact plenty of women there, but I was too shy to approach any of them. I sat in a corner, reading a book, and after twenty minutes I was ready to leave. But then Nabil came in, with a group of fellow students, and I stayed where I was. If he saw me, he didn't recognize me. He and his friends settled in at a table across the room, and I studied him as he joked with the girl beside him, a short-haired blonde with high cheekbones who looked enough like my ex-fiancée for me to feel an ache in my chest when she laughed and touched his arm. He was wearing sweatpants again, and a long-sleeve pullover that showed off his bulging forearms, and the same fingerless gloves. A backpack was stretched across the handles of his wheelchair, a sticker in its center printed with the words "Mad Rock."

I didn't know what Mad Rock meant. Later I'd look it up on the internet and discover that it was a company that sold rock climbing equipment, shoes and gloves, harnesses and ropes, crash pads and carabineers, and I'd be amazed at the thought of Nabil halfway up a cliff, those fingerless gloves reaching for a fissure, legs in baggy sweatpants dangling beneath him. At the time, though, I guessed it had something to do with music, and I pictured him instead with a guitar in his lap, its body resting on his lifeless legs, neck propped on the arm of his wheelchair. For some reason, the image made me unbearably sad, and also more ashamed than I already was. Nabil had suffered and survived, had accommodated himself to life's impossible challenges, had carried on with a dignity I envied but could never aspire to. I'd not only passed up on telling his story, I'd failed to honor his strength. That he was a Palestinian who'd once thrown rocks at Israelis was beside the point.

I considered going over to him, apologizing for bailing on the film, explaining the mixed emotions I hadn't been able to express to Laura. The possibility that he'd understand them brought far more relief than I'd felt after I'd quit the class. But before I could get up the courage to approach him, the girl beside him leaned close and whispered in his ear. Once again the baristas were banging on the counter, the students were laughing and clicking their keyboards, the bell on the door kept jingling, but Nabil was in a world apart, his movements slow, his expression placid. The girl's fingers were long and slender, pale against his dark pullover when she lay her hand on his shoulder. Her lips brushed the skin beside his earlobe, and her eyes, adoring or infatuated, briefly closed.

I should have been happy for him, but I wasn't. I wasn't even jealous. What I felt on his behalf was only dread. I wanted to call out and warn him. I wanted to tell him to run while he had the chance. There was danger ahead, heartbreak and pain and clouds of despair. Those were the only things I could imagine for him, the only things I could imagine for myself when I'd pictured being with Laura, with the Japanese film student, with the women I met on the internet, with any of the lovely ones around me in the coffee shop now, whose sweet-sounding voices made me cower in the corner.

It would be some time yet before I'd stop being afraid to live.

Nabil laughed at whatever the girl had said to him and whispered something back, his nose buried in her soft hair. I snapped my book closed and left as quickly as I could.

3

Scavengers

IN THE MID- TO LATE-1980S, THERE WAS AN UNOFFICIAL tradition at my high school. It played out every year or two, usually in late winter or early spring. Some senior would die drag racing or joyriding on his father's motorcycle or waterskiing drunk at three in the morning on Indian Lake. Then the entire senior class – and those freshmen, sophomores, and juniors lucky enough to call some seniors their friends – would gather in the gym, on retractable bleachers usually pulled out only for pep rallies and basketball games. For three or four days, even a week, they'd skip class and grieve their fallen comrade, passing around photographs and newspaper articles, making posters and wreaths, listening to the dead kid's best friend or prom date or cousin from Parsippany relating his last words before he'd walked off into the fatal night.

It was a big regional school, and half the students in the class wouldn't have known the dead kid or each other. But this was their opportunity to bond. A lot of hugging and crying, and inevitably someone would bring a boom box and play the kid's favorite songs, or the songs someone imagined might be the kid's favorites but were in fact the songs that made the class most sentimental and nostalgic, songs that were popular when the seniors were freshmen and triggered wistful memories and colored the previous four years in a dreamy, haunted light. People sang along, a few couples slow-danced under the basketball hoops, and a few others drifted into the shadows behind the bleachers to make out. The principal would show up and make a speech, encouraging everyone to keep the kid's memory alive, to carry his spirit inside us, but also to forge on with our lives, as the kid would want us to, and return to class. Before he'd said more than two or three sentences, he was drowned out by shouting and jeers.

The dead kid's picture and biography would appear in a two-page spread in the yearbook, but by the time it came out most of the class had forgotten him, thinking instead about their own futures, the parties they'd have over the summer, the friends they'd miss when some went off to college and others stayed behind to work at their father's gas station or pizzeria. At graduation, someone would talk about the kid again, listing off his accomplishments, or the accomplishments he might have had had he lived past his eighteenth birthday, and there would be a moment of silence, but by then his name would have taken on new meaning, standing in for transition and community and growing up, a blessing of sorts, or magic words with which to send the survivors off into the rest of their lives.

At the time it didn't occur to me that this was an especially violent or reckless period, that we were suffering an unusual number of premature deaths. I guess I didn't know any better. Now I wonder if the spate of losses was a by-product of late-'80s malaise, when we were bored sick with Reagan optimism and awful pop music. More likely it was just bad luck. Whatever the reason, for half a decade or so, I came to expect tragedy as a natural occurrence, an ordinary texture of life or a routine rite of passage. We lost a kid both my brother's junior and senior years, when I was still in junior high, and again my freshman year. There was a hiatus my sophomore year, and though that class was spared any grief, they struck me as an especially dull and uninspired group, immature, even, unprepared to face the challenges of the outside world.

I should probably make it clear up front that I was a bit of an outcast in high school. Maybe that goes without saying. Why write about it if I'd been happy and well-adjusted, if it hadn't caused me torment and humiliation? I was short and pimpled and quiet, a terrible athlete, out of step with fashions and hair-styles, and for my first two years I was an easy target for those kids who got their kicks by slamming people half their size into lockers, and for big-haired girls – this was northern New Jersey, epicenter of teased bangs – who liked to laugh at other people's pain. I often ate lunch by myself behind the school to avoid being noticed and ridiculed, and in the hallways I kept my head down, reminding myself that in four years it would all be over. When I did stay in the cafeteria, I ate nothing for fear someone would dump a tray of food in my lap – it was all so unoriginal, as if no one could come up with acts of cruelty we hadn't seen in movies a hundred times before – and I went home famished and lightheaded. And maybe as a result of all this, I was particularly acute to death and mourning, though I wasn't a terribly morbid kid and rarely entertained suicidal thoughts. Rather, I was grateful for any event that disrupted typical routines and distracted my cheerfully sadistic classmates. Death meant reprieve, less an escape for the poor soul who'd moved on than for the tormented ones who were left behind.

By my junior year, however, I'd learned how to keep a low enough profile to blend in, growing my hair long and wearing Led Zeppelin T-shirts to school – those safe, timeless fashions – and talking, like everyone else, about drinking and smoking pot, though the only way I could get my hands on illicit substances was to raid my father's mostly empty liquor cabinet scattered with unpleasantly sweet things, Amaretto, Triple Sec, Crème de Cacao. I did manage to make some friends and get invited to a few parties, and I began to imagine I might be able to salvage these years, that they wouldn't all be a waste. I even began to wish I could live those first two years over again, now that I knew how to survive them, and savor the full experience rather than praying for it to flash by. It seemed unfair that just as I was beginning to enjoy myself, I'd soon be moving on to something new.

In the spring of that year the tradition reasserted itself in a particularly gruesome way. Driving home from a neighboring school's prom, a girl's date fell asleep at the wheel and crashed into a concrete divider separating the east- and westbound lanes of Route 10. He died instantly, and the car burst into flames. The girl was trapped inside. The fire spread to her clothes before the first policeman to the scene could pull her free. Third-degree burns covered ninety percent of her body. For a week, she hung on in intensive care. Our principal gave us updates every morning over the loudspeaker. She began to show signs of stabilizing but then caught pneumonia, and within a few hours her lungs filled with fluid. She died the first week of June, less than a month before graduation.

I knew the girl, if only slightly. Her name was Debbie. Our families went to the same synagogue, and she was president of its youth group, whose meetings and outings and dances I attended sporadically, feeling as much an outcast among my fashion-conscious fellow Jews as I did at school. Debbie was pretty and smart and personable, and her death was unambiguously tragic. Though I'd spoken to her fewer than a dozen times, I was shaken by the loss and shed a couple of genuine tears.

But I was also, I'm ashamed to admit, grateful to have had a reason to join the senior class in the gym, to participate in the ritual of mourning and bonding. I talked to kids who'd never spoken to me before and hugged several of Debbie's pretty friends. We railed against Randolph High, already a sports rival, whose prom had killed one of our own. People exchanged stories of the last time they'd seen Debbie alive, and I told my story, too: Despite being its president, she'd served food at our youth group's Passover Seder, and though she hadn't yet had a chance to eat, she offered me a second bowl of matzoh ball soup. *Are you sure you don't want more*? Those were the last words I'd heard her speak, and when I accepted she smiled and nodded in approval. My story fit with the larger narrative of the week, which was that Debbie had been uniquely kind and humble, that she'd never uttered a petty word, that she was unlike anybody else we knew, that she was, in fact, not a person but a symbol of all the things we'd never be.

I was amazed to find how close I felt to kids I hardly knew. The moments we shared in the gym seemed to outweigh all the months and years they hadn't known of my existence. Now my face was one they'd remember when they went off to college or disappeared into the swamp of job and family and local bars. When I went back to class after three days, I was equally amazed to find that none of my teachers questioned me, none asked to see my missing homework or a note from the office. A number of my classmates who hadn't known Debbie offered condolences, and I nodded somberly, with what I hoped came across as an expression of wisdom and experience. I wasn't the same person I'd been before entering the gym, and I wanted everyone to know it.

Strangely, though, I returned to ordinary life dissatisfied, the whole thing feeling like a bit of a tease. I wasn't a senior. I wasn't going to graduate in three weeks. I hadn't been in classes with those kids in the gym, and I didn't get nostalgic for the same songs. I'd participated in the ritual only tangentially, and at best, it was a partial coming of age, a first step toward maturity – a trial-run for the real thing, maybe, which was due in just another year.

LET ME CLARIFY: I wasn't thinking about these things in such conscious terms. Or at least I wasn't actively hoping for anyone to die. But I was certainly aware of a distinct, buzzing sort of energy in the fall, a sense of danger and anticipation only partly connected to filling out college applications and taking the SATs. And I did find myself idly assessing kids in my class, wondering not only who would go to college and who would work at the mall, but who might not make it to graduation, who might be the object of our shared grief.

It's hard to believe now, from a distance of nearly twenty years, at a time when I spend most of my waking hours in terrified denial of mortality, that I could speculate about death so casually, that I could look on tragedy as something not only expected but necessary. It speaks, I suppose, to how badly I wanted a way to connect with the people around me, how desperate I was to leave my outcast days behind. Or maybe my fixation then had more to do with how I wanted to see myself, or how I wanted others to see me, as someone who was versed in the darker aspects of life, who didn't shy away from challenge but carried it with unusual dignity. I wanted to have stories to tell when I got to college, to show that I was a tough Jersey kid who had insight into the difficult workings of the world.

In any case, I had no trouble imagining the reaction some deaths would spur – the class president's, the valedictorian's, the star wrestler's – but others were harder to picture. Would everyone cry for Dirk, the skate-punk with blue hair who sold psychedelic mushrooms behind the school? What about for Teo, the wanna-be mobster with slicked-back hair and gold chains – guidos, we called his kind, with our boundless cultural sensitivity – who drove a Monte Carlo and kept brass knuckles in his locker and once shoved me down in the cafeteria, claiming, rightly, that I'd been staring at his girlfriend's legs? It didn't matter who the victim was, as far as I was concerned, so long as his loss brought us all together; if Teo was the one to go, I'd have forced myself to wear an expression of sorrow no matter how disingenuous it was, no matter how guilty it might leave me feeling afterward.

No one died in the fall. In early winter, a kid I knew wrecked his car and spent three days in the hospital with a pair of broken ribs and a punctured lung, but he was back in school the following week, holding his chest whenever anyone got him laughing. I felt excitement mounting by mid-February, when a pair of ice storms made the roads treacherous, but an unexpected warm front melted everything a few days later. In mid-April, when most college-bound kids found out where they were going next year, the first serious parties started, in the woods, at the end of cul-de-sacs, in houses left empty by permissive parents. But aside from a couple cases of alcohol-poisoning, and my friend Bill who broke his wrist punching a wall, there were no major casualties.

By May the energy and anticipation I'd felt in the fall began to turn toward impatience. Even if I was having a good time, making more friends, I was mostly ready to be done with my present life, to move on to more serious pursuits. I knew where I was going to college – North Carolina, a place I'd been only once and knew almost nothing about – and I'd lined up a summer job. But I also had the uncomfortable feeling that things were left undone, that I was missing out on something important, that I'd look back on this time with regret.

The prom came and went. Afterward, most of the class spent the weekend at Seaside, a trashy boardwalk town halfway down the Jersey shore. Drunken kids swam in the Atlantic, but no one drowned. There were no riptides or undertows, no shark attacks. Several football players got roughed up by the local police after trashing their motel room but came away with nothing more than bruises and black eyes. On our last night there, I watched one of our guidos get into a fight with a sailor, who pulled a four-inch switchblade out of his starched white pants and, in a flash, nicked the kid's chin with the tip of the blade. I waited for more, feeling nothing but elation – I was drunk, too, after downing a pint of peppermint schnapps stolen from my father's liquor cabinet – and when the guido turned and took off down the beach, I was unreasonably disappointed. "Anyone else want some?" the sailor called, but no one stepped forward. We all shuffled back to our motels, where we slept ten to a room.

The first week of June, little shivers of fear rippled through my excitement at the prospect of graduating, of leaving the stifling world of high school and home life, of turning my back on everything I'd known. I didn't want to acknowledge the change, but after a while I couldn't ignore it. I didn't feel ready for what was coming. I had visions of my future in which I was a different person than I'd been for the past four years – or rather, one in which I was seen as the person I'd always believed myself to be, clever and interesting and quietly adventurous. But the clever, interesting things I imagined myself saying never made their way out of my mouth, and the only adventure I managed to find was drinking myself to the point of vomiting. My long hair didn't make me look like the rock stars in the posters on my walls; it grew in a sort of bubble on top of my head, with curls to my shoulders, nothing like Jimmy Page's beautifully ruffled shag shining under the stage lights of Madison Square Garden. I worried that I wasn't mature enough to leave home, to survive on my own; I didn't feel I'd been prepared for it, and I spent a lot of time thinking about those senior classes that had come before me, those that had faced death and those that hadn't, and the differences I'd sensed between them.

In the illogical, anxious swirl of my adolescent mind, I believed that growing up didn't necessarily happen of its own accord, that I needed a boost to lift me into the next stage of my life. Why it had to involve some kid getting killed I can't say, except to guess that I was overwrought and unsubtle, that my imagination couldn't encompass anything more complex. I needed big markers to point my way forward, weeping and gnashing of teeth, nothing less than melodrama. Most of all I didn't want to be a sheltered kid, thrust out into the world without experience to guide me.

The anniversary of Debbie's death came and went, too, and no one acknowledged it. There weren't any rallies or banners tacked up in the halls. It was as if she'd left with her fellow classmates, gone off to the University of Michigan, where she'd been accepted last spring, and for the past nine months she'd been sitting in classes and pledging a sorority and beginning a romance with a boy in Hillel. There was no hint of somberness in the air, nothing but the coming taste of freedom. There were only two weeks left in the school year.

AND THEN, SOMEONE organized a scavenger hunt. No one seemed to know who'd started it, but soon a whisper campaign spread through the cafeteria. Teams of four, ten bucks per person, winner take all. It would start at ten o'clock on Saturday night, on a dead-end street near Green Pond, and end Sunday at dawn, in the parking lot of the Denville library. There'd be far more items on the list than any team could gather in a single night, and no one would see it ahead of time. Whoever had the biggest haul would win the prize. A girl with a twenty-one-year-old sister at Montclair State collected money for bottles of booze – for the passengers in each car, she said, not the drivers. By Friday afternoon, sixteen teams had signed up.

I told my parents I was spending the night at my friend Alex's house, and either they trusted me, or they'd resigned themselves by then to the fact of my growing up and moving away, of the independence I didn't yet believe was real. I can't quite describe the nervousness and exhilaration with which I left the house, which had nothing to do with the hunt, or even with the bottle of bourbon I'd bought, but with the sense that I was now heading off into uncharted territory, crossing a threshold far more important than graduation or even losing my virginity. Whether I was conscious of it or not, there was no doubt in my mind: Tonight, someone was going to die.

Alex was a math and science whiz with a big head appropriate to his big brain, and he had a passion for fast cars. He was going to Cornell in the fall, planning to study electrical engineering. For some reason, the smartest kids in my high school all wanted to be engineers; even then it struck me as strange that they didn't have greater ambitions, that they didn't dream instead of being astrophysicists or senators or foreign correspondents for *The New York Times*, that they'd settle for the same upper-middle-class lives their parents had and not, as I did, crave something new and exotic. Great wealth or utter poverty were equally attractive to me, though since I was already leaning toward an artistic career, fancying myself a poet, the latter seemed more likely and easier to achieve.

Sometimes I'd study Alex's big head and wonder how so much brain could want so little: cheap cars with light bodies and peppy engines that did tight, thrilling fishtails when he zipped around a corner. Since getting his license a year ago, he'd already wrecked his first car, a lime-green Volkswagen Beetle, with which he'd rear-ended our physics teacher on the way out of the high school parking lot. Now he had a tiny Hyundai that he drove as if it were a Porsche, weaving from lane to lane, menacing other drivers until they got out of his way. On straightaways he'd pushed it to ninety-eight miles per hour. In the fall, when he'd leave for college, he'd pass it on to his younger sister, but before then he was determined to make it break a hundred.

Tonight, though, he wasn't driving the Hyundai. He'd borrowed his father's Isuzu sports car, which broke a hundred easily. I'd met Alex's father only a handful of times, but it had struck me as equally strange that he, too, had a big head and big brain – he taught chemistry at Seton Hall – and liked fast cars. I couldn't help wondering if my indifference to all things automotive reflected a lack of intelligence.

On our team was Bill, the kid who'd broken his wrist punching a wall, and his friend Jeannie, a sullen-looking girl I hardly knew, who only nodded to me as I climbed into the backseat beside her and then went back to staring out the window. Bill, freckled and chubby, still had his arm in a brace, and he was already pumping it in the air when we left Alex's house, bouncing on the seat, singing along to a tape he'd brought – Mötley Crüe's *Girls, Girls, Girls*, maybe, or Guns n' Roses' *Appetite for Destruction*. He was a sucker for heavy metal ballads, their mournful introductions, their frenzied, ecstatic endings, and he always ignored me when I told him they were all just bad rip-offs of "Stairway to Heaven." Alex usually listened to synth pop, bopping along to Pet Shop Boys or Duran Duran while flying down quiet suburban streets. The rhythm helped him steer, he said. "Pussy music," Bill called it. There was no way we'd win the scavenger hunt listening to "West End Girls."

"We've got to get pumped," he said. "You pumped?" he asked Alex.

"Sure," Alex said, pulling on his fingerless gloves.

"You pumped, Jeannie?" Jeannie twirled a finger in the air and kept looking out the window. "You pumped, Scott?"

I said I would be, as soon as I drank some Jim Beam. We stopped at a 7-Eleven on the way to Green Pond and each bought thirty-six ounces of Coke to mix our booze into, all except Alex, who instead bought a six-pack of Jolt, which had enough caffeine and sugar to keep him awake for a month. "I've got to stay sharp," he said, though he relented when Bill insisted he take a sip from his enormous cup, for good luck.

By the time we made it to Green Pond, two dozen cars already lined either side of the dead-end road, engines revving, kids walking around in confusion, asking where the list was, who we were supposed to give our money to. For a minute I thought the whole thing was a hoax, or just a rumor that had gotten out of hand, and found myself unreasonably disappointed to think that these cars wouldn't be tearing around the county all night, that this would most likely turn into nothing more dangerous than an ordinary Saturday party, all of us standing around guzzling our drinks and stumbling around the fringe of the woods until the cops came and chased us away. If I'd known there'd be nothing else, I told myself, I wouldn't have bothered coming.

But then a girl appeared in the street with a megaphone in one hand and a thick envelope in the other, a walkie-talkie clipped to her belt. I knew her, though I've since forgotten her name – she was in my English class, a pretty, popular, undistinguished girl I never would have expected to organize something so ambitious and illegal and potentially deadly. She reminded me of Debbie, wholesome and congenial, the type to lead a youth group, though not a Jewish one. Of all the things she could have spent her time on, why a scavenger hunt?

She was stiff, unsmiling, not looking like someone enjoying herself as she called instructions into her megaphone and then whispered into her walkie-talkie. She was dressed in pants and long sleeves, though it was balmy out, and her clothes were black, as if she were going to break into houses and swipe jewelry or head to a funeral. As other kids with walkie-talkies came around to each car to collect our money, I felt, despite the shouting and revving engines, a solemnity in the air, a looming sense of catastrophe. Even then I was pretty certain I was the only one who noticed, and I was proud of myself for being the one person to acknowledge the reality of the world and all its dangers. But maybe the organizer was aware of it, too, I thought; maybe her grim expression suggested ulterior motives in gathering us here. I imagined she'd set out to avenge Debbie's senseless death, assuring that this time it would happen to someone who deserved it, someone stupid enough to get into a car with bottles of booze and an over-caffeinated teenager behind the wheel.

I got out of the car to survey the scene, to take note of my fellow travelers, and yes, to decide who was most likely to go. There were the obvious choices: the wrestling star in a black Mustang, the class president in a jacked up pick-up. Teo in his Monte Carlo, big-haired girls in a Firebird, straight-edge skinheads in a '69 Skylark. So much car pride. Was I the only one who'd seen *American Graffiti* too many times to take all this seriously? The future I dreamed of was one in which no one cared about what they drove.

Soon I found myself focusing on a kid in the passenger seat of a nondescript blue Honda. He was a friendly guy, liked by almost everyone, but not showy or clownish. He played sports, baseball, and maybe hockey, but wasn't a star or even a starter. He was a decent student but not stellar, and was going to

Rutgers or Penn State or one of the SUNYs. His name was nondescript, too. John, or maybe Jim.

I didn't want him to die. Even thinking about it made me sad, though we weren't especially close. He wasn't someone who'd be easy to mourn. The process would be painful, and no one would take it lightly. And that was exactly what we all needed – what I needed, that is, or thought I did – something to struggle with, something to complicate what were otherwise relatively privileged and comfortable lives, something to make our experiences rich and full enough to lift us into a world bigger than Denville and Rockaway, bigger than Morris County, bigger than New Jersey. The only thing I knew about North Carolina was that it was far away. How was I supposed to survive there if I couldn't toughen myself up, if I didn't learn how much I could stand?

John or Jim was smiling, waving to people, drinking out of a plastic cup, one arm dangling out the window. He didn't know what was in store for him, and I felt badly for singling him out, though I didn't believe his coming death would be my doing – I didn't think I had such power, or any power, for that matter – but rather an act of fate or God or simple odds. He caught me staring, pointed a finger, and called, "You don't stand a chance, Nadelson."

By then the girl who'd organized the hunt had reached our car. She was just as stiff and serious as before, her walkie-talkie crackling on her belt, sweat gleaming above her black collar. I wanted to know what she would do all night while we were driving around. Would she stay in the dead-end street at the edge of the woods, or would she wait for us in the library parking lot? I preferred to imagine her sitting in the cemetery, beside Debbie's grave, though as far as I knew she and Debbie hadn't been friends or even acquaintances. I passed her our money, and she handed me a paper sheaf thicker than I'd expected, ten sheets, maybe twelve, printed with tiny letters, single-spaced, no margins on top or bottom.

And then she called more instructions into her megaphone, after which she began a countdown. I took one last look at John or Jim and slid into the Isuzu, where Bill was drumming the dashboard, and Alex was adjusting his rearview mirror and turning on his radar detector, and Jeannie was slumped down in her seat, staring sullenly out the window, her enormous cup of bourbon and Coke balanced on her knees. Somehow she managed to keep it from spilling when the girl with the megaphone reached "One," and shouted, "Go!" and Alex spun his tires and peeled out into the street. I lost a few drops of my drink, and a quarter of Bill's sloshed onto his lap, which made him shriek and squirm and shake his broken wrist.

But Alex was all concentration now, his big head tilted forward, leg pumping clutch, hand jerking gearshift, that enormous brain, I thought, putting all its power into a single thought: fast, fast, fast. We were five miles down Green Pond Road, nearing the barbed wire fences of Picatinny Arsenal – behind which the army built and stored enough weaponry to annihilate the continent of its choice – before any of us thought to consult the list.

There were maybe four or five hundred items, in an order that followed no apparent logic but rather the spontaneity and concrete randomness of dreams. Paper clips. Cough drops. Flavored condoms. A birthday card from Grandma. A dead skunk. Licorice. Ten maple leaves. A bowl of cooked rice.

I called out an item – feather pillow – and Bill shouted that he had one at his house. Alex gunned the car, winging around a corner, tossing me into Jeannie, who, to my surprise, didn't push me off but clung to my arm and to the door handle, her drink between her knees. It was only then that I realized how terrified she was, justifiably, and that this whole time she'd been imagining her own death tonight, no one else's. How strange that this possibility had never occurred to me, that we were just as likely – or more likely, the way Alex swerved around parked cars and garbage cans and the occasional screeching cat – to be the ones to skid into an embankment, or collide with a semi, or plunge off a bridge.

And I wondered how the school might mourn one of us. Alex, I had no doubt, would be lauded. He was so unapologetically smart that everyone respected him. In four years, as far as I knew, no one had ever picked on him, not even when he'd had terrible acne or when he'd had to wear his marching band uniform to class. He was our great hope, the one who made up for the rest of our failings, who'd go to Cornell and become an engineer and design the electrical devices of our future, who'd drive faster cars than we could imagine. If he died, people would cry for a week straight. The administration would name a classroom for him. The yearbook had already gone to press, but the staff, of which he was editor-in-chief, would add a four-page insert detailing his achievements.

Bill, who had his head out the passenger window, hollering song lyrics at the darkened windows of every house we passed, was a more dubious figure. He had plenty of friends, but a lot of people couldn't stand him. He got into fights. He had two ex-girlfriends who wouldn't speak to him, one of whom had written on his locker, in lipstick, "I HAVE A TINY PRICK." The kid whose wall he'd punched had threatened to sue him. Still, he was known by almost everyone; not a single person in the class would have to ask what he'd looked like. Volatility made him interesting, and his loss would be a loss to everyone.

Jeannie was another story. She was quiet and morose and no one knew much about her. She hung around with Bill, and she seemed to show up at every party, but if I weren't looking at her, I wouldn't have been able to describe her. Even sitting next to her I found her somewhat indistinct, though I studied the top of her head as she crouched beside me, the part in her dirty-blonde hair, the little white hand that clutched my arm. People would do their best to grieve her, but it would be difficult, I thought, like grieving a ghost or air, though now I was sure I'd be the one person to truly miss her, the feeling of her shoulder against my chest, her fingers through the fabric of my shirt, the little squeal in my ear as Alex flew around another curve.

I hoped she would feel the same about me, if I were the one to go. And with the car's tires skidding beneath us I was suddenly sure it *would* be me, that it *had* been me all along, and that I'd been blind not to realize it – or maybe I had realized it, and that's why I'd been fixated all year on the idea of someone dying. But I couldn't picture how the gym would look with my face on the poster. Who would show up, and for how long? What would the principal say about me in order to get people back to class? I'd been as invisible as Jeannie, as quiet and unassuming, trying to call as little attention to myself as possible, and still I'd been picked on relentlessly for two years, bullied by Teo and his friends, slammed against the locker every couple of days. Would the guidos cry over me and say they wished they'd known me better, that they'd miss the sound of my back crashing into metal?

The whole episode might raise me in everyone's estimation. People would remember me as smarter than I was, kinder, funnier. They'd recall some interesting thing I'd said in English class, though for the life of me I couldn't remember anything I'd ever said in class, and I berated myself for not saying interesting things, things that would have made me sound brave and principled and perceptive. "End apartheid!" I shouted now, imagining my final words being recalled in the gym, but either no one could hear me over the roar of the engine and the stereo blasting "Paradise City," or no one cared what I said, even if those were my last words, which I was now quite certain they would be, because the car seemed to be spinning out of control. My head was down next to Jeannie's, and I could see that her eyes were closed, that her mouth was moving, and she had a more striking face than I'd ever realized, a sharp nose and dimpled chin and soft lips, and if I knew for sure that I was going to die I would have kissed them, and she could have reported my final, bold action to everyone. But a degree of doubt must have lingered in my mind, because it occurred to me that Jeannie might still be the one to die, and what a terrible last moment it would be for her, to have some jerk kiss her without even asking.

But before I could make up my mind whether to kiss her or not, or find out which of us would die, the car screeched to a halt. Bill threw open his door and ran across his front lawn. Alex stretched his arms above his head. Jeannie and I straightened, and I slid back to my side of the seat. Both of us took long gulps from our drinks, and Jeannie looked out the window, turning her face from me so that I couldn't tell whether I'd been right about its appeal, or whether adrenaline – or bourbon – had distorted my perception. In a minute Bill came stumbling out his front door, with a feather pillow hugged to his chest, and Alex started rolling down the street before he'd gotten back into the car. As soon as the passenger door slammed, we were off again, two miles down the road before I called out another item – electric toothbrush – and Bill shouted that he had one of those at his house, too. Alex hardly touched the brake when he made a U-turn in the middle of the street.

WE CROSSED THE county half a dozen times that night, from Ledgewood to Parsippany, from Boonton to Mendham, stopping at 24-hour convenience stores and diners, at each of our houses, into the woods and down to the riverbank, gathering a single item at each place, only to realize we could have gotten two or three things while we were there. I snuck into and out of my house three times, certain that my parents could hear me, that they'd given up worrying about what I was doing, that they'd already let me go. At a Quick Stop in Morris Plains, we made Jeannie go in and buy the flavored condoms, and when she came back, her color was high, she was breathing hard, and if not lovely, she looked at least spirited, full of life; but then Bill asked if she preferred grape or cherry, and she tossed the condom box at the back of his head. Later, all four of us stopped to pee in the woods, and though Jeannie was behind a tree a few yards from us, I could hear her rustling in the leaves, and I was aware of her pants being down around her ankles at the same time that my fly was open, and I decided that this was the most alive I'd ever been, even if I was soon going to die.

Every leg of the trip Alex seemed to make the car go faster, and Bill howled louder, and Jeannie and I flopped against each other, until finally we just huddled together in the middle of the seat, our bodies touching from shoulders to ankles. I don't know if it was the proximity to death, or the Jim Beam, but Jeannie even made eye contact from time to time, and smiled at me, and when we skidded around a particularly terrifying turn, she took my hand, though as soon as the car straightened she let go.

And maybe I'd resigned myself to dying by now, or was too drunk to care, because I no longer thought about my last words and how I'd be remembered. I just called out whatever was on my mind, insulting the town and the state and the people who lived here, saying I couldn't wait to get out and never see the place again. "I'm a Tar Heel now!" I shouted. "What the fuck's a Tar Heel? I don't know, but I am one." I sang along with Bill and the tape we'd heard eight times over, and called to Alex, "Can't this thing go any faster?"

When the first faint glow lit the horizon, I counted our haul. Thirty-seven items. We cheered ourselves, and Alex tore off toward downtown Denville. On the way I remembered the ten maple leaves, which we collected from a tree on Franklin Road. Alex's radar detector went wild when we passed the baseball diamonds of Gardner Field, and for the first time all night he slowed down. "Wait a minute," I said. "It's on the list. A speeding ticket. Go! Go!"

But he wouldn't. Maybe he knew I was lying.

We were the first ones to make it to the library parking lot. Dawn was still ten minutes from breaking. It hit me only slowly that I'd survived the night, that Jeannie had, too, and Bill and Alex, and I was relieved for all of us, happy for our lives to go on, for our futures to unfold, no matter how dreary or difficult they might be, no matter how mysterious. It occurred to me that I didn't know where Jeannie was going to college, or if she was going at all. She eased away from me and looked out the window.

The organizer of the hunt showed up a few minutes later. She'd changed out of her burglar outfit. Now she was wearing an oversized T-shirt, pink pajama bottoms, and slippers. Her hair was in pigtails. She hadn't waited for us at all. Instead she'd returned home and gone to bed. Why was this the one thing I couldn't have imagined? She came over to chat with us, and her serious expression was gone, replaced by a groggy cheerfulness. She asked if we'd had a good time, if we liked her list. It amazed me to think she could have slept while we were zipping all over town, and I was pretty sure now that she'd had no intention of killing us off. She'd just wanted to entertain us, knowing we had nothing better to do with ourselves than search for things we didn't need. She had us line up our items on the pavement beside the car. She seemed surprised when she counted them, though whether she was surprised by how much or how little we'd found she didn't say.

A few more minutes passed, and still no one else arrived. Only then did I realize that while thinking about my own death, I'd forgotten about anyone else's. That we'd made it didn't make others' chances any better. And for a second I imagined that we were the only survivors, that everyone else was dead, the occupants of all twenty-three cars. And I thought, too, that maybe it was my fault after all, that I'd wished disaster onto us, and I decided I no longer wanted the tradition, I no longer needed to sit in the gym and cry. I was grown up enough, or maybe I no longer cared about growing up; in either case, I'd face my future without mourning and bonding, though I did like the idea of listening to music with Jeannie and sneaking away, not behind the bleachers, but out of the school and past the football field and down the hill behind it, to a soft patch of grass at the edge of the woods where I'd eaten lunch by myself freshman and sophomore years, where we'd no longer be hemmed in by bleachers and lockers and cafeteria tables, where we'd be free of all those things that for so long had kept us from being ourselves.

But then the first cars began to trickle in, Teo in his Monte Carlo, the class president in his pick-up, the wrestling star in his Mustang, the trashy girls in their Firebird. The organizer went around to each, counting items, making notes on a clipboard. Jim or John and his friends rolled up next to us in their blue Honda, looking tired and content, and I was relieved to see them alive. There was a dent in their front fender, but I couldn't be sure it hadn't been there before. Jim or John asked how many items we'd found, and by his smirk I knew we shouldn't answer. But Bill did answer, and Jim or John laughed. How many had they found? Eighty-three.

The organizer started calling out numbers. The wrestling star and his friends had gotten seventy-six. The class president ninety-eight. The trashy girls a hundred and fourteen. I stopped listening. Jeannie, as sullen as at the beginning of the night, lay her head against the window. Bill stomped around the parking lot, accusing people of cheating, trying to pick a fight. Alex shrugged and yawned. "No one found less faster," he said.

The last car to arrive was the Skylark. The straight-edge skinheads began to line up their items, and soon people gathered around to watch. It was unbelievable. Feather pillow, flavored condoms, a bowl of cooked rice, an electric toothbrush, orange Gatorade, a butterfly hair clip, a bamboo garden stake, a birthday card from Grandma... The objects kept coming, one after another. Even a dead skunk, tied up in a plastic garbage bag. Two hundred and five items. They took the prize. When someone asked how they'd done it, one of them shrugged. They'd spent half an hour in the dead-end near Green Pond, poring over the list, making categories, plotting their course. All night they'd made only four stops. Most of the stuff was sitting around in one of their garages. Finding the skunk was a lucky break.

My team had come in dead last. Alex rolled slowly back to his house. When we arrived, Jeannie got into her own car, a

Ford Taurus or a Chrysler LeBaron, something appropriately unassuming and invisible. She didn't look at me as she drove away. We hadn't said a single word to each other the whole night.

I slept all day. In the late afternoon, my mother asked what had happened to her crystal candlesticks and her good soap and the block of cheddar cheese she'd bought last week.

THREE HUNDRED AND twelve of us graduated without incident. The only kids not to join in the procession were those who'd flunked a class, and one who'd gone to jail two days after his eighteenth birthday for selling acid to an undercover cop. No one died during the parties the week after, or the ones that followed all summer, and by the middle of August we began scattering to our various colleges and jobs. When I got to North Carolina I found that I was as prepared as anyone for a new life, and I immersed myself in it without hesitation, quickly abandoning the New Jersey accent I hadn't even known I'd had, eating grits and biscuits, lusting after beautiful Southern girls.

I quickly forgot about high school and the mostly miserable time I'd spent there, about Teo and Bill and Jeannie. I forgot about Debbie and the week in the gym, about Jim or John, whom I'd wanted to die. And when I came home the following summer, feeling content and confident and as distant from the person I'd been a year ago as possible, I went with Alex to a party at a house near Green Pond. I'd hardly known the girl whose house it was, but she acted glad to see me. And so did everyone else there, the wrestling star, the class president, all seeming to forget that for four years we'd passed in the halls without speaking, that some of us had had to creep in the shadows to survive, afraid to show our faces. But to my surprise, all of us had grown up, even those who'd stayed behind to work crappy jobs. Everyone talked about the year that had passed, and asked me questions, genuinely interested in my stories of college debauchery, particularly the one about my friend who, in a drunken rage, pissed on his sleeping, fundamentalist Christian roommate. We were all relieved, it seemed, to have passed through that terrible time of adolescence, to have taken the first tentative steps toward adulthood. And no one had to die to make it happen.

About halfway through the night, a kid asked me if I'd heard about Pete. It took me a moment to figure out who he was talking about. Pete had been one of my few friends freshman and sophomore years, another outcast who'd figured out how to survive by recreating himself, growing his hair long, too, and taking up guitar. By the beginning of junior year he'd started a heavy metal band popular enough around the school to keep him from getting harassed. We'd drifted apart by the time we'd graduated, though we'd always greeted each other in the halls. I hadn't thought about him for more than a year.

He wasn't doing well, the kid told me. He had Crohn's disease, and there'd been complications. He'd lost a third of his body weight. He was in the hospital. Things were up and down. I should go visit him.

I said I would, and then said I needed to refill my beer. I refilled it again and again, all night, and drank from a whisky bottle someone was passing around, until I could hardly stand up. If Alex broke a hundred in his Hyundai on the way home, I was too far gone to notice. He had to help me into my house, where I threw up loudly enough to wake my parents.

In the morning, I was too sick to think about Pete. I managed not to think about him for the rest of the summer, either, and didn't visit him before going back to school. In the fall, his name would pop into my head from time to time, but I'd quickly push it away. Over winter break I considered calling the kid who'd told me about him but found excuses not to. I wanted to believe Pete was fine, out of the hospital, back in college, moving on with his life. I wanted to think that he'd forgotten me as completely as – or more so than – I'd forgotten him. I wanted us all to be whole and happy and a thousand years past those days when it mattered to me whether we'd bonded or not.

To this day, I don't know if Pete is alive or dead. I can't picture him as an adult any more than I can imagine his headstone on a grassy hill. When I think of him now, the only image that comes to mind is a long tiled hallway, bruised lockers on either side, Pete moving slowly down its center. His black hair masks most of his smooth white face. His baggy Motörhead T-shirt hides his skinny arms and chest. An electric guitar bounces against his back with every step. When the gym's tall double-doors appear at his side, he doesn't pause, doesn't wait for anyone to let him in. He walks past, keeping an easy pace, heading straight for the exit, for the bright cold light outside.

Melancholy-Mad in the Soft Night

I WAS MAYBE EIGHT OR NINE YEARS OLD, SITTING WITH my family at The Hunan restaurant in Morris Plains, New Jersey. It was a weekday evening in winter, the place raucous with kids and businessmen, no different than the dozens of times we'd been there before. We were in a booth beside a bank of windows, and outside it was dark enough for me to see my reflection in the glass. I enjoyed watching myself as I ate, making faces and tracing the movement of food down my throat. But then, just as I took a bite of spare rib, I heard a woman's voice behind me, not much more than a whisper: "I hope you *choke* on it."

The voice was slow and deliberate, full of anger, weighted with a bitterness deeper than any I'd encountered before, and this startled me even more than the words themselves. For an instant I was sure those words were directed at me, though I had no idea how I might have provoked them. I was sure, too, that I was the only one who'd heard them, the only one capable of hearing them, as if they'd been spoken directly into my ear, or only within my head. I chewed carefully and swallowed.

But then, beside me, my brother snickered. My father looked up, blinking, and my mother glanced over my shoulder with an astonished, stricken look, her jaw clamped on a mouthful of food. Not only had everyone heard the voice, I realized, but it had nothing to do with me. And for some reason I found this so disappointing that I set down my rib and began to turn. "Mind your own business," my mother said, but it was too late.

In the glass I caught sight of the couple behind us, their reflection framed by the red velvet uprights of the booth. The woman was in her early forties, with curly hair and a bony, bloodless face, lips pressed so tightly they disappeared. Her eyes were sunken and dark, and even then I recognized them as the eyes of someone who'd hardly slept for days. She had a plate in front of her, but her meal looked spare and unappealing, several chunks of crispy, glazed chicken surrounded by soggy broccoli, and in any case, it hadn't been touched. Her hands were under the table, her back stiff, her entire body still except for an odd twitch in her cheek that made her slender nose alternately sharpen and dull.

The man across from her I could see only in profile, and it was strange to think that he and I were back to back, separated by a few inches of fabric and foam. He was a little older than the woman, with gray hair over his ears, a trim mustache, a pinch of loose, rough skin under his chin. He wore a suit that seemed tight around his shoulders, and his face was flushed, as if his collar were squeezing all his blood into his face. His plate was nearly empty, only a few bits of pork and onion and pepper remaining in a pool of dark sauce. He sipped from his wine glass, then bent close to the table and scooped a mound of rice into his mouth. His jaw moved a couple of times and then stopped. He dropped his chopsticks. His hands went to his throat. But I knew he wasn't choking. He pretended for a few seconds, then laughed, and went back to eating.

The woman's mouth parted, but she didn't say anything. Her shoulders went limp. Her face no longer looked hard but beaten. Her tired eyes left the man, and before I could turn away, they caught my own.

There was no doubt that she'd seen me looking, no doubt that she knew what I'd seen. There was embarrassment in her expression, and shame, but also a hint of pleading, a desire for understanding and sympathy. She was glad to have someone else witness her torment, I can guess now, glad not to suffer alone.

When I turned back, my mother was looking at me with disappointment and reproach. I wanted to tell her she didn't need to scold me, that she was right, I shouldn't have looked, and that what I'd seen was punishment enough. There were three untouched ribs left in front of me, but I'd lost my appetite. I pushed the plate away.

I WAS RECENTLY reminded of this incident while re-reading "First Love," Ivan Turgenev's brilliant early novella, in which a boy discovers that his father is having an affair with their beautiful young neighbor, Zinaida. The sixteen-year-old narrator, too, is in love with Zinaida, but as yet he has no experience of love other than longing and fantasy. When he secretly follows his father to his rendezvous with Zinaida, he knows he shouldn't look, but he can't bring himself to turn away. Already he is in the grip of some kind of mystery, held fast by "an odd feeling, a feeling stronger than curiosity, stronger even than jealousy, stronger than fear." And what he sees he can hardly believe. The two argue quietly, Zinaida at first resisting her lover's advances. Then she holds out her arm, across which the narrator's father delivers "a sharp blow" with his riding crop. This horrifies the narrator, but what he sees next shocks him even more: "Zinaida quivered – looked silently at my father – and raising her arm slowly to her lips, kissed the scar which glowed crimson upon it." After this, her resistance is gone, and the narrator's father runs into her waiting embrace.

The narrator doesn't understand what he has seen any more than I understood what I saw in the restaurant, and his thoughts are "in a dreadful whirl." What he does realize, though, is that "however long [he] lived, [he] should always remember Zinaida's particular movement – her look, her smile at the moment." He has witnessed the ugliness and cruelty of adult love, the violence of desire, the wildness of passion, all of which he is years away from experiencing for himself. But he recognizes that this moment has aged him. His own love "now seemed ... so very puny and childish and trivial beside that other unknown something which [he] could hardly begin to guess at, but which struck terror into [him] like an unfamiliar, beautiful, but awe-inspiring face whose features one strains in vain to discern in the gathering darkness."

His glance has thrust him deeply into the mysteries of the world, and while this immersion terrifies him, it also transforms him. A few years later Zinaida dies in childbirth, and by then the narrator is prepared to face what lies before him: "Even in those lighthearted days of youth," he tells us, "I did not close my eyes to the mournful voice which called to me, to the solemn sound which came to me from beyond the grave." He is now open not only to the mysteries of love but also to grief and suffering and loss. He has entered the realm of truth, and there he remains, as much as it may pain him.

EXAMPLES OF SUCH forbidden looking abound in Western literature. None, I suppose, is better known than the story of Lot's salty wife, but close on its heels is that of the poet Orpheus, who, upon descending to the underworld to rescue his wife Eurydice from an untimely death, receives an injunction from the inhabitants of Hell: Take your wife back to Earth, but as you go, don't look behind. Of course Orpheus does look, and Eurydice falls back into the darkness, never to return.

In Ovid's version of the story, Orpheus casts his forbidden glance in order to make sure that Eurydice is still with him, "fearful that she'd lost her way." I read this less literally than metaphorically: What Orpheus fears is that his wife is in fact still dead, that she can't really return to the world of the living. When he turns, he sees the face of death behind him and knows that his wife is lost to him forever. She is taken from him a second time not because he has abandoned the prohibition but because his attempt to rescue her from death was futile from the start, because death is always final. Orpheus's forbidden glance brings him face to face with the fact of mortality, a fact he can no longer deny, and when he returns to the world he is inconsolable, "melancholy-mad," sitting in "rags and mud," living on "tears and sorrow."

But something else happens to Orpheus in the midst of his renewed grief, something, as with Turgenev's narrator, profound and transformative. Before being torn to pieces by "raging women" made wild by his beautiful singing and his refusal to sleep with them, he sits on a grassy hill to play his golden lyre. "A lovely place to rest," Ovid tells us, but one that "needed shade." And no sooner than Orpheus sings his first notes do all the trees of the world crowd around him, from the "silver poplar" to the "swaying lina," from the "delicate hazel" to the "spear-making ash."

His singing now isn't just beautiful but metamorphic, magical, an art form that transcends pleasure and enjoyment to literally change the landscape. According to Ovid, before visiting the underworld Orpheus was "poet of the hour." Now, having faced death and the horrible truth of mortality, he brings trees to a barren hillside. Informed by the knowledge of death, his art is lifted from momentary, passing fancy into legend. Despite what it cost him, his forbidden glance brings him greatness, and more important, infuses his song with a beauty that reshapes the world.

ORPHEUS REMAINS ONE of our most powerful archetypes of the artist, not because of his solitary brooding, but because of the way he captures his ineffable encounter with the unknown and gives it form, translating it for those who'll never experience it for themselves. In his image, the role of the artist is to see what we can't or don't want to see, and to present it to us in a form that doesn't allow us to look away.

No one, to my mind, has embraced this act of exposing the forbidden more fully or successfully than Chris Burden, the notorious performance artist of the 1970s, best known for pieces in which he has collaborators shoot him in the arm or crucify him to the hood of a car. When I first learned about Burden in an art history class in college, my professor spoke about him as an art world pariah, someone who took experimentation too far, who was reckless, sensational, exploitative. But when I finally viewed clips of his work, I was surprised to find how quiet they are compared to the sensationalism that surrounds us on every mediated front, how spare and simple and restrained. While his pieces often involve danger and self-inflicted pain, they resist the sensationalism of their subject matter in order to explore some of our most fundamental questions: How do we relate to the bodies that contain us? How much can these bodies bear? How can we live in the face of our vulnerabilities and the violence that constantly threatens us?

In 1973, the year I was born, Burden bought a month's worth of advertising time on a local TV station. After a highly produced ad for a dance music record anthology, video of one of Burden's performances appeared in black and white, with only a simple graphic, the artist's printed name followed by a handwritten title, "Through the Night Softly." For ten seconds, TV viewers watched Burden, wearing only underwear, with his hands held behind his back, squirm across pavement covered in broken glass. The only sound was Burden's heavy, grunting breath and the crunch of glass shards under his chest. And then the screen went blank, and he was quickly replaced by another highly produced ad, this one for shower soap.

I can only guess what viewers might have made of Burden's ad while awaiting the return of a sitcom or baseball game, when they were staring at their TVs with the half-consciousness that advertising demands. The image passed so quickly that they might have wondered if they'd really seen it, or if they'd only imagined it. They might have believed that someone at the TV station had made a mistake, that they'd glimpsed something they weren't supposed to see, that they should have turned away.

But that image of a man crawling through glass must have burned in their minds; they must have carried it around with them for the next few days or weeks or months, and even if they wanted to forget it, it would show up in their dreams.

When Burden placed "Through the Night Softly" on TV, American involvement in the Vietnam War was winding down, after many gruesome years, and certainly the piece evokes images of soldiers crawling through mud and debris, images that must have been all too familiar to viewers by 1973. But what Burden seemed to intuit – decades before reality television and 24-hour cable news – is that ours is a culture in which looking isn't really seeing. The images produced for us by advertisers are meant to lull, to erase thought rather than to provoke it, and the constant marketing of products drains meaning from even the hard facts of the nightly news. By slipping his ad between images of laundry detergent and motor oil, Burden ruptured the trance of his viewers, making them confront not only the horror of war and the ever-presence of mortality, but also the body's incredible resilience, its fragile beauty. He cut a small slit in the surface of our mundane daily existence and gave us a brief, irresistible glimpse of what lay behind.

The TV was his hillside, broken glass his lyre, ten seconds of video his song.

IT WOULD BE disingenuous to trace the start of my writing life to that evening at The Hunan restaurant when I was eight or nine years old. Another decade passed before I picked up a pen and tried to write a story, and certainly other experiences contributed to the genesis of those early efforts. But now, whenever I sit down to face a blank page, I try to remind myself what, above all else, I'm supposed to do: Look at what you don't want to see, even if you don't understand it, even if it causes you discomfort or confusion or pain.

I couldn't have guessed what went on between that couple in the booth behind me, what might have made the woman say those bitter words or look at me with such despair. Even now I can only wonder at the cruelty of the man's laughter as he scooped rice into his mouth. All I knew then was that I'd glimpsed something I shouldn't have, that I'd peeked into an adult world of misery and meanness I wasn't ready for and didn't think I ever would be. I'd seen something terrible and profound and mysterious, and like Turgenev's narrator, I knew it was something I'd never forget.

The couple left before we did, and I kept my head down as they passed our table. Soon after, my father paid the bill, and I followed my family outside. It had grown darker since we'd gone in. But now my eyes were all the way open. They took in more light. They made the darkness brighter.

The Two Lances; Or, Self-Portrait with Flames

THE SUMMER I SHOULD HAVE HIT PUBERTY BUT DIDN'T, I went to a Jewish sleep-away camp in the Poconos. My counselor was British, and in the showers, where I refused to take off my bathing suit and expose my hairless genitals, I was confronted by an enormous uncircumcised dick, which in my imagination grew as long as my forearm and twice its girth. To make things worse, the boys in my bunk held daily masturbating contests, and more than once I walked in to find four of them lined up on a bed, arms chugging, faces screwed up – in pleasure or agony, I couldn't tell – while a fifth knelt in front, squinting, to judge who came first. When they asked if I wanted to join in, I made whatever excuses came to mind: I couldn't get it up in front of other guys, I'd say, or I'd already jacked off in the bathroom and wouldn't be able to go again for another hour.

Needless to say, it was an uncomfortable summer for me, full of insecurities, and not only because of my slow development. Most of the kids in camp came from Westchester and Long Island, and even if their families weren't much wealthier than mine – we were solidly upper-middle-class – they showed off their wealth in ways that mine never did. Their parents dropped them off in Mercedes, BMWs, even the occasional Ferrari. Around their necks they wore 24-karat gold Chais and Stars of David. They were obsessed with brand-name clothing, Guess, Polo, Benetton. They talked about vacation homes on Nantucket,

Cape Cod, Hilton Head. They had rolls of cash to spend at the camp store, which sold shampoo, toothpaste, soda, and candy.

Now, of course, I can see that such displays of wealth were signs of insecurity in their own right. These parents were the tacky rich, desperate to prove how high they'd climbed, and their children were spoiled and snobbish, nothing to envy. And how rich were they really if they had to ship their kids off for eight weeks of every summer to a camp subsidized by the Young Men's Hebrew Association?

At the time, though, I was newly ashamed of the off-brand clothing my mother bought me on excursions to the Secaucus outlet malls, shirts with little giraffes and poodles embroidered on the chest instead of alligators or men on horseback. I was ashamed, too, of the decade-old Plymouth Valiant my father refused to give up and, worse, whose passenger door he refused to repair after denting it on a lamp post while backing out of a parking lot. "It still opens, doesn't it?" he'd say. They were both children of working-class families and cautious by nature, and frugality was a value they tried to instill in me early. But when they dropped me off at camp, and my father handed me a twenty-dollar bill that was supposed to last until they picked me up in August, I thought only, Cheapskates. I couldn't wait for them to take the Valiant away, praying that no one had seen me step out of its dented door.

Being invisible was the fantasy I indulged most consistently at thirteen.

THE TWO KIDS I remember best from that summer, strangely enough, were both named Lance, and both were the sons of doctors. Lance Berman was a tall, charming kid with a surf haircut and a sadistic streak, who had no respect for authority and no fear of consequences. He was late to every morning reveille and every Friday night service, usually because he had a hard time deciding what to wear. He'd stand in front of his cubby for forty-five minutes, pulling out one designer shirt after another, utterly deaf to our counselor's admonishments. He'd spend another half hour in front of the mirror, arranging his bleached curls with a wet brush and pick, dabbing cologne on his neck, under his arms, in a streak down his belly that ended just inside his shorts.

And as far as I could tell, his vanity paid off. Every few days he had a new girlfriend, with whom he'd rendezvous late at night, sneaking out of the bunk as soon as he heard our counselor's first snore. Most couples found secluded spots around the lake, but Berman always took his girls through the woods on the far side of the baseball diamond, to a clearing known as Devil's Meadow because some kid had spray-painted the number six on the trunks of three trees at its edge. "Jewish girls go wild for Satan," he'd say the next morning, showing off purple hickies on his neck, bragging about his fourth handjob of the summer. One of the other boys would say, "Doesn't count if you shove her hand down your pants," and Berman would answer, "It does if she keeps it there."

Aside from girls and clothes, what interested Berman above all was contraband. At the bottom of his trunk he'd squirreled away two stale packs of Winstons, a pint of peach schnapps, and four knives – one Swiss Army, one Bowie, one butterfly, and one Rambo-style survival, with built-in flint and fish scaler. He also had half a dozen butane lighters, which he'd pull out those nights he didn't go to Devil's Meadow. He'd lead a few of us to the middle of the soccer field, build a little teepee out of twigs, with dried leaves in its center, set it blazing, and tear back to the bunk. At morning reveille, the camp director asked anyone with information about the mysterious fires to step forward. It was only a matter of time before he found out who was behind them; the longer it took, the steeper the punishment. A kid from another bunk raised his hand. "I know who it is," he said, and everyone went quiet. A few of us snuck furtive glances at Berman, whose face was impassive, even amused. "Jason," the kid went on. "You know, from *Friday the 13th*? He's going to kill us all."

To be friends with Berman meant high adventure and constant risk, but the risk was greater if he didn't like you. At Friday night services he'd sit behind a girl who hadn't sparked to his advances and flick his lighter a few times, leaving burn marks in a hundred-dollar Benetton sweater. When he heard that some boy from another bunk had badmouthed him, he showed up in the middle of the night with his butterfly knife, waking the kid with a gentle poke on the cheek. "Pissed himself in two seconds," he bragged the next day. Others he'd pick on for no reason, except that he didn't like the look of their nose or teeth or bowed legs, and then he'd hound them relentlessly, making up dozens of nicknames, each more derogatory than the last – Pizza-face, Zit-face, Volcano-face, Puss-face, Diaper-rash-face – until they made the mistake of trying to fight him, or else wisely avoided him, taking the long way around to the cafeteria and swimming pool.

I should have been an easy target for him, hairless as I was, small and quiet, with cheap, ill-fitting clothes, but for some reason he left me alone. Maybe it was because I liked the thrill of danger, though I was never one to instigate it myself, happily joining in with lighting fires on the soccer field and throwing mounds of skunk cabbage through the window of a rival bunk. Or maybe it was because I covered for him early in the summer, when our counselor came in late from a rendezvous of his own – the female counselors loved his accent and, I guessed, his uncircumcised dick – and found Berman's bed empty. "He's out looking for you," I said, and made up a story about how Berman had heard the director walking around outside and wanted to make sure our counselor didn't get into trouble.

Whatever the reason, he soon treated me like a little brother, or a mascot, even though my birthday was three weeks ahead of his. He called me Baby Nadel. He gave me advice about girls – "They always want to go farther than they say they do" – though I couldn't bring myself to talk to any, much less make arrangements to meet them in the woods. Before the first all-camp dance, he gestured at my Fruit of the Loom crew-neck and said, "You'll never get any action in that." Then he handed me a collared Polo that came down almost to my knees.

LANCE ENGELBERG'S PARENTS must have spent just as much money as Berman's did on their son's clothes, but Engelberg wore only camouflage. Camouflage shorts, camouflage T-shirts, camouflage hunting cap. He had a buzz cut, thick glasses, pasty skin. He was pudgy. His voice was high-pitched and nasal. On the first day of camp he stayed on our counselor's heels, rummaging through his backpack, saying things like, "Got my mess kit, my bug spray, my compass, my magnifying glass. If I get lost in the woods, I can survive till winter." He was completely oblivious to the snickering around him, and also to our counselor's smirk, which slipped into a look of disgust when he turned and bumped into Engelberg for the third time in an hour.

That night, as soon as our counselor turned out the lights and slipped away, there was a sound – whump! – followed by Engelberg's nasal cry: "Who threw that? Whose shoe is this?" Then another whump! and Engelberg shouting, "You guys are asking for trouble. You don't know who you're messing with." Whump! whump! whump! The barrage lasted for a few minutes, the sound of leather slapping skin soon lost beneath Engelberg's howling. I should have felt sorry for him, but mostly I was grateful that the shoes weren't flying at me. In the morning our counselor scolded us for the mess, and Engelberg turned away as we gathered our scattered shoes. I'm not proud of it, but one of them was mine – a rubber flip-flop that couldn't have done much damage, other than add to Engelberg's humiliation. When Berman saw me retrieve it, he gave a smile and wink, wiping away whatever shame I might have felt, whatever regret.

Engelberg's torment was only beginning. We hid his hunting cap, broke his compass, threw his mess kit into the lake. Berman was particularly hard on him. He was offended that they shared a name, afraid, maybe, that someone would associate them together, though no one called Engelberg Lance. To everyone except our counselor, who called him Mr. E. (he called all of us by our last initial, and we all envied Judah Zelinsky: Mr. Zed), he was Engelbutt. Almost every day Berman dumped the clothes out of his cubby and then yelled at him for being a slob. When the pool lifeguard wasn't looking, he held Engelberg underwater until his arms began to thrash, and then let him up just long enough to cough and heave a new breath before plunging him back down.

One night, when Berman came back from Devil's Meadow, he pounced on Engelberg in bed, pinning his arms with his knees, and held his fingers under Engelberg's nose. "You want some action, Engelbutt? You want to smell some pussy?" Engelberg bucked and flailed but couldn't dislodge him. "Smell the pussy," Berman whispered. By then the rest of us had gathered around, and we all began to chant, "Smell the pussy, smell the pussy!" Engelberg howled, "I don't want to smell the pussy!" and soon he was crying, his nose so clogged that he most likely couldn't have smelled anything, even with Berman's fingers halfway up his nostrils.

Now, imagining myself standing at the edge of that circle, chanting softly, I can only shake my head. You don't have to do this, I want to call out to that scared, skinny kid in ugly clothes. This isn't really you. At the time, though, it wouldn't have occurred to me to stand up for Engelberg, to tell Berman to leave him alone, or even to stay in bed, in silent protest. I didn't see myself as someone who had the luxury to speak his mind, to voice judgments about right and wrong, not when Berman's fingers could just as easily have been up my own nose. That was something left to adults, or at least to kids with hair between their legs, and any time I found myself growing uneasy over Engelberg's treatment, I told myself he had plenty of other people he could turn to.

To my surprise, though, Engelberg never once reported his sufferings to our counselor or to the camp director. He didn't ask to move bunks or call his parents to take him home. He didn't quit talking about his mess kit and compass or telling us we didn't know who we were messing with. He took his punishments and quickly seemed to forget about them, walking around in a haze of obliviousness that cleared only the next time Berman tried to drown him. And every time, he was equally astonished to find the world so cruel, indignant to discover that the rest of us enjoyed watching his torture, and his tears always seemed to carry more disappointment than pain, anger, or embarrassment. I wanted to shake him, to tell him he could avoid all this if he'd just put his head down, as I did, to sink inside himself and make himself as little noticed as possible. At the same time, I couldn't help but admire his stoicism or stubbornness or stupidity, or whatever it was that kept him from retreating.

He was tougher than any of us expected, more resilient, and he did have genuine survival skills. On an overnight canoe trip on the Delaware River, our counselor forgot to bring matches, and Engelberg got a fire going with his magnifying glass. I hadn't read *Lord of the Flies* by then, but now, every time I picture Piggy, I see Engelberg's buzz cut, his pale, pudgy cheeks, his glasses reflecting flames. We cheered him as we made roasting sticks for our hot dogs and marshmallows. Even Berman clapped him on the back – he could have started the fire himself, but that would have meant having his lighter confiscated afterward – and for the rest of the night, instead of Engelbutt, he called him Daniel Boonedick.

At first I tried to keep my distance from Engelberg, for fear that I'd suddenly find myself within his sphere of suffering, but if we ever happened to be alone together, he'd confide in me, as if he recognized a fellow victim of circumstance. "That wasn't pussy, you know," he said once, out of the blue, when we stood on the lakeshore waiting for the rest of the bunk to come in from sailing lessons. He skipped a stone across the water, eight or nine hops before it slipped under. "He stuck his finger up his own ass." I must have given a look he took as skeptical, because he went on, "What? You don't think I know what pussy smells like? I got a girlfriend back home." I didn't say anything – not because I doubted him, but because I was feeling sorry for myself, worried that I'd never make it to puberty, that I'd stay a hairless little boy forever. But then Engelberg shrugged. "Okay. Maybe I don't have a girlfriend. But I got sisters."

It turned out that he was as obsessed with girls as Berman was, but he said he wouldn't waste his time on flat-chested Jewish thirteen-year-olds. He was in love with a movie actress, Kim Cattrall, who'd recently played a mannequin that came to life at night. "Think about it," he said. "It would be the greatest thing ever. You could keep her in the closet and suck on her tits whenever you want. Who cares if she's plastic?"

Another time, he claimed that his neighbor walked naked in front of her window every day, that she knew he watched and liked it. Before long he admitted that he didn't know for sure if she saw him, because he hid behind the curtain and kept his lights out, and only let his eyes peek over the windowsill. And then he admitted that she wasn't actually naked but in a bathrobe, and he didn't know if he wanted to see her naked anyway, because she was maybe fifty years old and fat, and he was pretty sure she wore a wig.

He told me that he and his father had built a go-cart together, and then admitted that it wasn't officially a go-cart because it didn't have an engine, it was more like a soap-box derby racer, and actually they hadn't built it yet but were planning to when he got home from camp, only his father worked all the time and never really did what he said he'd do, and in the end he'd probably just buy him a go-cart because that was easier.

Engelberg never seemed ashamed of the lies, nor of the truths he revealed shortly after. Rather, he seemed content simply to talk, and despite knowing I was supposed to spurn him, I found myself content to listen – that is, until Berman saw us together. Then I'd say, loud, "Later Engelbutt," knock his hat off his head, and get away from him as quickly as possible.

IF I'D BEEN conscious of such things then, I might have seen the Lances as representing two potential paths for me, two modes of living – like something out of Proust, the Berman Way and the Engelberg Way. Berman's may have been the more appealing, but it was also by far the more challenging. I was neither tall nor charming nor terribly sadistic. I would never have a cubby full of designer clothes or expensive cologne. Whenever I was with him I was nearly sick with anxiety, afraid he'd turn on me, suddenly decide I wasn't worth his time or effort, that he'd get more pleasure from torturing me than from taking me under wing. But Berman himself radiated anxiety, too. It was always painfully obvious how much he wanted people to think highly of him, or to fear him, and he was constantly glancing around to confirm that all eyes were on him. If I didn't comment on his newest hickey, he'd point it out, making sure I took note of the teeth marks around its edge. I didn't understand why my approval mattered to him. The idea that he could need something from me I found incomprehensible and somehow troubling.

To be Engelberg, on the other hand, meant taking some blows, but on the whole his was the path of ease. He didn't worry about what other people thought of him, or even, really, what other people did to him. He lived in the moment, without fear, and as a result he could say what he wanted, wear what he wanted, do what he wanted. He could get interested in hornets or poisonous mushrooms or the healing property of spider webs and talk about it for hours, without worrying that he was boring anyone, that someone might soon strangle him with a vine to shut him up. And he was more relaxing to be around than Berman was. I never had to have my guard up around him, and I found myself avoiding him less and less as the summer went on, allowing those moments we happened to be alone together to stretch out into entire afternoons, when we skipped some activity neither of us could stand – rope course or volleyball – and instead wandered into the woods, where he'd teach me to whittle sticks into spears and talk about a letter he'd written to Kim

Cattrall, professing his love and detailing the nasty things he did with her in his dreams – only he hadn't really written the letter yet, but he was going to as soon as he got home and looked up the address of her agent, but probably he wouldn't write the letter at all, because she'd never actually get it, and even if she did she'd never write back, and maybe instead he'd just buy himself a mannequin.

I became increasingly aware of the freedom in the Engelberg Way as I drifted in its direction, and I might have chosen it outright if paths stayed separate, if they didn't take sudden turns and unexpectedly converge. But sometime around the middle of summer, to everyone's surprise, Engelberg won over Berman and the rest of the bunk with fire. He showed us how to make a flame-thrower out of a lighter and bug spray, and we watched in amazement even when he explained, in his tedious, nasal voice, that you had to spray a little extra after the flames went out, or else the fire might get sucked back into the can and make it explode. "You could lose a whole hand," he said. "I bet none of you guys know how to make a tourniquet." Then he squirted some bug spray on his arm and touched the lighter to it. Blue flames danced over his pasty flesh. Several of us shrieked, and one kid tried to bat out the fire. But Engelberg just waved his arm until the flame sputtered out. A pink streak showed faintly on his white skin. "Jeez," he said. "You guys don't know anything about fire."

Berman snatched the can from him, made a flame-thrower of his own, and chased Engelberg around the bunk. When he took his finger off the trigger, the flame did indeed suck into the can. "Baby Nadel," he called. "Catch!" I jumped out of the way, and the can rolled beneath our counselor's bed. We all tore out of the bunk and took cover in the surrounding trees. I don't know what we expected – for the roof to blow off, a fireball to rise a thousand feet into the sky? After a few minutes we went back inside. The can had split open along its welded seam, and a gummy mess covered part of the floor. "You guys owe me a new can of bug spray," Engelberg said. "I need it. I'm allergic to chiggers."

We all pooled our money – all except me, who had only eight bucks left and was running out of soap – to buy every can of bug spray the camp store carried. And after that, the bunk became an unpredictable, perilous place for everyone. You'd come in to find a pool of liquid flames in the middle of the floor; or sometimes, it would be in the middle of your bed, and you had to leap on it and slap it out before it singed your blanket. You'd step out the door, and a three-foot stream of fire would come roaring at you, and then Berman would hoot with laughter when you dropped to the ground and crab-walked away.

But there were also unexpected moments of beauty. One night, Engelberg stood for a good half hour on another kid's top bunk bed, spraying the ceiling. None of us knew what he was doing, and Berman kept shouting at him, "There's no chiggers up there, Engelbutt." But when he flicked the lighter, a pattern of stars and moons spread across the rafters, and all of us, even Berman, were awed into silence. The furiously rippling night sky cast a soft, magical glow over all our faces. None of us cared if the bunk burned to the ground. We watched until the last star winked out and then went to sleep without a word, not a single insult or dirty joke, entirely at peace with each other and the world.

WHAT SURPRISED ME most, though, what seemed least predictable, was how seamlessly Engelberg integrated into the group, as if all of us had forgotten that he was supposed to be an outcast, as if we hadn't persecuted him for nearly a month. Everyone still called him Engelbutt, and Berman still dumped his clothes out of his cubby from time to time, but there were no more shoe barrages or attempted drownings or soiled fingers stuck up his nose. In the cafeteria he'd argue with Berman and the others about different brands of skateboards and compare notes about favorite Nintendo games. They'd talk about go-carts and soap-box derby racers, with the genuine expectation that they'd own one or the other soon after they got home.

What surprised me, in other words, was how much Engelberg and Berman had in common. While they discussed the spoils of being doctors' sons, I sat silently, eating my Salisbury steak. My parents bought me plenty of things I wanted – which mostly included baseball cards – but all I could focus on now was that I didn't have skateboards or Nintendo, and that I'd never have a go-cart in a million years. And rather than being envious, I was disdainful. Things came too easily to the Lances. They didn't have to struggle through the summer with twenty bucks, doling out quarters for Red Vines and using a bar of soap until it disintegrated. For the first time in my life I adopted a sullen, underclass pride, which came with a large dose of sadness: No matter how much Berman and Engelberg vied for my friendship, I'd always be the real outcast among them.

Soon, Engelberg joined Berman's late-night outings, participating in fire-setting on the soccer field and skunk-cabbage raids on other bunks. It was as if he'd always been there, stifling giggles and giving advice about how to set the blaze – or as if I were the only one who remembered that he hadn't always been there, that the idea once would have been unthinkable.

But the unthinkable was now the rule. One night, Berman brought Engelberg along to Devil's Meadow, where he hid among the spray-painted trees while Berman and his newest girlfriend – who, to Berman's consternation, wouldn't let him touch anything below her neck – began their nightly struggle. At Berman's signal, Engelberg came running out of the woods in nothing but shorts, arms outspread, flames dancing from his shoulders to the tips of his fingers. The Devil himself, come to claim the young lovers. The girl ran off shrieking, leaving her shoes behind. The two Lances could hardly breathe from laughing when they made it back to the bunk, both flopping onto Berman's bed and sputtering, "Did you see – " "Her face! Her face!" "He kept – he kept – " "I – I – " " – kept shouting, 'Six six six! Six six six!'"

When they finally calmed down, I could see Engelberg wincing when he shifted his weight. Red welts were rising on his arms. "Next time, my hand's up her shirt like nothing," Berman said, and snapped his fingers. He leaned back on his pillow, with both hands behind his head, and stretched out his legs. "Get the hell off my bed, Engelbutt."

I was jealous, there's no denying it. Berman had never asked me to play such a prominent role in his pranks, and even though I knew the whole episode would have been far less frightening for the girl – and funny for us – if I'd been the one on fire, still I felt slighted.

But even more, I was bewildered. Maybe I still am. After all he'd suffered at Berman's hand, how could Engelberg laugh with him, how could he go along with his practical jokes and act as if he'd never been pounced on in the middle of the night, never had shit-stained fingers shoved up his nose? Did he have no memory? Was he some kind of saint, full of forgiveness? Or had he simply been seduced into the Berman Way, now so desperate for people to like him that he excused all past transgressions against him?

I tried to ask him about it the next time we were alone together, tramping along the lakeshore to a little beach where Engelberg thought we might catch spring peepers. I don't remember what I said exactly, but it was probably something along the lines of, "You must still hate Berman's guts, even though he's nicer to you now."

Engelberg gave me a puzzled look and shrugged. "He's okay." When I pressed him further, reminding him of the hurled shoes and the near-drownings, he shrugged again and said, "I got an older brother."

If I'd thought I was strong enough, I would have pushed him into the lake and held his head underwater. I'd never been angrier in my life, or so confused. "He put his finger in his ass and stuck it up your nose," I said.

He shrugged once more. "I breathed through my mouth."

It was the least satisfying answer he could have given, but he didn't offer anything more. Now I have a pretty good idea of why it bothered me so much, and even then I had an inkling. His shrugs, if not his words, suggested that whatever pain he'd experienced didn't matter now that he was free of it. They even seemed to imply that suffering was worthwhile if it brought you to a place of contentment, if you ended up happy, and this, above all, I couldn't accept. Avoiding pain and humiliation was the primary goal of my waking hours, and even if I wasn't always successful, I couldn't imagine approaching life any differently. Wasn't it better never to be seen at all, rather than to be seen, kicked, and then embraced?

One afternoon a few days later, I came into the bunk after swimming lessons to find another masturbating contest in full swing. Berman was in on it, and so was Engelberg. A magazine lay on the floor in front of them, opened to a picture of Kim Cattrall riding on the back of a motorcycle. I felt something stirring in me, though not in my swim trunks. What would have happened if I'd taken them off and let everyone see what was really there? Would I have felt any less lonely? The Lances didn't pay me any attention. They were side by side, arms moving in perfect rhythm, mouths open, eyes glazed.

Now, once again, as I picture my younger self standing in that doorway, so small and unassuming, hair tangled with cowlicks, shirt marred with grass stains, I have a terrible urge to call out. Go on, I want to tell him. Get it over with. If you can stop hiding now, you'll save us so much trouble later on. I can hardly watch as he turns, trunks still on, and walks away.

Another day, soon after, Berman laughed and hooted as Engelberg, arms on fire, flapped through the woods like a phoenix and belly flopped into the lake. Steam rose around him. Berman dove in after, and the two of them swam out to a nearby dock, where they tipped over a canoe full of girls, who squealed and splashed around them.

On the shore, I held the can of bug spray and the lighter. I don't remember what thoughts went through my mind, exactly, but I know that I wished for a different kind of pain than the dull, hollow ache of longing that left no mark on my body, that had no starting point and no end.

I gave a few squirts into my palm, flicked the flint, and held the flame an inch away. But that was as close as I could bring it.

The Secret Well

IN SEPTEMBER OF 1987, I DIDN'T THINK LIFE COULD get any worse. I was fourteen, a freshman in high school, and lonelier than I'd ever been. My brother had just gone away to college. My parents lived a life apart from me, lost in the politics of their jobs, which they discussed at length during dinner while I picked silently at my food. The last week of summer vacation I'd come down with chicken pox, which I'd somehow avoided as a child, and started the year emaciated and scabby. Malicious sophomores, eager to show off their cruelty, kicked my books down the hall and made me do push-ups in front of their cheering girlfriends, who were strangely alluring even as they laughed and shouted insults, in their tight Judas Priest T-shirts and short skirts and fringed leather boots. My friends from junior high, all more athletic and savvy than I, quickly learned how to navigate the new school's hierarchies and promptly dropped me, pretending not to know me when we passed in the hall, making sure no seat was left for me at their cafeteria table. I ate my lunch alone, on a concrete slab behind the school, hoping no one would see me. Usually no one did.

At night I watched baseball, hoping for solace, but found none. My team, the New York Mets, were reigning champions, but their playing was lackluster, unenthusiastic, without a hint of the previous year's heroics. Dwight Gooden, our star pitcher, had sat out the first two months of the season after his urine tested positive for cocaine. I felt alternately neglected and betrayed.

Didn't Doc know how much I needed his fastball? Couldn't he have waited until after the drug test to take a snort? The Mets ended the season three games out of first place, and I didn't bother to watch the playoffs.

And then, at the end of the month, my favorite uncle killed himself. The news came as such a shock that I felt myself falling off my chair as my mother told me, though I remained upright, staring at the computer in my brother's empty room, where I was typing a paper for English class. I still remember that feeling, of tipping backward and to the side, beginning to tumble, and then being startled to realize I was sitting up, rigid, staring into my mother's face, which was fraught with concern and confusion. This is the worst month of my life, I thought, and immediately felt guilty for thinking only of myself.

Uncle Mitch was my godfather, husband of my father's sister. I'd known him as a cheerful bald man, always making jokes and smoking cigars, though later I learned that he had a terrible temper and a tendency to brood. In other words, I hardly knew him, though he'd been a straightforward, benevolent presence in my life since the day I was born. He'd left no note, and to this day no one knows for sure why he did what he did. He'd been separated from my aunt for almost a year, living alone in a Manhattan apartment, but his daughters lived nearby, and the younger had just gotten engaged. He may have had legal or financial trouble. He suffered from frequent kidney stones, and the pain may have been more than he could bear. Whatever the reason, he cleaned his old army-issued pistol – he'd been a colonel in the Reserves, one of the only military men in the family – and shot himself at his kitchen table.

At first, I didn't care about the reasons. The fact of what he'd done was enough. It was inconceivable to me, but at the same time I was awed by it. As miserable as I'd been that month, I'd never once contemplated something like suicide. The thought hadn't even entered my mind. It didn't enter it now, either, though I was suddenly terrified. What did dawn on me was that as bad as things were, they could always get worse. It was hard to believe, but I had to confront the possibility that I could be even more miserable than I already was, so much so that death seemed like the only option. And if this weren't really the worst month of my life, then there was another worst month out there waiting for me, one that might be my last.

What I glimpsed in Uncle Mitch's death, I can see now, was the well of potential suffering we all live with but rarely acknowledge. At the time I couldn't have put it into words, but in the days after hearing the news I glanced down that well again and again and again, just beginning to realize how deep it was, deeper than I could have imagined. But as much as this scared me, it also had a strangely disorienting effect, making my present misery seem far away, as if it were something I'd lived through years ago and survived unscathed.

At the funeral I watched my cousins cry but couldn't do it myself. I was too mystified by what had happened, as puzzled and curious as I was sad. I pretended to wipe my eyes, felt guilty again, and stopped. Instead of wondering what had driven Uncle Mitch to this, I wondered instead what would drive me to it, what precise combination of pain and despair would be too much for me to take. If I could imagine the breaking point, I could avoid it. I could live through one month after another, each worse than the last, but never reach the final one, the worst of all.

But no matter how hard I tried to picture that hypothetical suffering, I could see only what was right in front of me: eating lunch alone on a concrete slab, spending evenings in my brother's empty room, struggling to do push-ups in front of lovely, sadistic girls in heavy metal T-shirts who squealed in delight at my debasement. And I felt guilty once more for thinking Uncle Mitch had done this for my benefit, that there was a lesson in it for me. Why couldn't I focus instead on the suffering of his wife and daughters, or on my own sadness, which was slow in coming, stalled by astonishment and self-pity? Why couldn't I linger on the plain awfulness of it, the simple tragedy and loss?

I studied my aunt, who looked stunned and furious and, I suspected, worried that people would blame her. I wanted to comfort her, to tell her I knew this wasn't her fault. If I could have explained what I'd begun to intimate about the depths of that secret well, maybe it would have helped her. But the best I could do was stay close to her, hoping she could read my mind, and after the service, I overheard her say to my father, "No one should ever get that lonely." The words weren't meant for me any more than Uncle Mitch's suicide was meant to send me a message, but I couldn't help taking them as further warning. Get it together, my aunt seemed to be saying, or look what might happen to you.

By then my chicken pox scabs had fallen off and my scars were beginning to fade. I'd gained back some weight, and color had returned to my cheeks. As we pulled away from the cemetery I scrutinized myself in the rearview mirror, once again feeling as if my present struggles were behind me, settled long ago and remembered only vaguely, with mild anguish and mild relief. If I didn't want this to be my last month, was it really so bad after all? My father caught my eye and held it. Now I guess that his look was meant to reassure me or at least to acknowledge my confusion and grief, but at the time I thought that the longer he observed me the greater the possibility that he could hear my selfish thoughts. I turned away and hunched down in my seat.

Despite the itchy suit and the tie I told myself I shouldn't loosen until we made it home, I felt myself relaxing a little, easing back from the brink. What was it, exactly, I began to wonder, that had made me so miserable? My brother was gone, true, and I missed him, but now I had his room to myself and his old computer and the stack of dirty magazines he'd stashed in the back of his closet. And though no one at school talked to me, I did have friends from summer camp, from a youth group, from my baseball team, and on weekends I wasn't always lonely. And though the Mets had stumbled this season, they still came in second place and had a strong lineup for next year. Even missing a third of the season, Doc Gooden, my broken hero, managed to win fifteen games. Now he was clean and focused and poised for a comeback. No more cocaine. No reason for despair.

Every day for the next week, I returned from a long, silent day at school, sat at the kitchen table in the empty house, and imagined holding a gun to my head. And every day I thought, No, not now, not a chance. This wasn't as lonely as I could get. This wasn't as much as I could suffer. And then I'd get up, trembling, with equal portions terror and relief, as if the bullet had grazed me. I'd grab a box of cookies, plop on the couch, and watch TV, relief turning almost to levity, and after a while I'd find my brother's stack of dirty magazines and entertain myself until my mother came home from work.

A week or so after the funeral, my brother sent my aunt a long, heartfelt, sympathetic letter, which she read to my father over the phone. "He's really grown up," my father said. "When did he get so mature?" I felt ashamed for not having expressed my sympathy, too, but mostly I wondered why my brother hadn't sent me a letter, why it hadn't occurred to him that I also needed comfort. Again I began to feel sorry for myself, abandoned and forgotten. At the kitchen table I tuned out my parents' frustrated talk about their jobs and tried to imagine what had gone through Uncle Mitch's mind as he held the gun to his head, what thoughts might have been his last. But of course I couldn't. I didn't know what the sorrow of his separation might have felt like, or the fear of legal or financial trouble, or the pain of kidney stones. The only thought that came to me was no, no way, not a chance. If I couldn't imagine the pain, then maybe I'd never have to feel it.

At school, the malicious sophomores let me pass without incident. They'd forgotten my scabby face or moved on to other victims. Their girlfriends no longer laughed at me, or noticed me at all, and I was left to stare at their legs and imagine them replacing the women in my brother's magazines, their bodies contorted, their eyes closed, their mouths parted and glistening.

One day at lunch I went back to the cafeteria and sat with some kids from my French class. No one seemed surprised to see me there, and no one told me I belonged elsewhere. At home I hurried past the kitchen table, going straight for the couch in the family room, watching TV with cookie crumbs sprinkled down my chest.

Sometime in early November, I cried, genuinely, over Uncle Mitch's death. It finally struck me that I'd never see him again, that I'd miss his jokes, his smirk, the smell of his cigars. I recalled that tumbling sensation again, that feeling of going down and down and down, but I no longer felt it directly, and I wasn't surprised to find myself sitting up. This month was better than the last, and the next, I had a feeling, would be better still. I continued to spend long days on my own, but I did so with a certain contentment, a half-formed notion that I'd been saved from a terrible fate and set on a safer path. I wished Uncle Mitch could have known what he'd done for me, though I doubted it would have eased the suffering I couldn't imagine.

I remained aware, however, that the worst month was still out there, lurking, ready to catch me unprepared. And for the next seventeen years I was braced for it, treading carefully around the edge of my secret well.

WHY, THEN, WAS I so surprised to find myself plunging in headlong, tumbling for real? Why was I astonished to discover that the well was deeper even than I'd suspected?

While living in a beautiful neighborhood in Northwest Portland, engaged, my wedding a month away, I had the feeling – well-entrenched if unconscious – that happiness and contentment were things I deserved. I didn't see the world as a terribly forgiving place but one in which I'd received my appropriate share of good fortune. And when good fortune turned out to be fleeting or illusory, I was suddenly stricken with knots in my back, headaches, a mysterious, burning rash that sprouted from groin to chest.

When I moved across town into the attic whose rent I couldn't afford, I thought again, This is the worst month of my life. It was far worse than what I'd suffered at fourteen, worse than all intervening months, some of which had included a measure of heartache and disappointment and despair. And I thought how naïve I'd been at fourteen, to imagine I could escape this fate, to think that Doc Gooden and the Mets could return to their former glory, that Gooden's career wouldn't be a story of unfulfilled promise, drug abuse, and prison time. I was naïve, too, to imagine that Uncle Mitch's suicide could have taught me anything, though I felt that now I could finally sympathize with him as he sat at his kitchen table, facing the pistol he'd cleaned and loaded. I could finally understand what he'd done.

My closest friends in town were musicians, all away on tour; other friends had families, pregnant wives, stressful jobs; they offered sympathy but had no time to see me. I went days without speaking to anyone or getting out of bed. I took up smoking for the first time since college. I drank alone in bars or in my attic and then drove fast through crowded streets, back and forth across Portland's half-dozen bridges, the dark water swirling below. One night I crawled out a window onto my roof, carrying a bottle of Scotch, and sat with my feet dangling three stories above cracked concrete. The old eaves, rotted in spots, creaked beneath me. If I fell, I fell, I told myself. If I didn't, I didn't. I'd leave it up to gravity and Famous Grouse.

Now it's hard to imagine being in such a state, and if I didn't recall it so clearly I might think it was something I'd dreamed, or something I'd made up for a story. But I can see myself up on that rooftop, a cigarette burning on the shingle beside me, bottle between my knees, warm breeze rustling the leaves of nearby cherry trees. Streetlamps. Dark rooftops. The voices of people passing on the sidewalk below. A world that had shrugged me off. I lay back and stared at the sky made orange by the city's glow, not a single star in sight. My feet dangled in the abyss, and when

I think of it now I shudder, knowing how easily the rest of me could have followed.

But of course I didn't fall, and at the end of the month I was still alive. And to my surprise, I found that that was how I wanted it. Once again I imagined the gun to my head and once again thought, No way. Even if my body were nothing but a container for grief and anguish, I preferred it intact. My friends came back from their tour, and though I was no less drunk, now I didn't drink alone. I walked to bars and stumbled home, staying clear of my car and of bridges. Sickened by the stench of tobacco on my clothes, I threw away a pack of Camels with three cigarettes unsmoked. I put a screen in the window that led to my roof. My rash went away, and my headaches eased.

By then it occurred to me I still didn't know Uncle Mitch at all. His pain remained unimaginable to me, as did his action. The well of suffering wasn't just deep. It was bottomless. But how far down you had to go before you couldn't take it was something I still hoped never to discover.

The date of my wedding came and went. I cried a bit, drank, went out with friends. The following morning I woke to face another day and thought, with relief, It could be worse. And then I thought, with a chill rising from the very depths of my being, It could be worse.

4

First Fees

I DISCOVERED ISAAC BABEL THE YEAR MY GRANDFATHER was dying. At the time it struck me as more than coincidence. Both men had grown up in the Russian Pale of Settlement, the great short story writer in Odessa, my grandfather in a shtetl near the Polish border. Both had experienced the terror of pogroms early in their lives, and both had been faithful communists during the ecstatic, hopeful years following the Revolution. My grandfather was too young to ride with the Red Cavalry as Babel did, and he left Leningrad for New Haven just as Stalin was beginning the purges that would eventually make Babel disappear. Still, in my mind they'd led parallel lives, and I was certain that if my grandfather read Babel's stories, he would have loved them as much as I did.

But my grandfather didn't read Babel or Chekhov or Turgenev or any of my other literary heroes, not in his native language or in his adopted English, which he'd spoken with a heavy accent for the past seventy years. He'd worked as a house painter, starting when he was seventeen, and in the evenings he was too tired to read books. He played cards or listened to the radio or watched TV. On weekends he took his children to the beach and fished for sea bass and snapper. His business did well, and he retired early. By the time I knew him he was one of dozens of big-eared old men in a retirement complex outside Fort Lauderdale, a shark on the shuffleboard court and at the gin table. He never talked about his childhood or about Russia.

What little I knew I'd heard from my mother, who herself had heard only snippets from her own mother and from her reticent Russian aunts. Everyone in the family seemed to agree that the past was best forgotten, and as I grew up, I developed a roving curiosity that didn't require satisfaction; I had the sense that while there were secrets waiting to be discovered, most mysteries would stay mysterious. Partial illumination was the best anyone could hope for.

Only during his last years, when his short-term memory was failing – doctors would eventually discover a tumor the size of a baseball in his brain – did my grandfather tell me a few stories about his early life. On the phone, or even when I was visiting, he'd forget who I was, mistaking me for a long-dead brother or cousin or card partner, and he'd say a few words about his first crossing to the States (his sister came down with chicken pox on the way over, and the whole family was sent back) or about his years in Leningrad, attending art school, painting factories, and chanting work songs (the happiest time of his life, he said).

These stories only whet my appetite – could secrets be revealed after all? – but soon my grandfather's health deteriorated further, and he could no longer talk much. By then I was in graduate school, trying to learn how to write fiction, and one of my teachers introduced me to Babel. How was it possible that I'd never heard of him before? His stories were revelatory, not only for their mastery of the form, their gorgeous sentences, but for the lost world they shed light on: one, I felt strangely, I'd known my whole life but of which I was only now becoming fully conscious. It wasn't just the time and place that felt familiar – Russia and its satellites from 1905 to 1925 – but the elegiac tone, the exhilarating voice, the yearning for a life lived fully, ripe with experience and passion.

At the same time, the stories were full of mystery of a deeper, more complex sort than the kind I was used to. Unlike in my grandfather's stories – both the ones I'd heard and the ones he didn't tell – what happened in them was clear and richly detailed, but their meaning was elusive. "My heart, stained with bloodshed, grated and brimmed over," one of Babel's narrators says after killing a poor woman's goose to prove how tough he is; "My heart contracted as the foreboding of some essential truth touched me with light fingers," another says, after nearly sleeping with a married woman. Intimations, hints of illumination, but nothing concrete, no solid answers. This was what made them so haunting, and also, I decided, what must have lain behind my grandfather's stories. He kept them secret not because he no longer wanted to think about the past, but because the past was full of mystery and passion, the horror and exhilaration of living – and for a modest man, these things were best kept to himself.

Both Babel's and my grandfather's stories thrilled me, but they also made me doubt myself. I hadn't ridden with the Red Cavalry; I hadn't killed anyone's goose or seduced a married woman; I hadn't been sent back to Russia after crossing the Atlantic or painted factories or joined the Communist Party. How could I write about the mysteries of life if I'd never experienced its exhilaration, its passion, its horror?

To compensate, I ripped off a line from Babel and started a story about my grandfather. I invented whatever I didn't know about his past, and the character I ended up with had almost nothing in common with the person I knew, a loving, stern old man with a mischievous sense of humor and an unpredictable temper, someone whose approval I craved more than anything else and whose judgment I feared just as much. Before I could finish a draft and send it to him, he died.

A YEAR OR so later, I was still struggling to write the story. By then I'd finished school and had gotten my first job teaching composition at a community college in Vancouver, Washington. This was in the fall of 1999. Everyone else was getting rich on the internet bubble, buying houses and cars and boats, but I proudly made almost nothing. Poverty was payment for the life I wanted, for the stories I hoped to tell. My basement apartment was straight out of a Babel story, freezing and smelling of mildew, with dingy carpets and sketchy wiring that often shorted and left the place in darkness. I imagined that Babel would have respected me for the hours I spent in there, scribbling and typing and pacing, and I wanted to believe that my grandfather would have admired me, too, though he may have frowned on my borrowing money so often from my parents.

My students were a mix of suburban kids right out of high school, working-class adults looking to change careers, and recent immigrants. The adults were far more motivated than the kids, many of whom weren't mature or studious enough to go straight to a four-year college, but they often had difficult home lives and disappeared for weeks at a time. The kids turned in most of their assignments, but their priorities were elsewhere – sports, romance, video games – and they showed up for class only when they had nothing better to do.

The immigrants were the most reliable and dedicated, though many struggled with English. There were several students from Southeast Asia, a few from Mexico, but the biggest group was Russian and Ukrainian, some of whom had come during the early days of Gorbachev's perestroika, some more recently. Because their accents reminded me of my grandfather, I had a special affection for them and often let their grammar mistakes slide. "In essay about environment, writer fails to mention concerns about economy," a student would write, and ignoring the dropped articles, I'd scribble in the margin, "Good point." Who needed articles anyway? The sentence was perfectly comprehensible, with the efficiency and punchiness of a headline. And there was music in it, too, that made the language come alive, far more so than in the awkward, butchered sentences of my native speakers: "In Annie's essay, 'Living Like Weasels,' she talks about a time when she saw a weasel at the lake and she thinks about what it would be like to live like a weasel."

Taking attendance the first day of the term, I found great pleasure in reading out names I'd read before only in Chekhov, Turgenev, and Babel: Dmitry, Pavel, Katya, Yulia. But when I stumbled over "Stanislava," a husky, heavily-accented voice said, "You can call me Stacey if you vant." The voice belonged to a girl in the front row, who was looking at me skeptically, I thought, with a touch of condescension. She didn't sound like a Stacey, or look like one, either, with a broad face and small features, hair done in an early '80s feathered job, parted down the middle.

"Do you prefer Stacey?" I asked. She shrugged. "Stanislava's fine with me," I said, careful this time to enunciate each syllable. She shrugged again. Her skeptical look remained.

And it didn't remain just for the rest of that class period, but for the rest of the term. When I talked about grammar, syntax, the function of the paragraph, the structure of an argument, she stared at me as if I were trying to sell her a used car with a missing engine or a piece of real estate in the middle of a swamp. And in truth, I was skeptical, too. I was just twenty-six, uncertain of myself not only as a teacher but as a figure of authority. I did know something about grammar and syntax, but I hardly believed myself when I insisted that those things were important. I'd never been formally trained in composition and taught the class from another teacher's curriculum. And though I didn't say this to the department chair who'd hired me, I secretly believed that composition classes were a waste of time. I'd learned to write by reading other writers and by writing about things that mattered to me. I had my students writing essays on race relations, poverty, conservation, but what really interested them were stereo systems and hubcaps and spoilers for their souped-up Hondas. How could they learn anything from me?

What I really wanted was to present myself as a renegade artist like Isaac Babel, someone driven by passion and devotion, who'd forsaken an easy life in favor of one full of meaning, content to remain unknown and unrewarded so long as I was free to pursue my calling. I thought the students should understand that writing wasn't just about sentence structure and paragraphs, that those things were important only as tools to express the hidden secrets of their souls. Occasionally I'd set aside the curriculum and give little lectures, or pep talks, encouraging them to write about whatever moved them or terrified them, whatever kept them up at night or haunted them through their waking hours. I quoted Babel as if his thought were my own: "No iron can stab the heart with such force as a period put just at the right place."

But even then Stanislava gave me the look that suggested she didn't believe a word I was saying, or maybe that she only half-believed me, but would wait to decide whether or not to take my advice under consideration. She seemed to know that renegade artists didn't teach at community colleges.

Her look chilled me. As soon as I caught a glimpse of it, I stammered and lost my train of thought. Then I had to give up any hope of inspiring the class and instead go back to drilling them on comma splices and sentence fragments. At least part of what unnerved me was Stanislava's appearance. Her clothes were as out of date as her haircut, relics of the '80s, or more likely, cheap Russian knockoffs of the early '90s: loose dresses that fell off the shoulder and bunched around the waist, shiny flats or pumps, black leggings or skin-colored panty hose. I figured she and her family couldn't afford more fashionable clothes, but she wore hers without embarrassment, even with an air of haughtiness.

In fact, she reminded me of girls from my high school, and maybe that's what really threw me: Her clothes, her indifference and poise, knocked me back a decade and sent me three thousand miles east, made me the pimpled, awkward sixteen-year-old I never wanted to be again. The girls she recalled had set my teachers then on edge, too, and I'd always admired the way they'd file their nails in class, fail tests without caring, date only rich kids or drug dealers because they wanted to be seen riding in hot cars. They were all still in New Jersey, I guessed, living miserable lives, with bratty kids and abusive husbands, but still I sometimes had a pang of regret when I thought about them, wishing I could have been bold enough to sell coke and buy an old Camaro, though I knew nothing about cars, and in fact couldn't even drive a stick shift.

After I handed back the first assignment, Stanislava stayed after class to talk to me. She wanted to understand her grade – a B+, despite dozens of dropped articles – and now her expression wasn't skeptical but wounded, as if I'd let her down. I spoke quickly, defensively, saying that writing wasn't like math or chemistry, there was no right or wrong, but that I was looking for a deep engagement with the subject matter, an in-depth analysis of texts, a logical structure and competent handling of language. Then I talked more specifically about her essay's ending, explaining that she'd wrapped up her argument too tidily, oversimplifying her conclusions. She'd be better off acknowledging the full complexity of the subject, I told her, and allow for ambiguity. "The way Chekhov does," I said, hopefully. She gave me a blank look. "Do you know Chekhov?"

She shrugged. "So you vant I should rewrite ending?"

Normally I didn't allow revisions after I'd recorded the grade, but I said yes, she could rewrite it, and turn it in next week. Then her old look returned, critical and scrutinizing, maybe even mocking. What a sucker I was, it seemed to say. How unethical of me to treat her differently than my other students. But she lingered as I packed my bag and then walked me out to my car, as if it were the only courteous thing to do, and the most natural thing in the world. Her presence made me nervous, and to cover it, I asked questions about her family and her background. She'd come to the States five years ago, when she was fourteen. Her father worked for the power company. She had three brothers, two still in high school. The oldest drove a cab in Portland. And where exactly did she grow up? I asked.

"Odessa."

"Odessa!" I said. "Like Isaac Babel!" Again she looked at me blankly. "Do you know Babel?" Again she shrugged. He was my favorite writer, I told her, and I'd read his stories so many times I felt I knew Odessa as well as I knew my own hometown, though of course it was the Odessa of 1905, or more properly the Odessa of Babel's imagination, an exotic place crawling with criminals and quaking with the threat of pogroms. As we crossed the parking lot I got carried away, describing Babel's humor and fierceness, his mastery of the sentence, and I had to cut myself off as Stanislava's gaze drifted away. "My grandfather spent time in Odessa," I said. He'd never told me so, and I knew it was unlikely, but the mere possibility – the fact that I knew almost nothing – seemed to justify embellishment. "He said it was beautiful."

Whether it was true or not, Stanislava didn't seem to hear me, or wasn't interested. We'd reached my car, a decade-old Camry my father had given me, with a busted taillight and a ding in the driver's door, badly in need of a wash. The sight of it filled me with shame.

"So I'll give you new ending next week," she said, and shook my hand forcefully, as if concerned that I might have second thoughts and try to back out.

I WASN'T ATTRACTED to Stanislava, exactly. For one thing she was too young for me, and she was my student. Plus her expression was sour, and she had a swath of acne on her neck, and her '80s clothes made her look silly. Nevertheless I felt drawn to her, a desire to connect competing with a desire to please, and even then I understood at least in part that what I really longed for was my grandfather and the world that was lost to me now that he was gone.

And here it was in a nineteen-year-old composition student. Dark, mysterious Russia, the Revolution and civil war, the communist experiment, the thick accent and air of struggle.

Stanislava, too, had lived a life I couldn't quite imagine, and like my grandfather who was born Moshe but always went by Morris, she, too, tried to hide it by calling herself Stacey and wearing clothes that were supposed to make her look American, though she was wearing them in the wrong decade. And maybe what I wanted was for her to recognize that we were alike, that I was someone who had more to him than he revealed on the surface, whose day job was a mask for depths of feeling and intellect he'd reveal only to a few chosen and worthy.

In any case, I thought about her more than I should have, and after talking to her in the parking lot, I scrapped my lesson plan for the following class. Instead of discussing topic sentences, I handed out my favorite Isaac Babel story, along with a new assignment for the next essay. The story was "My First Fee." In it, a young writer, lonely and tormented by the sound of neighbors making love through his wall, hires a prostitute. But when he follows her home, he's so disgusted by the sordidness of her lodgings, so disappointed by the lack of romance in her bearing, that he hesitates. When she prods him, he makes up a story about himself – he, too, is a whore, he says, "a boy with the Armenians" – and the prostitute is so moved by his tale that she offers him the passion he has been dreaming about, teaching him all the secrets of her trade. When he tries to pay her, she refuses. And he realizes that what she's really doing is paying him for his story. It's the first time he's been rewarded for the work of his imagination, and it's a transformative moment for him. Even years later, after various successes and disappointments, he still values this first fee, "from the hands of love," as the most valuable of his career.

In class I tried to lead a discussion about the story, asking questions about character and voice, about the power of storytelling and the passion of a life dedicated to art. No one answered. I pointed out a particular passage that excited me, one that gave me hope that I could write about human experience without having experienced much of it – "A well-devised story needn't try to be like real life," the narrator says. "Real life is only too eager to resemble a well-devised story" – and asked if anyone had a sense of what it meant. Again, no answer.

Finally one of my adult students raised her hand. I called on her and waited, smiling. "I can't believe you gave this to us," she said. "This is pornography."

I was too flabbergasted to say anything. I waited for someone to come to the story's defense. But then another student agreed that she found it offensive. Yet another began a speech about the exploitation of women, and soon the class devolved into a debate about whether or not prostitution should be legalized, whether it was better for society to keep its dirty secrets hidden or to flaunt them out in the open. They talked about Bangkok and Amsterdam, about disease and the new slave trade, and the whole time Stanislava fixed me with that bemused expression that suggested she'd known all along what a bad idea it was to break with the safe curriculum and branch out on my own. Only when a kid in the back row, with a baseball cap shading his face, piped in, "Some dudes just got to have it," did I cut the conversation off and go back to talking about topic sentences and the use of quotations.

For the assignment I gave the students a choice: either write a close analysis of Babel's story or write a personal essay about their own experience with storytelling, a time when either telling or hearing a story affected them deeply. Most chose the former, though rather than analyze Babel's craft, the essays tended toward analysis of his narrator's moral depravity, and by extension, I gathered, my own moral depravity for having assigned the story. Others ignored both options and continued to argue for or against legalizing prostitution. Stanislava took a stance somewhere in the middle, arguing that prostitution should remain illegal but that only the men who hired prostitutes should be punished. Much of her essay was a discussion of supply and demand. Her conclusions were no more complex or nuanced than the first essay's, and she had just as many missing articles, but this time I gave it an A-. Still, she stayed after class to discuss her grade, looking wounded again, and again I allowed her to rewrite the ending.

"Didn't you like the story?" I asked as she walked me to my car. She shrugged. "Did he capture the spirit of Odessa?"

"Story took place in Tbilisi," she said. "I never went there."

In front of my car, newly washed, she shook my hand and turned away. As she walked off, I wondered if my grandfather had ever visited prostitutes during his young, wild years in Leningrad, but as with most things about him, I could only speculate. What I knew for sure was that the old man I'd loved, the one who'd been a fiercely overprotective father to my mother, letting her go away to college only if she went to an all-girls school, would have thought it criminal to give such a racy story to a class with young women enrolled.

The only student to take my second option was a shy Vietnamese girl, to whom I hadn't paid much attention until now. She described a story her father had once told her when she was ten and wanted a dog. During the war, he said, when he was a teenager in Saigon, he'd adopted a dog he'd found in the street. The dog was skinny and full of fleas, but he loved it and cared for it. Then, during the Tet Offensive, the noise of gunfire scared it, and it ran away. He found it a few days later. Both its back legs were broken. It was in agony. He asked a soldier to shoot it for him. He had no place to bury the body, so he threw it in the river. He cried for days.

He wasn't trying to scare her, the girl wrote, or prevent her from getting a dog. He just wanted her to understand what responsibility really meant, the risks as well as the pleasures. But after hearing the story, she no longer wanted a dog. She didn't want a pet of any kind. She never wanted to love anything for the rest of her life. It took her years to forgive her father for telling her the story.

The essay was moving and complex, though nearly every line contained tense and pronoun problems. I gave it a B+.

I was young. Everything in the world was subjective to me then.

ON THE LAST day of class, after discussing details of the final assignment – I'd gone back to the regular curriculum, and everyone was to write arguments for or against capital punishment – I tried once more for inspiration. I gave my familiar speech about language's power to persuade, to evoke, even to infuriate, reminding the class that above all writing was a way to express what was most important to them, that structure and grammar didn't matter for their own sake but only as tools, etc.

And then, without having planned it ahead of time, I told them a story about my grandfather. In the 1920s, I said, when he was an art student in Leningrad, he'd had a real talent for painting cityscapes. He spent days wandering the streets for new angles and fresh views, and the leaders of the local politburo took notice, hanging several of his canvases in their offices and meeting rooms. But then his father moved the family to America. Here they had no money, and my grandfather had to go to work. He had no time anymore to paint pictures. Instead he painted houses and never touched a canvas again. But sometimes, when work was slow enough, he'd make little sketches on the siding he was painting and then cover them up before the owner came home. When he was dying, he told me, "Boychikul, anyone can make a living. Do something you care about, and you'll never regret it."

The story was sentimental, and hardly a word of it was true. Even before I'd finished speaking most of the students had begun packing their bags. It was the last time I'd see them, but no one said goodbye. Only Stanislava stopped to talk to me on the way out. Her expression was different today, not skeptical, I thought, not wounded, but worried. Maybe I'd struck a nerve this time. Maybe I'd finally broken through. Maybe she realized how much she'd miss seeing me every week.

"If ending of final essay needs more work," she asked, "can I rewrite over break?"

I hesitated. It wasn't a reasonable request. It would mean I'd have to put through a change of grade form at the beginning of the next term, and get it signed by the department chair and the registrar. I'd also have to make up a reason why the change was necessary. She smiled at me nervously. She was wearing a light blue cardigan over a dark blue turtleneck. Her hair was up in a high ponytail, flopping down on the right side of her head, and big earrings dangled to her shoulders. She was up against enough, I thought, moving to a new country and trying to fit in. She deserved a break wherever she could get it. "Sure," I said, and she shook my hand.

This time she didn't walk me to my car. There was a boy waiting for her outside the classroom. He was bright-eyed and pimpled, with a crew cut and baggy jeans, an oversized hockey jersey that came to his knees. Stanislava introduced him. Her boyfriend, Ivan. "I hear about your great class," he said. "Stacey tells me how much you help her writing." I was so choked with jealousy I could hardly respond. I mumbled something about what a pleasure it had been to have Stacey in the class. I wished them a good holiday.

"I'll send email to find out about ending," Stanislava said, and gave me a genuine smile, full of innocence and gratitude. I watched the two of them walk hand-in-hand to the parking lot, where Ivan opened the door of a brand new Mustang, bright yellow, with a black racing stripe down the middle of its hood and roof, hubcaps gleaming. It was the kind of car one of Isaac Babel's narrators would have admired and yearned for, I thought, wishing he could race it through the streets of Odessa, knowing he could never afford it.

And my grandfather? He'd driven a Camry, like me. Whatever life he might have lived in Russia, whatever experience of horror and passion he'd hidden from everyone who loved him, the man I knew wasn't a renegade artist. He wasn't Isaac Babel, who'd proudly boasted of his association with mobsters and Cossacks. His early struggles and triumphs were payment for a simple, ordinary life of work, family, fishing, and shuffleboard, which made up the bulk of his experience.

And only if I accepted this, I realized, could I finally write a story about him, which I did over the next few weeks. In it were no dramatic scenes of the Revolution, no prostitutes or slaughtered geese or drunken, married seductresses. Instead it was about an old man losing his memory and the grandson who desperately wanted his approval, its mysteries those that were – and are – most mysterious to me: the desire for connection and the fear of judgment that makes connection nearly impossible. It took place not in Leningrad but in Fort Lauderdale, in a mall, in a restaurant, at the side of a pool.

Before I finished it, I collected final papers from my mailbox and discovered an envelope tucked into the stack. It was addressed to "Mr. Scott." For a moment I felt renewed hope, imagining a letter from Stanislava, finally telling me that my words had meant something to her. Inside the envelope was a black and white photograph of a flower, a little out of focus and too dark, obviously developed by hand. On the back was a note: "Thank you for wonderful class. I love story about grandfather. Inspire me to make picture. Have happy break."

The signature wasn't Stanislava's. It was the Vietnamese girl's, the one who'd written the story about her father and the dog. Beneath it was a postscript: "By the way – anyone ever tell you look like Ross from *Friends*? (Compliment!)"

It was a payment of sorts, but I couldn't be sure whether or not it was from the hands of love. All I did know was that I hadn't earned it.

The Nothing That Is

MY SOPHOMORE YEAR OF COLLEGE I SIGNED UP FOR A comparative literature survey class that sampled the great works of the Western world from Goethe to García Márquez. I was fairly new to literature – I'd hardly read at all in high school but over the previous year I'd decided it was the most important thing in the world to me, something to which I'd swiftly and happily pinned my identity. This decision arose partly out of genuine passion; Dylan Thomas's poetry had moved me the first time I'd read it, and Chaucer's *Miller's Tale* had made me laugh out loud. But I also liked the idea of myself as someone who was passionate about literature, and even more, the idea of other people recognizing me for such passion, which struck me as unique and distinguished, a mark of my sophisticated and mysterious nature.

All this was part of a larger transformation I'd undergone over the past year, moving to North Carolina, quickly abandoning the New Jersey accent I previously hadn't even been aware of, taking my first tentative steps toward independence. It had never occurred to me before that an identity was something I could construct for myself. It didn't occur to me now, either – not consciously, at least – though as soon as I was gone from my parents' house I was aware that no one around me knew who I was, or who I'd been, and that, given a little effort, I could be whoever I claimed to be.

The comp lit course description stirred me, and I carried

it around in my pocket over winter break, as if to remind myself of the person I'd become. On it were big books I wanted to tell people I'd read – *Faust, Crime and Punishment, Madame Bovary* – along with others I'd never heard of but whose titles intrigued me: *Dead Souls, Death in Venice*. Yes, death caught my attention. What better subject for a nineteen-year-old obsessed with transformation?

Above all, though, I was excited about Kafka, who was then to me nothing more than a name. I knew he'd written a story about a man who turned into a bug, but I hadn't read that story or any others. Still, the name meant something to me. I associated it with mystery and weirdness and cryptic knowledge, and if anyone had asked I would have claimed to be a fan. That I hadn't yet read him was simply a matter of patience. I was waiting for the right moment. I didn't want to rush it, when I had so much to read for classes, though I did find plenty of time to read other writers, spending long hours in the stacks of the library, poring over *The Waste Land* and *The Cantos*, neither of which I understood and both of which I pretended to love.

Around the same time I signed up for the class, a friend introduced me to LSD. This, too, was something about which I'd feigned knowledge, though when I finally experienced it, I was surprised to discover how little my imagination held up to this new, distorted reality. The acrobatics and contortions through which the drug exercised my mind alternately fascinated and terrified me. I spent hours staring at the wiggling lines of my fingerprints, or at a textured ceiling crawling with neon death's-heads, and felt confirmed in my belief – copped from watching David Lynch films – that the world was stranger than I knew, that the reality I took for granted was shaky and porous, a mask for other realities lurking just out of sight. I was primed for further transformation, though a part of me resisted it, fearing I might not be able to transform myself back. Delaying reading Kafka may have been part of my strategy for keeping at least one foot in the world I knew.

On the first day of class, though, I was disappointed to find that Kafka wasn't on the schedule until early April. It was only January, but in the bookstore I'd already snuck a peek at the first page of "The Metamorphosis" – indeed, a man turned into a bug – and then forced myself to wait. Patience, I reminded myself, though for the next few months, every time I dropped acid, I found Kafka's phrase "uneasy dreams" at the forefront of my frantic thoughts.

The class was taught by a twenty-five-year-old master's student named Hugh, a small, sad-eyed young man with bad posture, who had a habit of pulling on his earlobes when he spoke. It was obvious from the first meeting that he was new to teaching and had no idea what he was doing. It clearly pained him to be standing in front of a room, stared at by thirty skeptical undergrads, and for the first half hour he didn't glance up at us. His voice trembled as he read out the attendance sheet and went over the syllabus. He muttered something about grading, then about not believing in grades, and then said, "Don't tell anyone I said that." He gained some traction when he read us a poem – Baudelaire's "Spleen," I think – but when no one responded to his attempts to provoke discussion, he let us go.

I knew we were in for a rough semester, but as excruciating as it was to watch Hugh struggle through the hour, I still found myself looking forward to his class – more so than he did, I imagine – and it wasn't only because of the material. I felt an immediate affinity for Hugh. For one thing, he was a fellow Jew, short and slight, with curly hair to his shoulders and soft, mournful lips. He, too, was from the Northeast – Rochester, maybe, or Buffalo – but he hadn't lost his accent at all, and every time he spoke I felt a pleasant nostalgia for a world I'd happily left behind.

Unlike me, however, who in moving to the South felt instantly freed from the constrictions, real or imagined, of my childhood, enrapt by the shining smiles and glistening hair and wild laughter of the North Carolina beauties lounging languidly all over campus (the first girl I slept with in college was the daughter of a Statesville preacher, who to my delight and exhilaration and utter terror, told me that if her Daddy caught us in bed together he'd shoot me in the belly with his Winchester), Hugh was clearly uncomfortable in his new surroundings, or more accurately, disdainful of them. He cringed every time one of my classmates read lines of *Faust* with a drawl. He often had to ask one kid, who came from a little town up on the Blue Ridge, to repeat himself, as if he were speaking another language. "When Faust *cowls* the dog? What do you mean?" To him they were all hicks and rednecks and yokels, no matter how well they could write an essay, and he soon began calling on me more than anyone else. And though I didn't have very interesting things to say – "I thought it was cool when the dog turns into Mephistopheles" – he appreciated my participation, always responding enthusiastically, pulling on one of his earlobes: "Yes! Yes! It *is* cool!"

What we shared above all was a love of literature so inarticulate that it had no place in the classroom, and certainly not in a classroom full of skeptical sorority girls, one of whom thought to ask why in the world Faust would make a pact with the devil in the first place.

Hugh only looked at her blankly. I imagined we were thinking the same thing: Who wouldn't?

DURING THE SEMESTER I'd occasionally run into Hugh outside of class, in the cafeteria, up on Franklin Street, and he'd greet me with a weary, sarcastic smile, one eyebrow raised, as if we were sharing a private joke built on mutual suffering. He was usually with a group of scruffy international graduate students, all of whom smoked and muttered indistinguishably in heavy French and Italian accents. "I don't know how you can stand it down here," he'd say, jerking a thumb at a restaurant he'd just left. "Nothing but hillbilly food. Their lasagna tastes like grits."

Away from the podium and blackboard, Hugh was far more eloquent about the books he loved, telling me why he'd always found the end of *Madame Bovary* so sad, what made the opening of *Dead Souls* so funny. He was more relaxed, too, making fun of one of my classmates, who didn't know the difference between *there* and *their* and wrote a paper about the potential for Faust's salvation, if only he would accept Jesus into his heart. It was clear that Hugh wanted something from me: to recognize that he was more intelligent than he seemed in class, maybe, that he reserved his true wisdom for only those who deserved it.

I wanted something from him, too, though at the time I couldn't have said what. Approval, I suppose, acknowledgment that I was serious and curious and distinguished in my desire for understanding not just the world I could see around me but the one I could imagine only with the help of books and drugs. One night, my brain sizzling with acid, I ran into him outside the library, and though there was a swirling screen of color between us, I thought I managed to carry on a reasonably lucid conversation, saying something about how I'd seen Raskolnikov's spiritual awakening coming the moment he committed the murder. Then I said, "I can't wait for Kafka," and Hugh raised an eyebrow, smirked, and twirled his cigarette in front of me, its glowing end a racing comet in the pulsing universe around my eyes.

"I bet you can't," he said.

Around that time I got arrested for smoking pot outside a concert hall and sentenced to fifty hours of community service. Transformation was in full swing. I felt unhinged, not from reality, exactly, but from the kid I'd once been, the person my parents wanted me to be. It didn't matter whether I was a literature student or a criminal; either way, I'd stepped outside the boundaries of the familiar, and my dreams did, in fact, grow uneasy, filled with snake pits and snapping dogs and policemen waving guns, and occasionally with characters from the books I was reading: Emma Bovary choking on poison, writhing in pain, calling out to me for help. I began locking my bedroom door at night and hiding my drugs in the battery compartment of an alarm clock I didn't use. For my creative writing classes I composed paranoid, incomprehensible stories, rip-offs of David Lynch movies.

When April finally arrived, I was disappointed again to find that we were reading only a single Kafka story and that we would spend only two class periods discussing it. I devoured "The Metamorphosis" in one sitting, without taking in much more than its plot – which I felt I'd already known – and then started reading the rest of the collection, which included all the stories Kafka had published in his lifetime. "The Judgment." "A Country Doctor." "The Hunger Artist." I was in the middle of "In the Penal Colony" when Hugh's class started, and I skipped it, sitting on a low brick wall outside the foreign languages building, smoking half a pack of cigarettes, flipping pages.

I can't say that I understood the stories, or that I knew what made them significant, but I felt them in a way that made LSD and David Lynch movies seem like cheap thrills. Now I could go on for pages about Kafka's genius, his humor and strangeness, his evocation of old storytelling traditions, his modern sensibility, but plenty of other people have done so far more intelligently than I can. At the time, all that mattered was that I couldn't stop reading the stories, that they were showing me something I felt I'd been looking for, though I didn't know what it was or why it was important. I could have kept reading all day, but I finished the book just as Hugh's class let out.

"Shouldn't you at least stay home and pretend to be sick?" he said when he saw me on the wall. His voice was a rasp, the bridge of his nose creased. I couldn't believe how angry he looked. When I told him what I'd been doing, his expression softened, but only slightly. He ran a hand through his hair, oblivious to my classmates streaming around him, laughing and calling to each other in a language he couldn't understand. I could tell he was warring with himself, still furious at my abandonment on the one hand, admiring my passion on the other. He'd obviously been dying up there without me, and it disturbed me to know how much he needed me to salvage his class. "Read on your own time," he said, and hurried away.

The next class I did my best to help him limp through a discussion of the second half of "The Metamorphosis," saying how amazing it is that Gregor's sister transforms, too, at the end of the story. "Yes, it is amazing," Hugh said, in a sweat, glancing around the room, hoping for consensus.

One of the sorority girls raised her hand. "But what in God's name does it mean?" she asked, her lovely twang making Hugh wince.

He closed his eyes for a second, shook his head, and looked up slowly. "It doesn't *mean* anything. It means *everything*."

I agreed with him, or felt that I did, though I didn't really know what he was talking about. If I'd been braver, I would have said so out loud, but I only nodded discreetly. The sorority girl tossed her shining hair over her shoulder and said, "That doesn't make any sense." Hugh dismissed the class, twenty minutes early.

On the last day of the semester he read from prepared notes, summing up everything we'd covered, reviewing for the final exam. He hardly glanced up. He didn't leave time for questions. To finish, he read us another poem, Wallace Stevens' "The Snow Man." He rushed through the first two-thirds of it. He couldn't wait to be finished. But then, maybe realizing how badly he was mistreating Stevens' lines and rhythm, he slowed down for the final stanza: "For the listener, who listens in the snow / And, nothing himself, beholds / Nothing that is not there and the nothing that is." He didn't try to grapple with its meaning. With those words he let us go off into the rest of our lives.

One of the essay questions on his exam asked us to compare Raskolnikov's and Gregor Samsa's roles as antiheroes. I'd written my last paper on exactly that premise and felt guilty regurgitating the argument I'd already made. But I was also pleased to know that Hugh and I thought so much alike, that despite our difference in age, we were something close to equals. He was at the front of the room grading those papers and at some point glanced up and caught my eye. It was clear that he'd gotten to mine and realized what had happened. I gave him an apologetic look. He shrugged and smiled. It means everything, he seemed to be saying. Or else it means nothing.

THAT SUMMER I stayed in Chapel Hill to do my community service. Rather than work on a road clean-up crew, I chose to serve my time at the local animal shelter. For fifty hours I played with kittens and scooped dog shit and made friends with kids who'd been busted for shoplifting, for drunken driving, for buying beer with a fake ID, none of whom wanted to talk with me about literature. At night I read *The Trial* and *The Castle* and wrote more paranoid stories and took whatever psychedelic drugs I could get my hands on. One night I watched my roommate turn into a witch, her boyfriend into a cartoon dog. My lungs exploded with every breath. After coming down, I hardly left the apartment until school started again, spending my days reading Kafka's letters and trying to make sense of the sparse, erratic notes I'd taken in Hugh's class.

Over the next two years I'd run into Hugh every few months, and he always acted glad to see me, though also somewhat chagrined, his smile sheepish and tentative, as if I had something over him, a secret he didn't want me to share. He asked what I was reading and gave recommendations, offering far more sophisticated interpretations than he'd ever managed in class. He seemed genuinely interested in what I was writing and said I should give him a story to read sometime. In turn I asked his advice about master's programs, to which he always replied, "Don't waste your time." Graduate school was the place to kill off all pleasure in reading, he said. "Go travel. Work shitty jobs. Write stories. That's what I wish I'd done."

Eventually I did give him a story, about an ex-convict working in an animal shelter. It had what I mistook for a Kafka-esque flight of fancy: the ex-con can divine the future from the smell of dog shit. The next time I saw Hugh – which turned out to be the last time – he didn't mention the story at all, and I couldn't bring myself to ask about it. I didn't want to know if he'd forgotten to read it, or worse, if he'd read it and didn't think it was worth talking about. This was in a bar on Franklin Street, and he was with his scruffy international crowd, and he was drunk. When he saw me come in with friends, he slapped the seat beside him and raised two fingers to the bartender, who ignored him. "Scott, my man!" he called, slapping the seat again. "You're almost finished. I envy you."

When I sat, he asked what I was doing after graduation. I told him about my plan to go overseas, first to the U.K., where I had a six-month work permit, and then to the continent, where I'd travel for as long as my money held out. I hadn't given up on graduate school entirely; I planned to apply to writing programs in the fall, but I left that part out. "Fantastic," he said. "That's fantastic. I'll put you in touch with some friends. I know people. Spain. Italy. Well, shit. Valerie." He turned to a girl across the table, pretty except for her pinched nostrils and morose expression, who blew smoke up through the crisp bangs hanging over her eyes. "You'll be in Paris this summer, won't you? You can put my man up for a few weeks." She shrugged, blew more smoke through her bangs, turned away. "She'll show you around," he said. "The real Paris. No tourist bullshit. I wish I could go with you. We'd have a blast."

His drunkenness embarrassed me. Not because I wouldn't soon be drunk myself – later that night I'd pass out on my bathroom floor – and not because I thought he was too old for such behavior, though I did consider twenty-seven old then, an age at which I envisioned myself mature and accomplished, no longer flailing for direction. The problem, rather, was that this picture of him – sloppy smile, flushed cheeks, wandering eyes – didn't fit with the image of Hugh I wanted to take away with me as I left college and traveled and contemplated graduate school, the one that provided some sort of guidepost to my future. I didn't want to be him, exactly, but I wanted to believe that it was okay to love literature so much you couldn't speak about it in front of people who didn't love it as much as you did, that being inarticulate didn't mean you were stunted in some way, doomed to remain in a childish state of wonder for the rest of your life. Above all, I wanted to believe that the identity I'd chosen was a noble one, and one I was worthy of.

But maybe what really bothered me was that he hadn't read my story, or didn't think enough of it to mention it, and as he swayed and blathered and failed to catch the bartender's attention, I felt a certain contempt rising, and superiority, thinking he was in fact stunted and childish, and that at twenty-seven I'd be far more confident than he was, more articulate, a better teacher.

"Oh man," he said, and slapped the table hard enough to slosh his friends' drinks. They grumbled, and Valerie swore at him in French. "You've got to go to Prague!" He said it as if no one had ever thought of such a thing before, as if it were the most original idea he'd ever had. I'd already planned to go to Prague; it was one of the highest priorities of my trip. I gave a shrug as dismissive as Valerie's. "You can go visit Kafka." He leaned away and scrutinized me, sizing me up. "You know," he said. "You look a bit like him. You've got a lot in common." Again I waited for him to mention my story, but instead he raised his fingers and called once more to the bartender. "A little help here? Cuervo shot for the soon-to-be graduate." Then he lowered his head, maybe embarrassed for himself, and now he looked more like the person he'd been in front of the classroom, shy and humble, trying but failing to maintain his dignity. "I wish I could go with you," he said again. "Get away from all these hillbillies."

Why didn't he? I asked, though now he was the last person I'd want with me. Wasn't he graduating, too?

"Not me," he said, without raising his eyes. "Signed on for another tour of duty. Ph.D., R.I.P."

His words infuriated me. All his disaffection was nothing

more than a pose, his identity, like mine, suspect, built on shady motivations and insecurity. Whatever transformations he'd gone through earlier in life had ended with dull resignation, with a career that didn't suit him, with friends who turned away in disgust. I couldn't wait to get away from him.

"Lay a stone on Kafka's grave for me," he said, as I began to rise. "And hey, keep in touch." He made me wait while he borrowed a pen from Valerie and scrawled an address and phone number on a beer-stained coaster. "Let me know what you're reading."

I stuffed the coaster in my pocket and rejoined my friends.

FIFTEEN YEARS HAVE passed since then, and now I don't often question the life I've created for myself. I glance around at my shelves crammed with books, at titles I still find thrilling, and have the feeling I was born into a world of literature, that these stories – Chichikov gathering his souls, Emma Bovary writhing on her death bed, Aschenbach yearning after young Tadzio on the beach – have been with me since I first managed to puzzle out the shapes of all the letters in the alphabet. That it might ever have felt otherwise I can hardly believe.

I've also gotten used to the smirks my own students exchange when I lose myself in a discussion of Kafka's humor, or Chekhov's minor characters, or Babel's intricate sentences, or the magical opening of *Mrs. Dalloway*, which sends shivers of excitement through me no matter how many times I read it. They roll their eyes and snicker, and I know what they're thinking: How can he care so much about words on a page?

Occasionally, though, I catch a certain expression on one of their faces, a fevered look of enchantment, sometimes even concern, and in that moment, however brief, the world feels less lonely. Most recently I glimpsed it on the face of a young woman who came to my office crying, after one of her classmates made a hurtful comment about a story she'd written. It wasn't the comment alone that made her cry, she said – she didn't really care what that asshole thought; after all, his own story was a rip-off of a bad action movie – but rather the difficulty of ever getting it right, of ever putting down on paper what you really felt, what you wanted other people to feel. Her hair was long and stringy, her teeth slightly jagged, her face puffy from crying. I regretted, not for the first time, forgetting to stock my office with tissues. "I just wish people could see what I'm trying to do," she said. "I wish reading my writing was like reading my mind."

After she gathered herself, wiping her eyes on her sleeves and giving me an embarrassed smile, we talked about *Lolita*, which had been the inspiration for her story, and especially for her slippery narrator's voice. She'd discovered the book a month ago and since then hadn't been able to think about anything else. She was mystified by it, alternately delighted and horrified at her delight, and now she was reading it for the third straight time. "I could study it for the rest of my life and not figure it out," she said, pushing hair out of her face. And that's when I caught the look, clear-eyed and determined and somewhat startled to find herself in the grip of something she didn't yet understand. You could, I thought, and judging by your expression, you probably will. "It's not like I could ever do what he does. I should probably just give up. It's a waste of time trying."

If I thought she believed herself, I might have suggested she pursue other interests. Instead I encouraged her, telling her not to be too hard on herself, to remember that writing is a difficult process and doesn't happen overnight. I pulled down other books from my shelves for her to borrow and said that above all she should try to enjoy the struggle, to recognize what a privilege it is to have writers like Nabokov as models, to have something so brilliant as *Lolita* towards which to strive. Then I offered a few suggestions for her story and sent her on her way. What I didn't tell her was that she was at the start of a long journey, that it would often be a solitary one, and that she should look around every once in a while to see who was beside her on the path. Instead I kept quiet, and she walked out of my office with her eyes set on her shoes.

If she had looked up, I might have told her the rest of this story:

A year after I ran into Hugh in the Franklin Street Bar, I was in Prague. Once again, I thought I'd known what to expect, and once again I was surprised to find how little my expectation matched reality. I'd read guidebooks and looked at pictures, I'd spent months in other European cities, but nothing compared to the alternating waves of strangeness and familiarity, an uncanny sensation of having been at once transported to another planet and having returned to a place I'd visited in dreams. Even the hordes of drunk American college students on the Charles Bridge didn't undermine the feeling of mournfulness and mystery with which I wandered the maze of alleyways and trudged up to the imposing castle and ducked into the synagogues of the Jewish Quarter. I was still primed for transformation, more so than ever, though I'd mostly given up drugs by then. I'd turned into a bug and back, and I wanted to stay in my human body. But I knew from watching David Lynch movies that the world was as bizarre sober as it had been through a swirling screen of color, and I was as ready for it to reveal its secrets as I'd ever been.

For most of a week I haunted the streets around the Old Town square, sat in dark basement pubs, listened to string quartets in ornate baroque chapels. I was aware of Kafka's presence, but once again I was holding off, savoring my anticipation. Finally, on my last day there, I rode the subway out to the new Jewish cemetery, in a quiet neighborhood away from the city center. The caretaker handed me a cardboard yarmulke. He was an old man with enormous ears, and he, too, looked familiar, as if he'd stepped out of an old photograph I'd seen years ago in my grandparents' apartment. For some reason I greeted him in Hebrew, and he smiled broadly and tried to sell me a cemetery map. "Kafka," he said, pointing to a fuzzy spot on a washed-out photocopy. Then he pointed at me. "Kafka, yes?"

I gave him a couple of coins, and he handed me the paper. Then he gestured for me to head in the direction opposite the one the map seemed to suggest. "Go," he said, shooing me with both hands. "Kafka. Go."

The stone was fairly simple, polished gray marble, chest-high, with a pyramidal top, Kafka's name followed by those of his parents. I don't know why I should have been so disappointed. What had I expected? A gravestone shaped like an insect, or the date of Franz's death inscribed in flesh, like the punishments in the penal colony? I suppose I wanted something that marked his uniqueness, that distinguished his from the rest of the stones, which might as well have been the stones of my relatives in the Jewish cemetery in Queens, so ordinary were they, so indifferent to their company. It seemed all wrong for the great writer – or for anyone – to be set to rest in a grid of graves as vast and listless as the bureaucratic offices in *The Trial*, noted only by a smudge on a badly photocopied map. I tried to place a pebble on his marker, but it rolled off the sloping top.

I rode back to the center of town, unexpectedly despondent, and if there was ever a moment when I might have stepped off the path I was heading down, when I might have sought out another identity, an easier one, one that would cause me less anguish, this might have been it. What futile business all this seemed to be, stories that so few people read or understood, words neglected between the closed covers of books, their brilliant authors left to rot in out-of-the-way cemeteries, visited only by the occasional disheveled pilgrim who tried but failed to put a stone on their grave. I felt myself turning away, putting a stop to the transformation just before it entered its final stage. But then, as an afterthought, I stopped at the Kafka Museum. An entire museum dedicated to the writer was a far more appropriate monument, I thought, one that made the world seem less cruel, though I guessed it was also one that would have bewildered Kafka, and maybe embarrassed him.

But the first thing I saw floored me completely. Printed on

a placard just inside the door was the date of Kafka's birth, which hadn't been on his gravestone. July 3, 1883. I was born on July 3, 1973. Kafka's ninetieth birthday. I read it, closed my eyes, opened them slowly, and read it again. Then I laughed out loud.

I wanted to share this with someone, but the only person I could imagine telling I had no way to contact. I'd lost the coaster with Hugh's address or thrown it away. I hadn't called him before I'd left Chapel Hill and hadn't looked up his friend Valerie in Paris. I'd tried to walk away from him as definitively as possible, hoping his influence wouldn't linger. But I knew he would understand how proud my discovery in the museum made me, and how absurd I felt taking pride in something I'd had nothing to do with. He would have understood that when it came to figuring out who I was, I'd take any help I could get. But I was left to stare at the date alone.

July 3. It meant nothing. It meant everything.

A Minor Character

I.

THE SUMMER I TURNED TWENTY-TWO, I HAD A TEMP JOB I hated and was dating a girl I didn't love. The work was mindless and agonizing. I spent all day making photocopies and stuffing envelopes for a marketing agency in Morristown, New Jersey, where none of the permanent staff paid me any attention or invited me to join them for lunch. I took my sandwiches to a bench on The Green, the old town square, and watched pigeons swarming around senior citizens who dropped bits of bread on the ground and groups of homeless drunks passing bottles in paper bags and shouting at cars stuck at traffic lights.

I was bored and lonely and impatient but tried not to be bothered, reminding myself it was all temporary, soon to be forgotten; in the fall I was heading to Scotland, where I had a permit to work for six months, and with luck I'd save up enough money to travel around the continent for another three. It was an adventure I'd been dreaming up for myself for more than a year, looking at pictures and guidebooks but mostly imagining all the fascinating people I'd meet, the conversations I'd have, the stories I'd tell afterward. I envisioned myself as someone with experiences others would envy, with connections that spanned the globe. Still, most days, as I ate my sandwich I vacillated between fantasizing about the year to come and brooding over how to end my relationship with the girl I knew I would never love, despite having told her I did more than a dozen times.

One afternoon, about a week into the summer, a man

appeared on the bench beside me. He was short and balding, in his early fifties, I guessed, wearing old stained chinos and a shirt that was too big for him. He said hello without looking at me, made some comment about the weather, and asked how my sandwich was. There was something off about his voice – too slow maybe, and without enough inflection – and the way his gaze wandered around the park without seeming to fix on anything specific. I assumed he was a resident of one of the nearby halfway houses for patients cycling out of the state's underfunded mental health system, and as a result I kept my answers curt, not wanting to open myself up to anything stranger than the interaction we'd already had. We sat in silence for a while, and when I got up to head back to work, the man looked me straight in the eye and said, "Take care, friend."

I didn't see him again until a few days later. He was shuffling across the park, muttering to himself, his gaze wandering again, and I was surprised when he glanced at me with real recognition, waved, and came to join me. This time he told me his name – Ernie – and I reluctantly told him mine. He talked about the weather again, and asked more questions, about my lunch, about the magazine in my lap, about my job. Again I didn't say much, thinking I needed to protect myself. I had the feeling he wanted something from me, but I didn't know what, and decided I didn't want to know. What I did tell him was that I wouldn't be here long, that in a few months I'd be across the ocean. At the mention of Scotland, his far-away look seemed to turn inward, and he began rocking back and forth, arms crossed on his knees. "In my family," he said slowly, in a kind of sing-song, "were twelve Scottish kings, three Swedish queens, five Danish princes, and the Emperor of China."

An out-and-out lunatic, I thought, and was ready to dismiss him entirely. But when I stood, he looked straight at me and gave a shy smile, perfectly lucid, and I had the feeling that he'd just been messing with me, that he wasn't crazy at all. "Take care, friend," he said, and I hurried back to work.

Two or three times a week for the rest of that summer Ernie sat with me as I ate my lunch, and the more time I spent with him the less I understood him. He told me he worked as a chef at a restaurant on The Green, but the name of the restaurant changed three times, and his hands didn't look like a chef's hands, soft and pudgy and free of scars. His clothes were always shabby and worn, but his face was clean-shaven, boyishly ruddy, his sparse hair oiled and neatly combed. He didn't show up for a couple of days, and the next time I saw him he had hair plugs. How in the world had he paid for them? He knew more about current events than I did, talking in detail about Bosnian Serb atrocities and the Midwestern heat wave that killed hundreds in Chicago. But whenever I mentioned Scotland, he hunched forward and began to rock, his eyes glazed, his voice going low and incantatory. "Twelve Scottish kings, three Swedish queens, five Danish princes, and the Emperor of China."

After a while I didn't care whether or not he was yanking my chain. I enjoyed his company after my long, dull mornings at the agency, and I found myself dreading the end of the lunch hour and my return to that indifferent, inhospitable office. I still wasn't sure what Ernie wanted from me, but I allowed myself to open up to him, complaining about my job, telling him I couldn't wait until I never had to live with my parents again. I even mentioned the girl I was seeing, who'd begun to talk about coming to visit me in Edinburgh after I found a job and settled in. I still hadn't had the guts to break up with her, and every time she said she loved me, I responded in kind.

To Ernie I said only that I wasn't sure we'd be able stay together after I left, and he gave a short, eloquent speech about how young people have to find their own path in life, sometimes sacrificing the feelings of others along the way. Then he invited the two of us to his house for dinner. "Stop by anytime," he said. "I'm home all weekend." He gave me an address in Randolph, in a ritzy neighborhood full of enormous brick-fronted Tudors with three-car garages. We'd try, I said, but I was pretty busy with my trip to Scotland coming up in just a few weeks. "Twelve Scottish kings," he chanted, rocking forward, "three Swedish queens, five Danish princes, and the Emperor of China."

He invited me again my last week at the agency, and this time I said I'd come. I was starting to feel nervous about heading overseas, about going to a strange city where I knew no one, where I'd have to rely on my shaky ability to make new friends. For the first time, it occurred to me I might be just as lonely there as I was here. Ernie and I talked about Bosnia and about the terrible traffic pattern around The Green, and before the end of the lunch hour, a pair of ragged drunks wandered over from a nearby picnic table. "Hey Ernie," one of them said, squinting, pushing stringy hair out of his eyes. "Who's this?"

"My friend," Ernie said. He shifted in his seat, embarrassed, maybe, or annoyed. The drunks gave him a knowing, conspiratorial look and staggered on. It was a brief, bizarre exchange, and though I didn't understand it, I was suddenly sure I was being played, that Ernie was trying to scam me. I'd eaten only half my sandwich, but I wrapped the other half, stuffed it in my bag, and stood. Ernie stood, too, and walked with me to the corner, where we waited for the traffic light to turn. "You'll stop by this weekend?" he said. "I'll make my specialty. Shrimp Creole."

"I don't know," I said. "We'll see. I've got a lot of packing to do."

"Take care, friend," he said, and put out his hand. His eyes were clear, his smile sad. We shook, and then he moved away, with that odd, mental-patient shuffle, his baggy shirt billowing with the first cool breeze of fall, his hair plugs looking like raw scabs beneath wisps of oiled hair. My certainty about his motives evaporated. Why would he play me? What could he possibly scam from me, a recent college graduate with five hundred bucks and a plane ticket to my name?

I walked away with the feeling that I'd been tested, that I'd failed miserably. I'd missed an opportunity of some kind, and now in front of me was nothing but an uncertain future I faced with growing dread. I no longer understood why I was going to Scotland, what I was looking for there, or whether I'd find it. All I did know was that a girl I didn't love would visit me, and that I'd tell her lies and hate myself for every one.

2.

IN DAVID MALOUF'S brief story "A Trip to the Grundelsee," four college students, two boys, two girls, are traveling in Austria. By the middle of the story's first page we have learned that the two young women, Cassie and Anick, are very different: "Anick was elegant, almost beautiful, and Cassie had never been either." But the two girls have both tried and failed to interest Gordon, one of their fellow travelers, whom Cassie has loved for years despite knowing they'd never be more than friends. She is comforted that Anick, a "spoiled and rather unworldly French girl would be no more successful with Gordon than she had been," but still she is utterly stuck in the pain of unrequited love as the trip begins.

What's unusual about the story is that Malouf never outwardly dramatizes its central conflict – Cassie's heartache – in interactions between the main characters. The drama of the story arises entirely from Cassie's observation of two minor characters, a pair of older women she and her friends are going to visit. Before we meet these characters, we learn about them first from Michael, the other traveling companion, who is himself hopelessly in love with Anick. He informs the rest of the party that the women had been in a Socialist group with his father, and that his father had planned to marry one of them; but while his father escaped before the war, Elsa and Sophie spent seven years in concentration camps. When Anick says, sarcastically, "They sound fascinating, these old women," Michael "failed to catch her tone." He replies, sincerely, "Well ... they're sort of special – you know what I mean? ... They've *suffered* a lot." It's an odd thing for him to say, but it begins to point us in the direction of what the story is actually about – the stamp of suffering and how one does or doesn't carry it. While Anick isn't impressed by Michael's words at all, they touch lovelorn Cassie in a way she doesn't yet understand: While riding through the beautiful scenery, seeing "the Alps … dazzlingly white along the skyline," she "wondered why she felt so depressed."

Cassie's depression follows her throughout the day and deepens during her brief encounter with Elsa and Sophie. The two older women have a surprising effect on her, pushing her anguish over Gordon to the point of real despair. There are several reasons for it, some obvious, others mysterious and profound. First is the physical appearance of Elsa, who "was still handsome, and still preserved the assurance of what must once have been a remarkable beauty." What Cassie recognizes in her is that while her looks have faded, in "learning to exploit her beauty [Elsa] had learned how to deal with power… In her ugly-duckling way [Cassie] valued beauty, had pondered the subject deeply, and was made aware of Elsa Fischer's great measure of that ambiguous gift in the effect it was having on Gordon."

Watching Gordon fall for Elsa's charms, Cassie "writhed in a dark and stolid silence." What troubles her most is that she "wanted her life, wanted it at all costs. But she despised the means she had to use, and had been using, to get it – the humiliations, the pretense that she had no passion, no ambition of her own, no sense of honor." She understands what is required of her in order to pursue her desire – to deny the things that make her most herself. What gives her pause, though, is that "she was afraid that if it came down to the point she might not be willing to suffer." This, then, is the impact Elsa has on her: Faced with someone who has suffered and survived, Cassie recognizes her own limitations. She knows that despite all of her effort she is still likely to fail in her pursuit of Gordon, and now – fearing that she may not be willing to suffer as Elsa has – she begins to imagine that she might one day have to abandon her desire.

And only then do we meet the second woman, Sophie, "who was smaller in every way than Elsa Fischer, had red hair rather inexpertly coloured, red-rimmed eyes and a drooping nose." Like Cassie, she is plain and forgettable, and after making one brief comment about how much Michael looks like his father, she disappears from the scene. Or almost does. While Cassie broods over Elsa's attentions to Gordon, thinking "that if she ever stopped being under [his] spell she would hate him," she sees Sophie slip away behind a partition. And then comes the strangest moment of the story, its quietly dramatic center:

> Cassie, who might have been able to see through walls, saw her, at a little shelf, put slices of meat on pumpernickel and stand there in the half-dark pushing the stuff into one side of her face; vigorously working her jaws and gulping, so that her scalp, with its shock of coloured hair, moved up and down and her throat muscles formed stringy cords. She ate one slice, then another, then a third. Cassie was mesmerized. At last, after swallowing a difficult mouthful, she composed her features, swept her hair with a light hand, and came back into the room looking dignified. She sat, and when she caught Cassie looking at her, produced a smile that was all innocence.

What an odd way for a character to behave, especially one we hardly know. But this is precisely what makes Sophie so fascinating, so mysterious, and so resonant. Despite a façade of dignity similar to Elsa's, her action betrays a desperation, the continuing presence of suffering or its aftermath.

Seeing this has an unexpected and unpredictable effect on Cassie, who suddenly wants to ask questions related to her feelings for Gordon but which are also much bigger than her heartache: "What about the suffering? How do you know if you can face it? Do you just go through it and come out the other side? Does time dull the pain and anger of it?" These two women have opened up something in her; they have shown her what's at stake in her pursuit of Gordon and have offered visions of what her life might become. She, of course, can't be Elsa, being neither beautiful nor elegant; the best she can hope for is to come through suffering as Sophie has, hiding behind a partition and stuffing herself with bread and meat.

Cassie's reaction stands in contrast to that of Anick, who is as unaffected by the suffering of the women and their attempted show of dignity now as when she'd first heard about them: "I was disgusted," she says of Sophie's bizarre action. "I found it insulting… 'Orreeble!" But Cassie "hadn't Anick's clear notions of how people should and should not behave. People were extraordinary or plain odd, that was all." For the rest of the day her "cloud refused to shift. Everything gave off a kind of blackness that added to it like smoke."

The visit to the Grundelsee is a turning point for Cassie, but what makes the story truly remarkable is where the turning takes her. Sunk so far into despair when she and her companions leave the old women, we might expect her to continue her downward slide. And she does, briefly, but the story doesn't linger there. Instead it jumps forward ten years, when, "married … and with three exuberant daughters who liked to sing in the car as she drove them to and from school, [Cassie] would not recall this particular gloom, or its cause." The long-term effect of the encounter with Elsa and Sophie is much different than was its immediate impact; it allows Cassie to escape Gordon's pull, and even more important, the pull of suffering. Instead she has "settled for a quiet, an ordinary fate." Anick, still beautiful and elegant, living alone, considers Cassie's life now "'orreebly provincial," but Anick is the one who still thinks of Gordon, the one who still lives a life in which despair might threaten. Cassie accepts her "flat, uninteresting" domesticity, thinking, "I almost lost my life. And then, by the skin of my teeth, I saved it." Having glimpsed the possible future that Sophie represented, stuffing her mouth behind the partition, Cassie rejects suffering altogether, choosing instead a life in which she has become unexpectedly, startlingly happy.

The minor characters in this story cross Cassie's trajectory in the briefest and gentlest way, but that brief crossing nudges her in a new direction, reveals to her what path she's actually been stumbling along. Elsa and Sophie don't know anything about

Cassie's heartache and struggle. They don't interact with her at all in the story; in fact, they don't even seem to notice her, but their presence alone sparks the drama of the story, spinning Cassie off into a life she might otherwise never have lived.

But while these two women act as bearers of possibility, they also bring into relief the impossibility of knowing what will come, the unavoidable mystery and uncertainty of living. Cassie can study the strange behavior of Sophie all she wants, but Sophie doesn't provide any answers; in the end, Cassie must decide for herself whether or not she can stand the suffering before her. Presented with a model of how or how not to live, she faces forward and heads on into the darkness.

The power of minor characters, then, lies at least partly in their limitations – they offer protagonists nothing concrete, just guesses, intimations. Only Cassie can decide to reject her suffering; only she can choose to turn away from desire and accept the blissful oblivion of a dull, uninteresting, happy life. But after encountering those mysterious beings who have wandered quietly into and out of her life, she can no longer avoid those decisions, or enter into them blindly. Malouf's minor characters have awakened Cassie to herself. She knows herself at her story's end in ways she hasn't before, and what's left up to her is whether or not she will act on that knowledge or let the opportunity pass her by.

3.

I STILL DON'T know if Ernie was crazy or not. I don't know if he was trying to scam me. I don't know how he paid for his hair plugs. I don't know if he was a chef or if he lived in Randolph or if his ancestor was the Emperor of China. And maybe it's this not knowing that was, and continues to be, the source of his power in my life. He was entirely mysterious to me, a complex surface upon which I could project all of my confusion about the world, all of my fear. He pushed against my weaknesses, my difficulty with connection and intimacy. He reflected back to me the worst in myself, and though his appearance in my life was brief, after he left it I could no longer quite go back to being the person I'd been before, one who happily ignored his limitations, who walled himself against the potential hazards of openness and never let his guard down.

Ten years later, living alone and struggling to envision a future for myself that wasn't governed entirely by despair, I found myself wondering about Ernie often, his strange chanting, his shabby clothes and knowledge of world events, and most important, the friendship he offered me, which I refused. Whether he was crazy or not, whether he was toying with me or trying to rip me off, none of that mattered now. What remained was what he revealed to me about myself: that I was terrified of what I didn't know, that fear kept me from discovery. I didn't trust anyone who wanted to get close to me, and as a result, few tried. That was my burden to bear; Ernie simply placed it in my lap, where I could no longer avoid it.

A few months after I saw him for the last time, I was sitting on another park bench, in Edinburgh, the place I'd dreamed about for so long, a city as bleak as it is beautiful. The girl I didn't love had just visited and gone home. On her first day there, Christmas Eve, I managed to tell her how I felt. For a moment I was proud of myself for finally being honest, for overcoming the fear that had held me back, but for the next two weeks, as she wept beside me in a bed that was too small for two people, in an apartment that was too cold not to crave another body's warmth, I felt nothing but shame and regret. I cried, too, when she left, and was overcome with a loneliness more profound than any I'd felt before.

Now I was eating another sandwich, watching pigeons that looked no different than the ones in New Jersey, these roosting on statues of Scottish heroes that looked no different than the statues of Revolutionary War heroes in Morristown. I was on my lunch break from another job I hated, scrubbing pots and pans in a hotel on the Royal Mile. It was cold out, dark and windy, and even wearing a sweater and coat, scarf and hat, I couldn't keep from shivering.

In front of me was Edinburgh Castle, where Ernie's ancestors may or may not have ruled, sitting atop an ancient volcanic plug. Behind me was Princes Street, crammed with tourist buses and frantic shoppers. Dozens of people hurried past without paying me any attention, but I huddled on one end of the park bench, leaving plenty of room beside me. If a shuffling old codger decided to stop and chat, I was ready to welcome him. If he detailed his complicated genealogy, I was ready to listen with interest. If he invited me to dinner, I was ready to consider accepting. I rubbed my freezing hands together and waited for someone to sit.

The End of the End of Desire

FOR A BRIEF TIME IN COLLEGE, I READ THE WORK OF Arthur Schopenhauer. I did so in part, I'll admit, in the hopes of impressing people with my intellectual sophistication and esoteric curiosity. Who're you reading? I'd ask a girl in the library, dreadlocked and artistic-looking, sprawled on a couch in the smoking lounge. Burroughs, she'd say, and shrug, as if only one answer were possible and the question not worth asking. You? Schopenhauer. I liked the sound of the name as much as the ideas in *The World as Will and Representation*, though it did strike me, as I watched the girl turn back to her book, as unimpressed with my answer as with my appearance, that Schopenhauer was onto something when he wrote that misery ends only with the end of desire.

For an even briefer time in my early thirties, just before I met my wife, I pared my life down to its barest essentials. The only things I owned in my furnished apartment were clothes and books, an old stereo and records, a few cooking utensils and a single pot. I finally had a full-time job and a real salary and was nearly out of debt; I could have afforded a place with higher ceilings and central heat, could have bought a used couch and armchair, but I spent only what I needed to survive, and squirreled the rest away in a savings account, with no thought as to what I might be saving for. I ate my meals out of the same pot I cooked them in, standing at the stove or perched on a stool at the kitchen counter.

This asceticism wasn't accidental, or some natural devolution into primitive bachelorhood. For the past two years, since the canceled wedding and dissolution of a future I'd once been counting on, believing it to be real just because it was something I could imagine, I'd been working to eliminate wanting from my life, along with hoping, those two futile pursuits that led inevitably, I thought, to disappointment and dissatisfaction. I'd been fighting off all expectation for happiness, particularly when it came to romance, though I had, during those two years, gone out with a number of women, and even slept with several. But I did so with an indifference to emotion – theirs and my own – that scared me and left me with an empty, sickened feeling akin to a hangover from cheap red wine. Now I'd sworn off not only romance but sex, too, and told myself it was preferable to cease imagining my future altogether rather than struggle to picture what was never more than shadows and haze, no clearer than the images obscured by static on the old TV that came with my apartment's shabby furniture.

This was in the spring of 2006. I taught three afternoons a week, and the rest of my time was unspoken for. A year earlier I would have frittered it away, brooding over my loneliness and lack of direction, my heartbreak and constant misfortune. But now I carved my open days into a regimented routine I followed religiously, with the specific intention of keeping my thoughts from straying. I woke every morning at eight, read the news for half an hour until I was filled with indignation, wrote until eleven-thirty, showered and masturbated, and ate lunch at noon. Then I went to a coffee shop, where I did my week's grading and prep work, walked around Laurelhurst Park or up Mt. Tabor or to the Powell's bookstore on Hawthorne Boulevard, came home and read for two hours, took a half-hour nap, made dinner while watching fuzzy reruns of *The Simpsons*, and read a little more while sipping a glass or two of Scotch. At nine or ten, if any friends thought to call me, I'd head to a nearby bar, but more often I just wandered the neighborhood, peering into the windows of people whose futures weren't as uncertain as mine, whose desires were evident in their remodeled homes, their flat-screen TVs, the strollers and playpens on their front porches.

I was surprised to find myself reasonably content with this routine, thinking only about the few hours ahead, satisfied with each new accomplishment – each page I wrote, each book I read, each meal I cooked – simply because I'd accomplished it. At worst I felt a mild undercurrent of longing that occasionally set me pacing my attic or made me scour the personals – followed by the ads for escorts – in the back of the *Portland Mercury* or the *Willamette Week*.

But usually I could keep this longing in check by reading a few lines from Schopenhauer's *Essays and Aphorisms*, which I pulled down from my bookshelf for the first time in a decade – "Each individual misfortune, to be sure, seems an exceptional occurrence; but misfortune in general is the rule"; or, "Not the least of the torments which plague our existence is the constant pressure of *time*, which never lets us so much as draw breath but pursues us like a taskmaster with a whip" – and heading out into the late spring drizzle, hunched down into the decade-old quilted jacket I refused to replace, its cuffs worn to threads. I strolled past restored Victorians and Craftsmans with reframed leaded windows, newly installed vintage cabinetry and light fixtures, meticulous grape arbors and rock gardens, thinking that time had nothing on me since I'd quit looking ahead, nor did misfortune, since I expected nothing else. Rather than envy the owners of those restored homes for the clarity of their flat-screen TVs, the hopefulness of their strollers, I pitied them: How deluded they were to believe in such bright, happy futures, to imagine that the unforgiving world could accommodate their dreams.

ON THESE NIGHTTIME walks I often encountered the neighborhood collectors, who pushed shopping carts down the sidewalks, gathering bottles and cans from recycling bins. They were almost always the friendliest people I passed, the only ones who acknowledged me, sometimes with a cheerful greeting, sometimes with nothing more than a grunt. I imagined myself as one of them, or rather, imagined that they were just like me, content with their limited needs, their suppressed desires. I also knew how ridiculous it was for me to identify with them, or how ridiculous they would probably find it. My apartment may have been spare and drafty, but I didn't sleep in doorways or under bridges, without a job or a salary or the luxury of deciding never to want anything again. Still, I was gratified whenever they gave me a few moments of attention, usually making comments about the weather, how they were glad the nights were growing warmer, or how they were ready for the rain to stop, or how they'd heard the coming summer would be the hottest on record.

One of these encounters was with an elderly Vietnamese woman, who wore stained khakis, a white gardening jacket, and a white sun visor. Her cart was neatly organized, cans up front, bottles behind, all standing and tightly packed. She was bending over a bin at the curb but straightened when I came close, and gestured to the flower beds in the yard next door. The peonies, she said. Had I ever seen them bloom so early? Her accent was heavy, her voice hoarse and watery. I hadn't noticed the peonies, and wasn't even sure which flowers she was pointing to, but she smiled at me so broadly, with a hint of impatience, that I shook my head and said that no, I never had. She bent back to her bin, and I moved on, comforted by her apparent contentment, when collecting bottles and cans was all she could do, I guessed, to keep from starving.

And I must still have been thinking about her when, half an hour later, I came upon something that startled me. On a quiet side street, where the ground sloped up abruptly and the houses were built into the hillside, an old Victorian had been lifted off its foundation and propped a dozen feet above the ground to make room for another full story beneath. This wasn't the most unusual sight in the world, I suppose, and during the real estate craze that followed over the next couple of years it was one I'd come upon often enough; but at the time, I'd never seen anything like it, and my initial reaction was outrage, which surprised me as much as the sight itself. Why should people want so much? I thought. Why couldn't they be satisfied with a beautiful house as it was?

Now it's strange to think that this of all things would have ruptured my serenity, or rather the serenity I was struggling to maintain. People did far more lavish things with their money, and why building an extra floor under the original house offended me so deeply I can only guess. Maybe it had to do with the age of the house, which had sat in one place for long enough that I believed it deserved to be left where it was. Or maybe it was because the house would now be tall enough to mar the view from my attic, which looked out over most of the rooftops in the neighborhood. Or maybe I'd just bottled up the bitterness lurking inside me for so long that almost anything would have triggered its release. Whatever the reason, lifting the house struck me as audacious, arrogant, even, and rather than pity the owners for their delusions, I found myself instead wishing them ill, hoping that their house jacks would fail and the entire structure topple into the street.

It was a spiteful, mean-spirited thought, one I knew even then I shouldn't indulge. There may have been perfectly good motivations for raising the house. Maybe the original foundation had cracked, and since the owners had to lift it to make repairs, why not put in an additional floor? Or maybe they'd just had their third child – or fifth, or twelfth – and needed the extra space. Or maybe they'd inherited a billiards table from a dead uncle and had nowhere else to put it. And really, what business was it of mine? Why shouldn't people do whatever they wanted, as long as they weren't hurting anyone else?

No matter what justifications I came up with, though, I wasn't satisfied. I couldn't help imagining what the Vietnamese bottle-collector would have made of people lifting their home in the air when she, I guessed, had no home at all. I couldn't help thinking about my own apartment, three stories up in a similar Victorian – though not a restored one – whose fir floors were splintering, whose window panes had rotted around the edges so that all winter the wind blew straight across my bed. I kept imagining one of the jacks beginning to tremble and then giving way.

From across the street I could see up into what I guessed was the house's living room, which had once been on the ground floor. The light was on, an intricate chandelier with a copper finish. Shadows moved on the ceiling. It infuriated me to know that people were living in the house while it sat on wooden supports that seemed far too flimsy for it, that they were walking around in their living room with no thought that they might come crashing down. I felt obligated to retract my earlier wish – I didn't after all, want them harmed – and hoped instead that the project would bankrupt them, or at least drain their children's college fund. Now that they were so much higher than the street, they didn't feel the need to close their curtains, not realizing or caring that I could see their chandelier and their shadows and, when they stepped close to the window, their faces lit by a nearby streetlamp.

It was a couple, of course, young and good-looking. They were in jogging clothes. They held glasses of wine. The man was my age, maybe a year or two younger, tall and fit, with a sharp jawline and precisely mussed hair. The woman could have been as young as twenty-five. Her ponytail bounced as she spoke, and her smile flashed on and off, a beacon above the street. Her slender arms gestured gracefully, the wine glass dancing, dark liquid sloshing, but as far as I could tell not a drop found its way over the rim. There was no evidence of children in sight, no aging parent they'd taken in, no one but the two of them to occupy a house that was soon to be three stories tall – four, if you included the attic, which itself was a perfectly adequate space in which to live, I thought, especially if the windows weren't rotting, the floor sanded and sealed.

The couple seemed unaware of the vastness of the house around them, of the empty space beneath them, unaware of any potential trouble in the world. Every desire they'd ever had had been fulfilled, and still they kept desiring more. But I wouldn't envy them, I told myself, I didn't want to be them, who were so blind to the misfortunes that could rain down on them at any moment. I tried to recall lines from Schopenhauer's essays, about the inevitable path to suffering, and wished I'd read them more often in the last decade, that my copy hadn't sat unopened on my bookshelf all these years, though I'd conscientiously dragged it from North Carolina to New Jersey to Oregon, from my first Portland apartment, a dank Eastside basement, to my ex-fiancée's immaculate Northwest condo, to my drafty attic. Wanting was painful, I reminded myself, and tried to detect a hint of suffering in the couple's cheerful, healthy faces, the dissatisfaction that came from wanting more than a person could have in a lifetime, in a dozen lifetimes, some sign that their desires had enslaved them, kept them from the peace and freedom Schopenhauer describes as the goal of suppressing the will, a peace and freedom I desperately wanted for myself, though, according to Schopenhauer, it was something to which only saints could aspire.

But the woman went on talking, swinging her wine glass, and the man returned her smile with a hungry, seductive look, and I could see no sign that they wanted anything more than they had at that moment. For now they, too, seemed entirely content, though an hour from now, I guessed, their clothes would be on the floor, the woman's slender hands gripping her husband's hunky shoulders, her ponytail bouncing in rhythm with the house bouncing on its jacks. Picturing it, I couldn't help also picturing myself in the husband's place, though my shoulders weren't nearly so hunky, my jawline not so sharp, and now I felt the first stirrings of a desire I wanted no part of but couldn't fend off. The woman finished her story, the man laughed, and they both looked out the window, in my direction. They couldn't have seen anything more than the orange glow of the streetlamp through their own reflections, but still I flinched and turned away. My hair was wet, rain dripping down into my collar. I hunched lower in my jacket and hurried up the street.

THE JACKED-UP HOUSE distracted me. It disrupted my routine. At the time I couldn't have said why, exactly, though now I can guess that a part of me craved distraction by then, that the comfort of my routine was already wearing thin. And as outraged as I was by the house, I was also fascinated by it, the plain wonderment of an enormous structure suspended above the ground.

In any case, I found myself thinking about it as I read the news and tried to write, as I graded papers and planned my classes, and instead of walking through the park or up Mt. Tabor, I went back to the house two or three times a week, and sometimes every day. There was no sign that the jacks were failing, though in daytime it struck me as even more impossible for those little stacks of wood – half a dozen, spread out around the foundation – to support something so large. There was too much air between the ground and the bottom of the house. One little earthquake would make quick work of it, I thought, though from certain angles it seemed as if the jacks were beside the point, as if the house were floating of its own volition, and as if nothing on earth could touch it.

A contractor and his crew were at work when I went by, digging away more of the hillside with a backhoe, building the forms for the new foundation, fastening bats of insulation to the underside of the raised floor, and I was amazed to see them walking back and forth under the house without a second thought, trusting their jacks and the ground beneath them so completely that they didn't imagine it collapsing on top of them. They worked without any urgency, as if they had all the time they needed, as if the house could stay as it was for as long as they wanted. They took frequent breaks, and joked with each other, and when it was raining, ate leisurely lunches on the dry ground under the beams.

Some days I stood watching them long enough that they acknowledged me with a nod or a little wave, and eventually I asked them about the work, what it took to get the house into the air, how they kept it balanced, how they made sure it wouldn't fall. I also asked how much something like this would cost, whether it was cheaper to buy a bigger house, and the contractor, an amicable squat guy with a pitted face and a nose that looked as if it had been broken in three places, glanced at the frayed cuffs of my jacket and smiled. "Let me put it this way. Most of us have better things to spend our money on."

I wasn't the only one who watched them. Often enough one of the neighborhood collectors would stop on his rounds, a haggard vet – or, who knows, maybe a draft-dodger pretending to be a vet – with dirty POW-MIA patches on his coat, a beard to his chest, and a cart overflowing with sleeping bag and clothes, on top of which he heaped his findings. If he resented the project or the people who were paying for it, he didn't let on. He seemed to have nothing but respect for the workers and awe at their accomplishments. "How high could you take the sucker?" he called out, and the contractor turned to me, as if I were the one who'd asked. He winked and said, "How high's the sky?" I wondered if he thought the collector and I were together, or if we were interchangeable to him, though I was twenty-five years younger, didn't have a beard, and looked generally put-together, I thought, despite my threadbare jacket and the fact that I didn't shave on the days I wasn't teaching. It bothered me to think that he couldn't tell our voices apart.

Occasionally I'd see the little Vietnamese woman, wearing her sun visor no matter the weather or time of day, a cigarette usually dangling from one corner of her mouth. She'd pass by the construction site without stopping, without even glancing over to see the house on its jacks. She pushed her cart with determination, as if her journey from one recycling bin to another required all her attention, though she did pause to look at the peonies in the yard next door, gawking at them, a show of pure wonder. I knew which flowers they were now that they were all the way open, enormous pink bundles that drooped almost to the ground.

By then I'd discovered she wasn't actually homeless. She lived in a ramshackle apartment building down the street from my own place, snuck in between a pair of Craftsmans by a cynical developer in the '70s, I guessed, when the neighborhood had been in decline. A few times I'd seen her coming and going from the parking lot usually swarming with shouting, unsupervised children, and it was a relief to know she had somewhere to go at night, and to imagine she collected cans only to supplement a social security check, or maybe just to keep herself busy, to keep from thinking about all she didn't have.

"Aren't they something?" she asked, palming a blossom, when she saw me standing in front of the house. I agreed that they were, though the truth was the flowers meant nothing to me then. I could have been looking at a piece of cardboard or a hunk of plastic, and I thought that maybe I really had suppressed my will. But I felt no freedom in it, no peaceful bliss, only an empty sickening indifference, similar to the one I'd felt after sleeping with women I never intended to love.

She asked the same question of the house's owner one afternoon, the young woman with the ponytail, who drove up in a sporty white Subaru with a "Kerry/Edwards '04" sticker on its bumper. Only she didn't have a ponytail this time. Her hair was loose to her shoulders, framing her face, which looked harder now in the fading gray light, the slightest bit gaunt, and rather than jogging clothes she was wearing a suit jacket and slacks. Her hands were red – chapped, I guessed – and so was the exposed skin of her neck and chest where her blouse opened in a wide V. "Aren't they something?" the Vietnamese woman called to her from the yard next door, bending a stem to point the blossom in her direction.

But the owner didn't hear or didn't think the woman was speaking to her. She clutched her purse close to her body, those red hands standing out brightly against black leather, and strode on heels that tilted her forward at a surprising angle, so that she seemed about to charge head-first into the broad chest of the contractor, who stood waiting for her, frowning, hands on hips, looking suddenly stern and defensive, but also paternal, as if he had to deliver an assessment of her behavior she wouldn't want to hear and that he was reluctant to give.

I'd moved off a short distance and crossed the street. I didn't want the owner to notice me, in case she ever glimpsed me standing outside her house at night; if she recognized me, she might mistake me for a stalker or someone casing her place for a burglary. But neither did I want her to associate me with the Vietnamese woman, one more of the neighborhood's shuffling underclass, gathering scraps from the blessed and fortunate. If she saw me at all, I wanted her to think of me as I thought of myself, a serious person with serious ideas – a little eccentric, maybe, but certainly someone to distinguish from the rest of the neighborhood's residents, from the yuppies like her and the hip kids with mod haircuts and perfectly tattered clothes, from the homeless and crazy and destitute, from the Vietnamese woman who was pushing her cart away now, leaving the peonies behind.

But the owner didn't look my way. She had eyes only for the contractor, who shrugged and jerked a thumb over his shoulder, in the direction of the backhoe and his crew, all of whom kept working, pretending not to notice what was going on around them. She squinted at him, and he went on talking, his eyes roving, hands moving, jaw working hard. Eventually he threw his arms up over his head, as if to say, How high do you want me to lift it?

How high's the sky? I thought, but by then he was staring at the ground. A single phrase reached me where I stood on the sidewalk. “If you’re going to do something, you might as well do it right.”

And then it was the owner’s turn to talk. This time she didn’t gesture gracefully with her slender arms. In fact, she hardly moved. Her hands stayed on her purse. I was too far away to see, but I imagined them whitening at the knuckles. Once or twice she let the purse swing freely from her shoulder in order to tap her palm insistently with the tip of a finger, but as soon as she was finished she grabbed the purse again and pulled it tightly to her side. Her mouth hardly moved, either, but the longer she went on, the lower the contractor seemed to crouch. His arms were now crossed over his chest. When the owner leaned toward him, he rocked back on his heels. He lifted his eyes from the ground only to look up over her head. I felt sorry for him, being badgered by a woman half his age, who got everything she wanted, who could never be satisfied. I wanted him to tell her to finish the job herself, but soon he was nodding, defeated, I thought, browbeaten into submission.

But then the owner turned, and to my surprise her face was no longer hardened and angry but trembling, streaked with tears, and instead of feeling sorry for her, I felt a little surge of joy at the sight of her crying. Exactly, I thought, as she stormed back to her Subaru and slammed the door. Desire led only to struggle, and hiring someone to jack up your house inevitably brought frustration and grief. So did supporting Kerry/Edwards in ’04, I thought as she drove away, something I, too, had done so hopefully, believing I could set aside the pain of my heartbreak for the sake of the world at large, donating what little money I had to the campaign, volunteering at a phone bank, canvassing the neighborhood, only to wake the morning after the election to find that my hopes had meant nothing, that my heartbreak was even more acute and devastating, not only my own future in question but the future of the planet.

As soon as the Subaru was out of sight, the contractor smiled again, joking with his crew, and they all quit working and laughed along with him, one of them imitating the woman's skeptical squint, finger tapping palm. And I laughed, too, feeling a sudden lightness come over me, a freedom like the one Schopenhauer described, I thought, and I made my way home convinced that I'd resisted temptation, that desire had knocked in the form of the owner's slender, elegant arms, her bright, hopeful smile, her adoring glance at her husband, and I'd successfully turned it away.

Half a block from my apartment I saw the Vietnamese woman again, and I waved to her enthusiastically, maybe I even called out, because I wanted to tell her something: I didn't think the peonies were something. I didn't care about the peonies at all. In fact, I didn't care about anything, and not caring, I wanted to tell her, was a great blessing, one everyone should strive toward, the only way to navigate a future riddled with pitfalls, with contractors who'd shrug and laugh behind your back, with earthquakes and wars and tragic elections, with fiancées who'd leave you for someone else a month before your wedding.

But the woman didn't see my wave or hear my call, because she was shouting at the other collector, the haggard vet or draft dodger with the beard to his chest, telling him to stay away from her street, to stay away from her bins, to give back the bottles he stole. "Yamhill Street is mine!" she cried. "I don't tell you again!"

The vet moved away from her, hunched down into his jacket decorated with POW-MIA patches the way I was hunched down into mine. The woman followed him, cursing and spitting, until he started to trot awkwardly, and then to run, his cart rattling, one of his cans falling out and rolling into the gutter. She threw her cigarette butt after him, and then pulled a can from her cart's neat stack and threw that, too. Only after he disappeared from view did she stop shouting and gather herself, straightening her visor, lighting another cigarette, re-stacking her cans.

Then, as if nothing had happened, she pushed her cart

forward to retrieve the can she'd thrown and the one the vet had dropped.

I SUPPOSE IT was ludicrous to have believed I'd suppressed my desires, that I'd arrived at some kind of blissful indifference, and it pains me now to think of myself laughing at the jacked-up house's owner's tears. I *had* wanted something – for the woman to be miserable – and I'd gotten it, and that was the sole source of my satisfaction. But as soon as I recognized it, it no longer gave me any comfort. If desire was as unavoidable as suffering, why waste it on something so empty as reveling in the misfortunes of others? This, too, was an idea Schopenhauer had written about, but I soon found myself spending even less time with *Essays and Aphorisms* and more time with the personal ads at the back of the *Portland Mercury*. By the time the jacked-up house had been lowered onto its new foundation, I was in love and hadn't taken the book down from my shelf in months.

I have it in front of me now. It's the first time I've looked at it in more than three years. On its front cover is a portrait painted when the philosopher was in his early twenties, a sensitive young man in a thoughtful, serious pose, with full lips and curly hair, and sideburns a little longer than mine – the type a dreadlocked, artistic-looking girl in a library smoking lounge might have fallen for. And maybe he would have known the right answer when she asked what he was reading: *Junky* or *The Soft Machine*.

The biographical note inside the cover claims that "Schopenhauer's belief in his own philosophy sustained him through twenty-five years of frustrated desire for fame."

It goes on to say that his "fame was established in 1851," with the publication of this very volume of essays and aphorisms.

Wanting ended in having.

Like Fire on My Skin

DURING THE TWO YEARS BETWEEN BEING LEFT BY MY fiancée and meeting my wife, I read a lot of books, watched a lot of movies, and listened to music obsessively. I didn't have much money then – in fact, I was often in debt – but there was a record store within walking distance of my apartment, and every couple of weeks when I was feeling especially down, I'd treat myself to something new. When I brought it home, I'd play a single track over and over until I could hear it in my head as I walked down the street or shopped for groceries or lay awake in bed, staring at my grimy skylight. It was a sort of meditation tactic, I suppose, a way of crowding out thoughts I didn't want to indulge.

The music I was into ranged from Eric Dolphy to Steve Reich to the New York Dolls, but more than anyone else, I listened to Townes Van Zandt. I'd been a fan for years, but since my life had fallen apart, and in the state of despair and slow recovery that followed, I had the feeling that his lyrics were addressed to me directly. "Everything is not enough, and nothing's too much to bear," he'd sing as I paced my attic's splintered floorboards. "The dark air is like fire on my skin, and even the moonlight is blinding," he'd sing as I huddled down in my frayed second-hand sheets. "Lay down your head awhile, you are not needed now," he'd sing, and I'd forgive myself for hardly having left my bed in months. His ballads were mournful, but his voice was casual, with a mixture of wisdom and resignation and reckless bravado, as if he couldn't take all this mournfulness too seriously. Life is tough, he seemed to be saying, but you can take it. At the time, that was the only message I wanted to hear.

When a documentary about Townes came out, about a year after I moved out of my ex-fiancée's condo, I went to see it alone – as I did dozens of movies during that time – in a rundown theater in Southeast Portland that showed only independent films guaranteed to lose money. I expected to have the whole place to myself, but to my surprise, the theater was packed, though half of its seats were broken. I was stuck sitting next to a young couple who held hands through the entire movie. They were maybe twenty-four, both pink and chubby as babies, the boy with a patchy beard, the girl in pigtails. They were too young to appreciate Townes, I thought, too happy to understand the songs. What could "Waiting Around to Die" – with agonizing lines like, "Sometimes I don't know where this dirty road is taking me, sometimes I don't even know the reason why" – possibly mean to them? But whenever a song came on, they sang along, too loud and too fast, making clear to everyone around that they had the lyrics memorized. Not fifteen minutes in I was ready to strangle them.

The film was unquestionably tragic, I thought, a story of missed opportunities, of disappointments and losses, of unrecognized genius, of life cut short. About a third of the way through, there was footage of Townes in the mid-seventies, at the height of his creative powers. By then he'd written most of his best-known songs, including those that would become big hits for other people: "Kathleen," "If I Needed You," "Pancho and Lefty." He should have been a household name, but he wasn't. He didn't play to crowds of thousands. He didn't ride in limousines or private jets or even a lavish tour bus. Instead he was living in a beat-up trailer outside Austin, drinking whiskey straight from a bottle, wrestling with a mangy dog, shooting at tin cans.

Here was easily the best songwriter since Dylan, completely neglected by the world, almost entirely unknown. His albums would never sell more than a few thousand copies, and all would go out of print. He'd be screwed by managers and record companies and die at fifty-two, his body ravaged by booze. Only after he was gone would he be rediscovered, his albums returned to circulation, his name mentioned in interviews with more famous songwriters, his songs played in hip coffee shops all over Portland, his lyrics memorized by irritating young couples in love.

Hunched down in my broken seat, with loose springs pricking my thighs, I could think only that the world was terribly cruel, that no one got what he deserved, that I shouldn't bother to hope for fulfillment. I was on the verge of tears, and if that couple hadn't been right next to me, the girl's popcorn balanced on the armrest between us, I might have wept openly during Townes's funeral, when his best friend and fellow songwriter Guy Clark walked to the altar and said, "I booked this gig thirty years ago."

At the movie's end, the two lovers looked into each other's eyes for a good forty-five seconds, in some kind of communion, as if the film had affirmed them in their love and happiness and bright future together. They kissed all the way through the credits, and I left the theater in a rage, believing I was the only one who'd actually *seen* the film, just as I often thought I was the only one who really *heard* Townes's songs. Back in my apartment I poured myself an enormous scotch, paced, and listened to Townes reassure me: "It's easier than just a-waiting around to die."

THE STRANGE THING is – or maybe it's not so strange – I didn't listen to Townes any less as my life began to turn around, as I left the apartment more and re-awoke to the world. Nor did his songs mean any less to me when I wasn't drinking or huddling in bed. "Heaven ain't bad, but you don't get nothin' done," he sang as I went through days with renewed promise and hope, throwing myself into writing and teaching and connecting with friends. "To live is to fly, all low and high," he sang when I met my wife and moved out of my attic. "If you needed me, I would come to you, I would swim the seas for to ease your pain," he sang at our wedding, two years later.

But as essential as the music was to me, I didn't want to watch the documentary again. Townes's life story was too heartbreaking, I decided, the film too focused on his addictions and gambling, his shortcomings as husband and father, his failures rather than his triumphs. It detracted from the beauty of the melodies, the genius of the writing. The real person was in the songs, I thought, not the one so drunk he could only mutter on stage, or the one telling stories about huffing so much glue his teeth stuck together and had to be shattered with a ballpeen hammer. The image of Townes that appeared on screen was just a weathered surface, lashed by the harsh winds of an indifferent universe.

And yet, something about this way of thinking didn't satisfy me. For years I was haunted by that image of Townes outside his broken-down trailer, and I was never able to separate it entirely from the songs, or from memories of the two bleak years I spent in that attic with squirrels scurrying overhead. There'd been something crucial about sitting in that rundown theater, about watching Townes's drunken antics, about wanting to strangle the happy young couple next to me, though I wasn't entirely aware of it at the time and couldn't quite put my finger on it now. Maybe because several years had passed, and because I'd now begun to look back on that dark period with a kind of bewildered scrutiny and disbelief, and even with faint nostalgia for the melancholy that shadowed me in my apartment and in record stores and in dark movie theaters, I found myself wondering often about how I'd react to the film if I saw it again. Whatever the reason, I finally rented a copy.

And even then I hesitated to watch it. It's terribly sad, I warned my wife. You probably won't like it. It sat on my desk for a few days, and whenever I glanced at it, I considered returning it. I knew what my reluctance was about. I no longer wanted to believe that the world was cruel, that no one got what he deserved, that life was a long series of disappointments and losses. Even if it was true, I'd rather remain in denial, to think of Townes only as a brilliant songwriter who was properly revered – by me, at least – and not as one who remained underappreciated and neglected.

Eventually, though, my curiosity outweighed my misgivings, and one night after dinner, I put the film on. About halfway through, I glanced at my wife, who gave me a look that suggested she didn't see what was so tragic about the story. Yes, Townes was a mess; yes, he'd had his childhood memories erased by insulin shock treatment; yes, he abandoned his first family for the road and drank himself into an early grave. But he also threw himself into life, with a passion and dedication that was impossible not to admire. He was drunk but charming, telling jokes, shrugging off disappointments. At times he wasn't lucid enough to remember which songs he'd written; at others he articulated very clearly how much he cared about language, how carefully and precisely he selected every word. There was still sadness in the film, and I still got choked up when Guy Clark took the stage at Townes's funeral. But there was also joy, and humor, and above all the incredible beauty of the songs.

A few years earlier I'd seen only half the film, my own sadness blinding me to the rest. The young couple beside me had likely seen only half, too, and sitting beside each other, we might as well have been in two different theaters. It amazes me to think what we carry with us into the world, the very air around us subject to our states of heart and mind. One day we "welcome the stars with wine and guitars," and the next, "even the moonlight is blinding."

This, above all else, is what I'd missed the first time around: Outside that broken-down trailer, Townes didn't care that his albums weren't selling, that he wasn't a household name. He didn't care about private jets or lavish tour buses. He had his songs, and his dog, and his friends, and his guns. He laughed a drunken laugh. He showed no sign of wanting to be anywhere else.

5

The Other Scott Nadelson

ONE AFTERNOON IN LATE OCTOBER, ABOUT A YEAR AND a half after my first book came out, and a year and a half after I moved out of my ex-fiancée's condo, I was walking through Laurelhurst Park in Southeast Portland. I'd just come from a record store and was heading home with a copy of *Born to Run*. I'd had the album once before, but during the move into my attic apartment it had fallen out of its case and gotten so scratched I could no longer play it. Replacing it felt like an important step in rebuilding my life, and as I left the store, reading familiar song titles on the back of the CD – "Thunder Road," "Tenth Avenue Freeze-Out," "Jungleland" – I was overcome with a sense not only of nostalgia but of reconstitution, as if I'd reclaimed a missing limb, or rather a crucial joint or ligament, some vital connection necessary to keep me from falling apart.

And I must have been so caught up in the feeling, so focused on those song titles, that when a woman stopped me on the path, I started, jumping back and letting out an awkward sound, half cry, half grunt.

"Are you Scott?" she asked.

I was so surprised to be spoken to that I muttered, "I'm *a* Scott."

She was attractive and stylish, with black bangs nearly covering her eyes, and dark scribbles on the back of her left hand. I didn't recognize her, but because of her dark eye make-up and frilly retro blouse, I guessed she might know some of my musician friends, that we might have met at one of their shows. "Scott Nadelson?" she asked, and this time I answered less hesitantly, "The only one I know of."

Her name was Corrina, and as it turned out, she didn't know my musician friends, and we hadn't ever met. Rather, she'd seen me at a literary event a few weeks ago, where I was one of several panelists charged with offering words of advice to aspiring writers. I didn't have much in the way of advice – work hard, get lucky – so instead I read from one of Flannery O'Connor's cranky letters, in which she admonishes a young correspondent,

> Experiment but for heaven's sake don't go writing exercises. You will never be interested in anything that is just an exercise and there is no reason you should. Don't do anything that you are not interested in and that doesn't have a promise of being whole… Nothing you write will lack meaning because the meaning is in you.

The event had taken place in a church downtown, the audience populated mostly by retirees, several of whom used the question and answer period to talk about their own manuscripts and complain about the publishers who didn't understand their work. While I was speaking I noticed one stocky old man in the front row, doing neck rolls and stretching his arms over his head, and after I finished reading Flannery's words, he stood up and said, in a thick Russian accent, "I write book about fitness. I am expert. What you know about how I write book. Are you fitness expert?" I glanced down at my bony chest, smiled, shrugged. He sat, crossed his bulky arms, and beamed at people around him, satisfied, it seemed, to have exposed my presumption. Afterward, the only person to come up to talk to me was another old man, who had a great idea for saving the publishing industry. All books should be printed in disappearing ink, he said. You read them once, and then you have to throw them away. No more used bookstores, no more libraries. Nothing to get in the way of sales.

I hadn't seen any attractive young women in the pews, and I didn't entirely believe Corrina when she said she'd been there.

But she recalled the Flannery O'Connor quote almost verbatim, and added, "You were the only one who said anything worthwhile." Then she laughed about the Russian fitness expert and said, "I felt sorry for you up there. What a waste of your time." She was new in town and had gone to the panel hoping to get connected with the local writing community. She'd been dabbling in fiction for the past few years, though mostly she was a painter. "If it weren't for you, the whole thing would have been a waste of my time, too," she said. "I bought your book afterward. I was going to ask you to sign it, but you were talking to someone else, and – well, I guess I got shy. But I just finished it last night. That closing story – oh, heartbreaking. And here you are, like magic."

She smiled broadly, and her teeth were charmingly crooked. I was too flattered to do more than thank her, shuffle my feet, and say I'd be happy to sign the book any time. Set against the trunks of nearby maples, her hair had a violet tint, and when a breeze stirred it, she shivered and rubbed her hands together, the black scribbles moving too fast to be legible. Only then did I realize I'd been hugging the Springsteen CD to my chest the whole time we'd been talking. Now I tucked it behind my back. There was a sparkle of recognition in Corrina's eyes, of admiration and undisguised interest, and I had the feeling that everything I'd struggled with over the past year and half, every moment of difficulty and suffering, had led to this.

We'd never met before, but here was someone who already knew me, I thought, the real me, the one who showed himself most clearly and honestly in his work, who was more than a gaunt, unshaven thirty-two-year-old who drank too much and barely made enough money to cover his rent, who spent whole days in bed and masturbated to pornography and occasionally burst into tears in public. The real me was intelligent and dignified and capable of deep feeling, and Corrina had seen this person in my book. She was imagining him in front of her now, and maybe he really was there; in fact, I felt him taking over from the mournful stand-in who'd been running my body for the past eighteen months, who'd kept me in hibernation all this time, who was no longer necessary to protect me from the dangers of living.

"I'm so glad I ran into you," she said. "Maybe we can get together and talk more. Can I maybe give you a call?"

She added my number to the scribbles on the back of her hand, and now I could make out an odd word or two – *envelopes, unwelcome* – and as I had when looking at the song titles on the back of the Springsteen album, I felt that things were falling into their proper place, my broken life repairing itself almost without my effort. While writing, she asked what CD I'd gotten, and I showed it to her with embarrassment, thinking how corny and nostalgic she'd find me, how incredibly unhip. But even after glancing at the cover, she gave me that look of recognition, a look that said our connection had already been established. "I'll call you," she said, and holding her hand beneath pursed lips, blew the ink dry.

WHAT I'D TOLD Corrina wasn't entirely true: I wasn't the only Scott Nadelson I knew of. And I don't mean that metaphorically. Ever since my book had come out, I'd been running searches of my name on the internet at least once a week. I didn't do so just out of vanity or inflated ego, but rather as confirmation that I really had written a book, that it really had been published, that a handful of people were really reading it. I had so little contact when I first moved into my attic – I went whole weeks without speaking to anyone – that any news of my precarious existence was not only welcome but crucial to keeping my heavy spirits afloat. I'd come across little reviews in obscure Jewish newspapers or on people's personal blogs and websites, and I'd convince myself I was still part of the world, that I hadn't faded entirely from view.

But about six months after the book's release, the news stopped trickling in. I suppose I no longer needed it by then; I was leaving the apartment more often, interacting daily with students and friends, even going on occasional dates, and enough people called or emailed that I didn't have to worry about being forgotten. Still, the sudden silence troubled me. It was strange to think the book had been read and written about by everyone who'd ever read and write about it. But worse was to think that I'd no longer receive those little missives that reminded me who I was and what I'd accomplished. I didn't like the idea that the task was now left up to me alone.

And then my searches started turning up websites that at first confused me. A local newspaper in New Jersey, just a few miles from where I'd grown up, listed my name not in a book review – the paper didn't even have book reviews – but on a roster of high school golf players. And then the high school's site named me as first trumpet in its jazz band. It didn't take long to figure out that these were referring to another person with my name, but even after I did realize I had the odd sense that this really *was* me, that all this time I'd been living a life parallel to my own, one in which I hadn't been a high school outcast, eating lunch by myself behind the school, getting slammed into hallway lockers when I was just trying to walk from one class to another, the idea of extracurricular activities unthinkable since they would have meant spending an additional moment in a building where I experienced nothing but misery.

Here I was, playing golf and trumpet, engaged with the world around me, presumably unafraid of what it might cost me to be seen by other kids, to call attention to myself rather than become as invisible as possible. It amazed me to think of myself at seventeen, swinging a nine-iron, taking a solo in the middle of "My Funny Valentine," standing on a stage in front of my peers and not worrying what they'd think of my suit and tie, how they'd punish me for showing off my talent and dedication – those ambitionless brutes destined to live dull, uninspired lives, stuck forever in the pit of suburban New Jersey, thinking back on high school days of fixing cars and slamming skinny, defenseless kids into lockers as the most fulfilling of their lives.

And it saddened me, too, to know that this wasn't actually

me, or another version of me, but rather a kid with my name, fifteen years my junior, who was probably related to me, since as far as I knew only one Nadelson family had ever settled in this country, all of us the offspring of a pair of brothers who emigrated from Minsk at the turn of the last century. Here was my fourth or fifth cousin, living just a few miles from where I'd grown up, a kid I'd never met, but who was far better adjusted than I'd ever been, who didn't feel shy about showing off his talents the way I'd been shy about showing off mine, though of course I'd had no talent for golf or music, and actually I'd never played golf in my life and had no interest in doing so now. In fact, I hated golf, thought of it as an elitist sport with no soul, a waste of perfectly good landscape. And though I did love music and would have chosen to be a musician over a writer any day if I'd had any ability, I'd never have played in some pansy high school band whose most radical playlist included Glenn Miller and Tommy Dorsey, but rather in an underground outfit that started with Coltrane and moved on to Ornette Coleman, Cecil Taylor, and Albert Ayler, and did free jazz interpretations of The Clash and The Damned. Or to put it in other words, even in my fantasies I ended up an outcast, though a more adventurous and admirable outcast than I'd actually been, one who made love to outcast girlfriends in a basement room decorated with punk rock posters and lava lamps and guitars I'd smashed on stage.

Still, I soon began to hunger as much for news of this other Scott Nadelson as I did for news of myself, torn between cheering for him and scorning him when he competed in a county golf tournament or played in a statewide jazz band competition. It was all so easy for him, I thought, with a large dose of bitterness and envy, this kid who was entirely free to be himself, who'd never have to work to discover who he really was. Sometimes I'd imagine that it was because I'd struggled so much that this other Scott Nadelson could live so freely, just as my grandparents claimed to have struggled through the Depression and the lean war years to make life so livable for my parents' generation and my own. I'd sacrificed so the other Scott Nadelson could thrive. And therefore I had a stake in his achievements, even though I knew they weren't actually mine. When he lost in the third round of the golf tournament I'd sulk for days, and when his jazz band took second place in the state I'd walk around with a pride I never let myself feel for my own accomplishments, that was elusive even when my internet searches turned up a new little notice about my book. And even if I wasn't entirely conscious of it then, I was grateful to this other Scott Nadelson for living his life while I was still making up my mind whether or not to do the same.

FOR A YEAR and a half, I'd spent far more time on the internet than I should have, not only searching my name or looking at pornography but reading the news, scouring the online personals, and working on my own dating profile. It was a strange thing to put into short, quippy phrases who I was and what I wanted in a romantic partner, and I revised what I'd written every couple of days. The ads I looked at were witty and suggestive and overflowing with confidence, and to read them you had to wonder how these women could ever be single. I tried to be honest when I filled out the online questionnaire, but when I finished I discovered that I'd created a person who didn't exist – one who shared my tastes and interests but who didn't have credit card debt or spend fourteen hours a day staring up at a grimy skylight or occasionally find himself crying in public and looking for a place to hide.

Even the photograph I posted was a half-truth. Taken in a bar a few days after I moved out of my ex-fiancée's condo, when I was fall-down drunk and in a state of frenetic denial, it made me look relaxed and friendly, a social guy with a welcoming smile. Before going on a first date, I'd study that photo and try to imagine other circumstances in which it had been taken – a birthday party, maybe, or the celebration of my book's release, some moment in which I felt self-possessed and content, excited about the direction my life was heading. Mostly, though,

I'd imagine I was looking at someone other than myself and wish he could go on the date for me.

The dates I did go on ranged from dull to downright disastrous. On one, a woman and I somehow got talking about movies, and within fifteen minutes of sitting down to coffee, we were arguing about *Mystic River*, which I'd just seen a day or two before. I said I'd found it manipulative and overwrought, simplistic in its portrayals of grief and the effects of child abuse, particularly disappointing because I was a fan of Clint Eastwood and Sean Penn. But before I finished speaking my date's face went hard. "You have no right to judge," she said. "You don't know anything about it." The severity of her voice stunned me, but it also brought out my stubbornness, or rather my belligerence, and I kept arguing. "Have you even seen it?" I asked after it became clear that she hadn't, and she shook her head. "Then how can you possibly have an opinion?" I realized my mistake too late. With an onslaught of tears, she told me she'd been abused by a cousin, from when she was five until she was sixteen. I spent the rest of the brief date apologizing, promising that I'd never make snap judgments again. My feeling about the movie didn't change.

The most promising date had been with a poet, a few years younger than I, who suggested beforehand that alcohol was the best salve for the anxiety of meeting someone new; why didn't we forgo dinner, she said, and go straight to a bar, preferably one that had a good selection of whiskey, as she'd recently become a convert from clear liquors and wanted to make a study of different brands to discover her favorite. She studied them seriously, with a look of concentration, while talking about obscure poets I'd never heard of and telling me about the awful break-up she'd gone through a few months earlier, with a guy she'd been with for eight years, since she was a senior in college. He was her best friend, she said, and she didn't know how she was supposed to live without him, but now she had no choice, and hey, how about another whiskey?

It turned out she was a fellow Jew, which she hadn't mentioned in her profile, and was also from the east coast, with a familiarly grim sense of humor, a brittle laugh that walked the tightrope between hysteria and despair. And it occurred to me that maybe my mother had been right all along, that there was a reason to date Jewish women – not because we celebrated the same holidays, but because we shared the instinct to joke through our pain. Her sadness had the effect of making me cheerful, and though I knew she was in no place to start a relationship a few months after breaking up with her boyfriend of eight years, I thought I had a good chance of at least getting her into bed. I felt my own somberness lift, replaced by a casual recklessness that made me reach out and squeeze her hand when her eyes started to redden. I told her about my own break-up, which was almost a year old by then, and said that though it might be hard to imagine now, in another six months she'd be in a completely different place, that time did incredible things. It was brave of her, I said, to start dating again, even if she didn't feel ready for it yet. The key was to find a guy in the meantime who wasn't in any rush to get serious, who just enjoyed being with her and sampling whiskey. Was she ready, by the way, to try another?

By the time the bar closed, she'd tried six or seven and had to lean on me to get to the front door. She'd taken a bus to the bar, knowing she wouldn't be able to drive home, and by now the buses had stopped running. "I'll call a cab," she said, making eyes at me, I thought, and I told her not to be silly, I was happy to drive her home. I was tipsy and giddy, feeling as reckless and free as I'd ever been. My somberness had lifted for good, I decided, and now I'd really become the person in my profile picture, relaxed and easy, with a welcoming smile. He was the person I'd be from now on, one who could cheer up a heartbroken poet and drive half-drunk through deserted streets and even get laid from time to time, one who understood the sadness of the world but didn't dwell in it, didn't let it consume him. When we made it to her house, the poet said, "I'm not going to invite you in. If I did, bad things might happen. Or good things. Things, in any case. I'm not ready for things."

"Things can wait," I said, feeling no less giddy and cheerful, giving her a smile that said I had no problem waiting, but one that also suggested I was already actively imagining the things she hinted at, and that those things might be just the things to ease her heartache. She hugged me and pecked my cheek, and before getting out of the car said she looked forward to sampling more whiskey with me.

I emailed her a day or two later, saying I'd heard about a bar with an even better selection of whiskey, and did she maybe want to check it out with me this weekend? This time we could even get dinner beforehand; on a full stomach, who knew how many whiskeys we could try. I expected to hear back from her right away, but more than a week went by without a word. I found my somberness returning even as I tried to fight it off, reminding myself that I was a friendly, easygoing guy with a welcoming smile, that I should just let the whole thing go, chalk it up to us being in different places – the poet too submerged in heartbreak to let me pull her out of it – and move on. Instead, I paced my attic, checked my email fifty times a day, and then finally wrote to her again, just as casually, just wanting to make sure my note had reached her. This time she did write back. "Dear Scott," she said, and the salutation alone told me that this was the last time I'd ever hear from her. "I'm sorry I didn't get back to you sooner. I've been really torn about it. I had a nice time with you the other night, and under different circumstances I'd be glad to go out again. But the truth is, you seem really sad right now, which, believe me, I totally understand – you have every right after what you've been through. But right now I need to surround myself with happy people, people without burdens. I just have to have fun, which is selfish, I guess, but I'm sure you understand. I've got to do whatever I can to keep it together. I wish all the best for you."

I stared at my profile picture and tried to figure out

whether I was wrong about that easy smile or whether the poet had just seen through it.

BECAUSE I HAD so much time on my hands following the breakup with my ex-fiancée, I found myself following the news religiously, in a way I hadn't before and haven't since, reading a dozen websites and blogs, picking up the local paper whenever I stopped for groceries. It wasn't a good period for news, especially not for someone with my political leanings. Abu Ghraib. NSA spying. The re-election of George W. Bush. Hurricane Katrina. These stories not only exasperated me but pushed me to the brink of despair. I couldn't help taking them personally. At the same time that my life had fallen apart, so had the country, the entire world. I felt that my own troubles were part of a global misalignment and therefore out of my control; so long as the news stayed bad, I didn't have much chance of getting my life together. With the planet in chaos, how could I possibly find a permanent job or make lasting relationships or pay off my debts or clean my filthy apartment?

One story, however, gave me hope that the world – and my life – might one day return to some semblance of normalcy, and I latched on to it as a potential turning point. Finally, wrongs would be righted. Justice would be served. The arrogant people who'd brought us into war and authorized torture and spying would be brought to their knees. I couldn't read enough about the outing of CIA agent Valerie Plame and the subsequent grand jury investigation, which was carried out mostly in secret, and as such, was for months the subject of wild speculation.

The case had been underway for more than two years by the time I met Corrina in the park, and any day now Patrick Fitzgerald, the federal prosecutor, was expected to announce indictments. Depending on the news source, the predictions about how far Fitzgerald's dragnet would reach was wide-ranging, from minor staffers to masterminds like Ari Fleischer, Karl Rove, and Dick Cheney. On TV I'd watch their smug, self-satisfied faces and try to detect signs of fear, some hint that they knew their fate was sealed. Driving to work, I'd listen to a report on the radio about possible links between Rove and the leaks and shout some variation of, "You're going down, motherfucker! You're toast! Sayonara, asshole!" and drum my fists on the steering wheel.

That fall I was commuting three days a week to a temporary teaching job, an hour each way, and I spent a lot of time talking back to my radio. Every time a commentator used the word "Plamegate," for example, I said, "Gate is not a suffix meaning political scandal, goddamnit." It was one thing, during the Clinton years, to refer to Whitewatergate. That had the logic of pun, a clever, if misleading, attempt to associate Clinton's scandal with a bigger, more destructive one. But to stick "-gate" onto the end of someone's name was just idiotic. "Be original, for fuck sake," I'd tell the commentator, and it wouldn't occur to me to wonder how anyone could do something for the sake of fuck.

Every day, speeding down I-5 from Portland to Salem, where I'd spend another fifteen minutes cruising the parking lot until someone pulled out – the college sold more parking permits than it had spaces – I'd wait almost breathlessly for Fitzgerald's announcement. The longer it was delayed, the more crucial it seemed to me. I was more than ready for justice by then, for order, for permanent jobs and lasting relationships. I could sense the end of this period of muddle, or wanted to, and by the time I pulled into a parking spot, I was desperate for the radio host to interrupt a story with breaking news about the grand jury's decision. I'd idle for five, ten minutes, waiting, and then have to sprint to class.

It makes sense to me now why this story gripped my attention so completely. There were clear villains and heroes – clear, at least, to me – and if nothing else I longed for clarity. It was easy to despise Rove and Cheney and Fleischer and columnist Robert Novak, who'd first printed the leak, those sneering bald men who professed loyalty to a phony Texas oilman and valued belligerence, secrecy, and tax cuts for the rich. Next to them, anyone would have seemed honorable. Patrick Fitzgerald, for example, was a tough New Yorker, now based in Chicago, and he spoke about the law and criminal activity in clipped, no-nonsense terms. Republicans tried to attack him, but he'd been appointed by Republicans, and he never publicly admitted any party affiliation. He'd investigated a Republican governor and a Democratic mayor. Earlier in his career he'd locked up mafiosos and terrorists. People compared him to Eliot Ness.

Even more appealing was former ambassador Joseph Wilson, Valerie Plame's husband, who was the real target of Novak's column and of the leak itself. Not only had Wilson exposed false claims about Iraq's pursuit of nuclear material, he'd spoken out publicly against a pre-emptive invasion, staking his reputation on his convictions. He also had a full head of wavy hair, spoke with thoughtful, studied eloquence, and shared a bed with a foxy secret agent fourteen years his junior.

And it was this agent, Valerie Plame herself, who garnered my highest admiration. A CIA operative made a strange hero for me, who normally associated the CIA with those very things I found most exasperating, that nudged me toward despair: subterfuge, torture, abuse of power. But in this case, Plame had stood up to lies and abuses. In sending her husband to Africa to investigate fabricated justifications for war, she'd risked not only her career but her life for what was right and honorable. I was in awe of the double life she'd been leading all these years, a former sorority girl with shining hair and a bright smile who wielded her power quietly, in the shadows. She'd infiltrated government and business circles around the world, gathering sensitive information about nuclear proliferation, and until now, no one had suspected her.

And I suppose it was this, above all, that made me identify with her, and why the story mattered so much to me. I wanted to think of myself as someone who was more than his appearance suggested, who could put on a front when it was called for. I did my best to keep my students from recognizing my heartbreak and loneliness, and I never let them know I was hardly making enough money teaching them to cover my rent. At the front of the class, I made a show of competence and engagement, talking intently about passages in books I loved, giving suggestions about character development and word choice, never revealing the truth of my muddled life. An identity was a person's most precious possession, as far as I was concerned, and exposing it to the world against one's will was an unforgivable violation. If someone had outed me the way Rove, Cheney, and their cohorts had outed Plame, I told myself, I would have spent the rest of my life trying to make them pay for the crime.

WHEN CORRINA CALLED me, two days after we'd met in the park, I was reading a blog that laid out a case against Rove and Cheney, giving them both life sentences, and listening to *Born to Run*. I had the stereo turned up loud, and because I knew my downstairs neighbor was at work, stomped on the floor to Springsteen's beat. The album *was* corny, and appealing mostly for the nostalgia it triggered, bringing me back to an earlier time, to a mindset I'd forgotten and wanted to recapture, to a place from which I could restart my journey, or any journey I wanted, any except the one I'd already taken. The songs were all about disgruntled kids trapped in small New Jersey towns and longing for escape, and when I'd been one of those kids – a little less disgruntled, maybe, my small New Jersey town a little less bleak than the ones Springsteen sang about, my dreams of escape having more to do with out-of-state colleges than the city's mean streets or the open road – they'd given me hope.

> Baby this town rips the bones from your back
> It's a death trap, a suicide rap

And now, after almost ten years on the west coast, I had the feeling that I'd never gotten as far from that town as I'd imagined. I was still one of those disgruntled kids, still fantasizing about my way out, and I wasn't playing golf or trumpet like the other Scott Nadelson but hanging out at the summer carnival across from Gardner Field, where the rides never went high enough or fast enough but just around and around in circles. I was standing beside a game booth, smoking a cigarette to look cool, my hair grown to my shoulders, watching girls in cut-off jeans throw darts at a wall of balloons, and in that moment I felt the promise of untold possibilities course over me like the warm breeze off the baseball diamond where I'd once pitched in Little League, erratically and without much power but well enough to win a championship game on my eleventh birthday. And now I wondered if that was the last moment my life had been on track, if I'd been distracted from my purpose by those girls in cut-offs, by those popping balloons. Or maybe it had happened after that championship win. I'd been too arrogant with the game ball in hand, too satisfied with myself and my accomplishments, and I'd momentarily quit longing for the escape that was necessary and elusive and that led mostly to dead ends.

> We gotta get out while we're young
> 'Cause tramps like us, baby we were born to run.

I was stomping manically when the phone rang, in a rage at Rove and Cheney, in a fever with the music blasting, and though I tried to answer calmly, turning down my stereo, the blood was pumping so loudly in my ears that I shouted hello. Corrina sounded nervous on the other end of the line, and I was so surprised to find someone else in the position of solicitude, to find myself sought after, the object of someone else's hopes, that to make her feel at ease I did most of the talking, breathlessly and maybe even a little madly, about Valerie Plame and Rove and Cheney, and then about Springsteen, saying that sometimes I had to fill myself with the old Jersey spirit, to connect with my roots and remember who I was. When she told me that she was from the Northeast, too – Connecticut, though she'd been living in Brooklyn for the past four years – it took all my effort not to break out singing, "Tramps like us, baby we were born…"

We made a plan to meet at a bar later that night, and though Corrina didn't say anything about sampling whiskeys, I felt that here was my chance to make up for the date with the heartbroken poet, who wasn't nearly as attractive as Corrina, I decided, nor as interesting. This time I wouldn't have to put up a front, pretend to be the friendly, relaxed guy with the easy-going smile, because Corrina already knew me as I wanted most to be known. She'd spent intimate time with me – I imagined her in bed, reading my book, the strap of a nightgown hanging off one shoulder – and was already primed to see me in all my complexity, to accept the sadness the poet had recognized along with the sporadic mania that set me stomping on my floor to the rhythm of the E-Street Band. To her I could rave about Rove and Cheney, or talk about the terrible break-up with my ex-fiancée, or laugh over the Russian fitness expert who dismissed my advice, and not have to worry that she was missing some essential part of me, that I was being mistaken for someone else. I could be my whole self, in other words, and not have to hide those parts I often felt were too precious or too vulnerable to expose to strangers, or even to my family and friends.

Corrina showed up wearing a long wool coat appropriate for New York winters, and her hair was pinned up, except for little wisps that fluttered over her white neck and jaw. Yes, she was far more attractive than the heartbroken poet, who had a horsey quality, I decided, too much teeth and chin, and Corrina was sweeter than the poet, too, giving me a hug the moment she saw me and saying, "I feel like we're old friends. Or like I grew up with your family or something." She had a familiar smell, fruity or floral and also vaguely recalling subways or Manhattan diners, and her way of talking with her hands fluttering around her face and shoulders and chest was familiar, too, a lovely nervousness that made me want to stroke her cheek and tell her not to worry, she could relax with me, she was in good hands. I went to the bar to get us drinks, and though she wasn't sampling whiskeys – vodka and cranberry, with a splash of soda – I still had the feeling of making up for past mistakes, of gaining important ground.

And I continued to feel that way as we found a table in a dim corner at the back of the room, a lit candle in red glass globe between us, flames glinting through our ice cubes, shadows dancing over the scribbles on the back of her left hand. My name was still there, a little faded now, but in a place of prominence between forefinger and thumb. We fell into conversation easily, as if we really had known each other for years, Corrina saying how much she identified with the characters in my book, how much we had in common, the dull suburban childhood, so placid from the outside but miserable and treacherous when you were living it. She'd rebelled in high school by sleeping with boys – "you don't want to know how many" – and then got into coke and heroin in college. She dropped out after her sophomore year, spent a few months homeless in Atlanta, where she'd followed a boyfriend who later died of an overdose, and then snapped out of the lifelong daze she'd been in after fighting off a rapist in a parking lot. "That's when I got clean, went back to school, discovered painting," she said, and I nodded along, as if we really did have all these things in common, though I'd never gotten into heroin and did coke only two or three times, never dropped out of school, never fought off a rapist, never actually did anything that threatened my existence, except to get engaged to a woman who'd change her mind about the wisdom of marrying me a month before our wedding.

When I asked Corrina what brought her to Portland, she shrugged, and a brooding look crossed her small features, those dark-rimmed eyes and naturally pursed lips. "Things just sort of started going wrong," she said. "You know how it is there. The place gets to be too much sometimes. And when personal shit goes down ..." She didn't offer any more detail, but I had no doubt what her look suggested: the whole city soured by lost love. And she'd done the appropriate thing, what I hadn't managed to do myself – pack up and head out, without looking back.

"I'm sorry things went bad there," I said. "But I'm glad you ended up here."

She smiled her broad smile, showing off those charmingly crooked teeth, and because she didn't seem to dwell in sadness as the heartbroken poet had, didn't seem to shy away from people with burdens, I told her about my own recent troubles, and how I, too, had considered picking up and moving away; only I explained my decision to stay not as one of inertia but rather of steadfastness, even courage. "I knew I'd only be running away from things I needed to face," I said. "And if I could just stay put and work on myself, I'd be better off in the long run." I told her how difficult the last year and a half had been, but said that I was in a new place now, at peace with myself and the world, and that I didn't regret a moment of it, because you needed to struggle to get anywhere in life, didn't you? And Corrina smiled and looked at me with admiring eyes, and I kept talking, in fact I talked more than I had for the past year and a half, saying that writing was what had kept me going all these months, and the fact of my book being published and finding an audience, even a small one; it made all the difference to have people like her, who connected with my characters and found their failings compelling. I even told her how desperately I'd searched my name on the internet, how I'd discovered this other Scott Nadelson who was living an alternate version of my life, and how comforting I'd found it to imagine there were other possibilities for who I could be. "Mostly, though, reading about him makes me glad to be who I am," I said, and in that moment I meant it.

Corrina gave me another look of recognition, though this time the look had a startled quality, as if she couldn't believe how much she recognized in my words. "A name doesn't mean anything, right? But it means everything, too." Her given name wasn't Corrina, she said. It was Carrie. But where she'd grown up, in a suburb of Hartford, there were maybe a dozen Carries her age, and a dozen more a year older and a year younger, all these Carries surrounding her, all belonging to a club of Carries she didn't want to join. They were cheerleaders or softball players or ballet dancers, chipper, spunky girls with swinging ponytails, and she couldn't stand them, not a single one, and it was just pure cruelty that her parents had given her such a horrible name. She changed it the day she turned eighteen, naming herself for a Bob Dylan song, because Dylan was all she listened to then; she carried a photo of him in her purse like a religious icon and treated his records like a bible, convinced that his lyrics contained a secret code to living.

And now the startled look of recognition was mine, because I, too, had discovered Dylan in high school, and he'd changed my life completely, opened me up to the possibilities of language and poetry, and if it weren't for him I'd never have picked up a pen. But more important was that all my adult life I'd fantasized about meeting a woman who loved Dylan as much as I did, who didn't say, as my ex-fiancée had on multiple occasions, that she liked his words but not his voice. His words and his voice were inextricably linked, I'd argued during our three years together, you couldn't have one without the other, they were basically the same thing, and I'd point to any number of covers to prove it. The Byrds' "Mr. Tambourine Man" was soulless and empty compared to Dylan's, I'd argue, as was Clapton's "Knocking on Heaven's Door," or Manfred Mann's "The Mighty Quinn." Sure, there was Hendrix's "All Along the Watchtower," which was a notable exception, but that was because Hendrix was a genius in his own right, and as long as his fingers were working the frets of his guitar, it didn't matter what song he was singing; he could have turned "Love Letters in the Sand" into a psychedelic masterpiece.

But no matter how convincing my argument, my ex-fiancée never agreed, and she never wanted to listen to Dylan. How could

I have considered marrying her? Here was the biggest mistake of my life, I decided, not to have set concrete standards, not to have drawn a distinct line. Never again would I get engaged to a woman who didn't appreciate Dylan's voice as a physical manifestation of his lyrics, I decided, but right here in front of me was one who did. Not only did she love the songs, but she'd named herself after one of them, a fairly obscure one at that, and not only did she appreciate Dylan properly, but she'd read my book and knew me well enough that I didn't have to hold anything back from her. And little wisps of her hair fluttered over her neck, shadows danced over her pursed lips, and yes, as soon as possible, I'd take her to bed. Tramps like us, I kept thinking. Tramps like us, baby.

When I brought our second round of drinks, Corrina started asking more about my book, specific questions not only about how I'd written it but how I'd gotten it into print. Did I have an agent? Had I written a query first, with a synopsis and a market statement? "Does your publisher happen to be looking for manuscripts right now?" she asked. While I'd been at the bar, she'd taken a pen from her purse, and now she made little marks in the few blank spots remaining on the back of her left hand.

She'd written a novel, as it turned out, based on her childhood and adolescence, up through her homeless months in Atlanta. It was similar to my book, she said, only a little sexier, with flashier language and more drama, and an uplifting ending, lots of redemption. She was sure my publisher would love it. "Don, my boyfriend, says I should keep trying big New York houses," she said. "But I'm through with New York. They won't even talk to you if you don't have two books out already. That's part of why we moved out here." She wanted to find a good small press that would understand her vision and honor her words. She didn't expect a big advance; five thousand bucks would be plenty. Would I mind talking to my editor for her, and maybe put in a good word?

"Of course," I said, staring hard at the flickering red flame between us. Of course, I thought. Of course. My smile was so wide and false it made my entire face ache. "I'd be happy to."

She reached around the candle, squeezed my hand, and said, "I knew I'd be able to talk to you. I could tell the first time I saw you. I thought, Here's the kind of guy you can really trust. What's your editor's name, by the way? Could I email her directly?" She added a few more scribbles to the back of her hand, put her pen away, and stood up. "Thanks so much for the drinks. And for everything."

Out in the street she hugged me again, and though I wanted her scent to repulse me now, it smelled just as sweet and familiar, the small bones of her spine just as inviting through the long wool coat that was far too warm for mild west coast winters. "I know you've been having a rough ride," she said. "But things are going turn around for you soon. I have a good feeling about it. Happier times are on the way." I wanted to believe her so badly that I nearly burst into tears. I hugged her harder, and she pulled away.

When I got back to the apartment, I took *Born to Run* out of my stereo and replaced it with *Blood on the Tracks*. Then I went to my computer and typed my name into a search engine. There I was in online bookstores and a few Jewish newspapers, all more than six months old. But there was also one site I hadn't seen before. The personal blog of a New Jersey high school student whose family, she announced in her most recent post, was moving to Florida. "Peace out, Milburn High," she wrote. "I'm outta this fuckin place, and you all can rot in hell." She then went on to eviscerate each of her classmates in turn. "Deborah D'Angelo: this bitch thinks she's hot, but you could show a double-feature on her ass. Mike Davis: I don't know which is smaller, his brain or his dick. Laurie Eggemeyer: whore whore whore whore whore whore whore." Eventually I got to my name. "Scott Nadelson: if what they say about this kid is true, I think he's sick. But if he made it all up, I think he's hilarious."

I read the line over several times but couldn't make sense

of it. Behind me, Dylan was singing, *We always did feel the same, we just saw it from a different point of view*. What had I done all the way across the continent, in those dreary New Jersey suburbs, in the shadow of New York skyscrapers? Was it sick or hilarious? How could it be one if not the other?

What a mystery I was, even to myself.

A WEEK OR so after I had drinks with Corrina, Patrick Fitzgerald announced his indictment of Scooter Libby on perjury charges. I'd never been so disappointed in my life, or so outraged. Who cared about Scooter Libby? Sure, he worked for Cheney, but he was small-time, especially for the prosecutor who'd taken down John Gambino and Sheikh Omar Abdel Rahman. Cheney himself was left untouched, as was Rove and Fleischer and Bush. I swore at my radio as I drove to work, and this time I was late for class.

When my anger faded, I was left mostly deflated. There was no justice served, no restoring of order. I should have known those things were too much to hope for, that no matter what, I'd be left on my own to get my life together. And in fact I'd already been doing so, slowly, over the past year and a half, and would continue to do so for the next six months before meeting my wife. By then I'd begun to pay down my credit card balance. I'd begun looking for permanent employment. I'd cleaned my apartment. And I was amazed to find that the gap between the life I was living and the one I projected to the world had begun to shrink, until finally there wasn't much open space between them.

Over the next few years I'd watch Valerie Plame on various news outlets, revealing how the leak had ruined her life. She'd been betrayed by her country, by the government she'd served so loyally. Her efforts to help prevent nuclear disaster had been undermined. She'd feared for her children's safety, but the CIA refused to protect her, told her she was on her own. She'd loved her job, and now she had to figure out what to do with the rest of her life. In the meantime she published a book and went on a speaking tour of colleges around the country. Whenever I saw an image of her, I was always struck by how strange it must have been for her, hidden for so long, now out in plain sight. What was most surprising, though, was how naturally she took to the spotlight, how comfortable she seemed in her new life, how perfectly content, in fact, without her secret identity.

When a movie based on her book premiered at the Cannes Film Festival, Plame appeared on the red carpet beside Naomi Watts, the lovely Australian actress who plays her in the film. I came across a photo of them together online, and in it they were both glamorous in strapless dresses, their blonde hair glittering in front of flashing cameras, and if you glanced quickly at the image you could easily mistake the former agent for another movie star. Plame's smile was clearly delighted, no sign of her shying away from the attention. She no longer had to pretend to be someone other than she was. She could be herself, in front of the whole world. Her outing was finally complete.

When I study the photo now, I wonder if she still regrets the leak, if she still believes it ruined her life.

I'VE LOST MY copy of *Born to Run*. As I began writing this, I wanted to listen to it, for the first time in several years. I was feeling nostalgic again, not only for the music or for my New Jersey childhood but for those two strange years between being left by my fiancée and meeting my wife, which I now look back on with a mixture of amusement and mild embarrassment and even, strangely, a touch of hard-won pride. The farther I get from them, the more they take on the misty, haphazard quality of dreams, and though in the broader spectrum of my life I know they'll one day seem entirely negligible, the briefest detour on a meandering journey, I feel the need to hang onto them somehow, to give them a place of prominence in my memory. I wasn't myself, I think when remembering how miserable I was, or how a giddy mood would overtake me and set me stomping on my floor. Or else, I think, I was more myself than ever.

But the CD wasn't where it should have been. There was

Nebraska, Springsteen's masterpiece, and *The Ghost of Tom Joad*, and even an illegal copy of *The River*, which I borrowed from the library and burned on my computer. But no *Born to Run*. I can only imagine that it must have gotten lost when I moved out of my attic into my wife's house, or later, when we bought a new house together and moved south, to Salem, where we both now have permanent teaching jobs.

And maybe it's appropriate that I've lost it, since I've lost track of the other Scott Nadelson, too, though I suppose if I searched my name on the internet I might find him easily enough. He must have graduated college by now, and maybe he's working his way up to the PGA tour, or maybe he's playing trumpet with an experimental jazz outfit, breaking new ground, exploding the boundaries of the form. Some mornings, though, I'll wake up groggy, and before turning to see my wife in bed beside me, I'll imagine he's in an attic apartment somewhere, staring up at a grimy skylight, frayed sheets pulled to his chin. He's a little more gaunt than I am, a little more passive, a little more apt to wallow in sadness, and he's constructing his life piece by piece, trying to discover what makes him whole.

Acknowledgments

BIG THANKS to David Shields, Dominic Smith, Rhonda Hughes, Adam O'Connor Rodriguez, Liz Crain, and the editors of the publications in which the following pieces first appeared:

"The Next Scott Nadelson": *Post Road*
"Three Muses": *The Southern Review*
"I'm Your Man": *Iron Horse Literary Review*
"Pal Man": *Crazyhorse*
"Scavengers": *The Pinch*
"Melancholy Mad in the Soft Night" (as "Go Ahead and Look"): *Oregon Humanities* and reprinted in *On Second Thought*
"The Two Lances": *New Ohio Review*
"First Fees" (as "The Odessa Writing Course"): *New England Review*
"The Nothing That Is": *Prairie Schooner*
"A Minor Character" (Section 2, as part of "What About the Suffering?: The Quiet Power of Minor Characters"): *The Writer's Chronicle*
"The End of the End of Desire": *Whitefish Review*
"Like Fire on My Skin": The *Ploughshares* Blog

I am also grateful for permission to quote from the following:

Acknowledgments